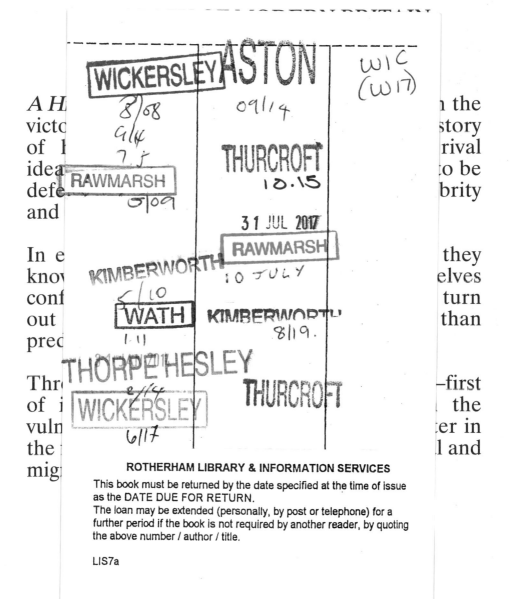

A H ... n the
victc ... story
of I ... rival
idea ... to be
defe ... brity
and

In e ... they
knov ... elves
conf ... turn
out ... than
prec

Thr ... –first
of i ... the
vuln ... er in
the ... l and
mig

WICKERSLEY
8/68
9/4
7.5

ASTON
09/14

WIC
(W17)

THURCROFT
10.15

RAWMARSH
5/09

31 JUL 2017

RAWMARSH
10 JULY

KIMBERWORTH

WATH
1.11

KIMBERWORTH
8/19.

THORPE HESLEY

THURCROFT

WICKERSLEY
6/17

A HISTORY OF MODERN BRITAIN

Volume 2

Andrew Marr

BBC
LARGE
PRINT

First published 2007
by
Macmillan
This Large Print edition published 2007
by
BBC Audiobooks Ltd by arrangement with
Pan Macmillan Ltd

Hardcover ISBN: 978 1 405 64879 0
Softcover   ISBN: 978 1 405 64880 6

British Library Cataloguing in Publication Data available

Printed and bound in Great Britain by
Antony Rowe Ltd., Chippenham, Wiltshire

PART 4

THE BRITISH REVOLUTION

Margaret Roberts, Superstar

In politics, if your tactics work and if you are lucky – then you will be remembered for your principles. Margaret Thatcher's tactics did work; she was shrewd, manipulative and bold, verging on reckless. She was also extremely lucky. Had Labour not been busy disembowelling itself and had a corrupt, desperate dictatorship in South America not taken a nationalistic gamble with some island sheep-farmers, her government would probably have been destroyed after a single term. Had the majority in her cabinet who disagreed with her about the economy been prepared to say boo to a goose, she might have been forced out even before that. In either case her principles, 'Thatcherism', would be a half-forgotten doctrine, mumbled about by historians instead of being the single most potent medicine ever spooned down the gagging post-war British.

Looking back more than a quarter of a century later, the epic events of the early eighties seem to have a clear pattern. Powerful ideas challenge the consensus and, after a nail-biting struggle, defeat the consensus. The early reverses of the Thatcherites, the 'New Right' promising 'a New Enlightenment', are turned into massive, nation-changing victories. Freedom wins. Yet if you stand back and ask what sort of Britain Mrs Thatcher, the grocer's daughter, the devout Lincolnshire Christian, hoped to create, the story is odder. She did not believe in privatizing industries or defeating inflation for merely economic reasons. She wanted to remoralize society, creating a nation whose Victorian values were expressed through secure marriages, self-reliance and savings, restraint, good neighbourliness, hard work. Though much attacked by church leaders she talked of God and morality a lot: 'I am in politics because of the conflict between good and evil.' Yet Thatcherism heralded an age of unparalleled consumption, credit, show-off wealth, quick bucks and sexual libertinism. That is the thing about freedom. When you free people, you can never be sure what you are freeing them for.

In the index to Lady Thatcher's memoirs of her years as Prime Minister, under 'monetary policy', 115 separate page references are given. For 'unemployment' there are fifteen. This is a fair clue to the economic experiment which began immediately after she took office in 1979 and provides the first, the most important, and still the most controversial part of her story. An attentive reader of the Conservative manifesto for the 1979 election would have missed it. After four years of her leadership the Tories were still talking about a wages policy and the importance of consulting with the trade unions, perhaps on the German model. There was talk too of the need to control the money supply and offer council house tenants the right to buy their homes. But other privatization barely featured. Only the comparatively insignificant National Freight Corporation was to be sold. As to unemployment, Mrs Thatcher herself had been vigorously attacking the Labour government for its failure there. In 1977, when it stood at 1.3 million, she had told the country it was absolutely wrong to associate the Tories with people losing their jobs: 'We would have been drummed out of office if we'd

4

had this level of unemployment.' And in case anyone had forgotten the message, the most successful Conservative campaign poster of the election, created by Charles and Maurice Saatchi, her advertising maestros, featured a long queue of gloomy-looking people (in fact Tory activists from North London) filing under a sign reading Unemployment Office, with the headline: 'Labour Isn't Working'.

If voters had studied the new Prime Minister a little more closely they would have noticed a more abrasive edge. She had been aggressive about the failure to control the trade unions – 'Never forget how near this country came to government by picket' – and had already won the insult from the leaders of the Soviet Union of 'Iron Lady' for a powerfully anti-communist speech in 1977. It was an insult that pleased her very much rather as the derisive cartoon lampooning Harold Macmillan as 'Supermac' had become a badge of honour for him and 'Tarzan' would for Michael Heseltine. Irony rarely works with politicians of the first rank. But the voter might then have looked at the people around the Iron Lady and noted just how many of them were old-style mainstream Conservatives in the Heath tradition. To the extent that she was radical, she was clearly completely surrounded and outnumbered. It was calculated that of the possible Tory cabinet members, just two (Keith Joseph and Norman St John Stevas) had actually voted for her in the leadership contest of 1975. There had even been a bizarre notion to lure the former Labour Chancellor, Roy Jenkins, back from Brussels, where he was in rather happy self-imposed exile from British politics, to take over the Treasury again as

Mrs Thatcher's Tory Chancellor. The mind boggles – as it presumably did in 1977, for the offer was never made.[1] A cabinet of ruddy-faced middle-aged Tory squires and former Heath supporters hardly looked like a revolutionary economic cabal. The man who did become Chancellor, Geoffrey Howe, was eye-rubbingly reassuring, blander than warm milk. Denis Healey had memorably compared being attacked by him in the Commons to being savaged by a dead sheep. A magazine competition of the time asked readers to think of a line to use if the door rang one night and neighbours you could not stand were on the doorstep keen to join a party. The winning answer was: 'Oh, do come in. Sir Geoffrey's on sparkling form tonight.' What could possibly be threatening about this lot?

The answer was buried in the personality of the Prime Minister herself, a far more determined woman than most people realized. The single most important influence through her life seems not to have been an economic theorist or even her husband Denis, but her father. Alderman Alfred Roberts was a self-made, austere, hard-working owner of a grocer's shop strategically placed on the main road north from London, the Al, at Grantham in Lincolnshire. He did not believe in fripperies or waste – there was no inside loo or hot running water in Margaret's childhood – and was a strong Methodist. Though an independent in local politics and keen enough for municipal action when he became mayor in 1945, Roberts was of Tory instincts. He was a pillar of the local community in an age when both pillar and community meant something – not only serving as mayor but chairing local charities, the Workers'

Educational Association and acting as a director of a local bank. He was a living exemplar of the kind of independent-minded local politics that would be devastated by the governments of his daughter and her successor. Meanwhile, he taught his daughter to argue. In this he was extremely successful.

Margaret Roberts was not only self-certain but clever. She won a scholarship place at the local grammar school. She went to Oxford to study chemistry, taught by among others the Nobel Prize-winning Dorothy Hodgkin, who rated her, and whose portrait hangs in Downing Street to this day. More significantly, she joined the University Conservatives, something regarded as eccentric in Attlee-era Oxford. Her early career was as an industrial chemist and she can be blamed for the waxy, air-filled texture of cheap ice creams sold from vans in summertime. She moved on to become a tax barrister, though not the kind who used the Bar as a training for politics. Tax law and chemistry meant an attention to facts and to detail. None of this was glamorous. At Oxford and in London, she was more the anonymous hard worker, like that other provincial Methodist who recoiled from public schoolboy flash, young Harold Wilson. But she was a Tory and ambitious; unlike Wilson who kept his Yorkshire accent as a badge of belonging, she lost her Lincolnshire burr as a passport in her direction of travel. In the words of her biographer Hugo Young, she 'was born a northerner but became a southerner, the quintessence of a Home Counties politician'.

Her two failed attempts to enter Parliament for Dartford in Kent brought her the other crucial figure in her life, her husband Denis. A divorced

Kent businessman who had had a good war, his political views were to the right of hers. A keen rugby coach and good golfer, he would become much satirized later as bumbling and henpecked, always with a large G&T in one hand a nervous glance for She Who Must Be Obeyed. In fact Denis was a highly successful executive, rising through the sale of a family paint and chemicals company to the top of Burmah Oil, and retiring very rich in 1975. He provided her with the money and the political, moral support which allowed them to have twins while Mrs Thatcher, as she now was, devoted herself to politics. In the eighties, he managed to keep out of the limelight so that his hard-right views on South Africa, immigrants, the BBC and the feckless working classes created no scandal.

It was a loving marriage which sustained her superbly. In the fifties there was nothing distinctive about the politics of his young wife. It was enough that she was fighting to win a seat as one of the very few women in the Commons, something achieved when she was elected for the well-off middle-class seat of Finchley in 1959. Her politics were formed, nevertheless, by the experience of the post-war years. Seen from above, the socialist experiment in planning and fair shares might have looked noble, she concluded. But from below it was a maze of deprivation, shortage and envy. The Housewives' League has been mentioned earlier in this book. Far later, Thatcher looked back: 'No one who lived through austerity, who can remember snoek, Spam and utility clothing, could mistake the petty jealousies, minor tyrannies, ill-neighbourliness and sheer sourness of those years for idealism and equality.'[2]

As we have seen, Thatcher had risen quietly through the party until as Heath's Education Secretary she had presided over a joyous, reckless slaughter of grammar schools and played her part in the high-spending consensus policies she later repudiated. When Joseph had his great conversion to free-market economics and monetarism she was with him but still several paces behind. She had won the leadership from Heath to general stupefaction and had been patronized and sneered at as Opposition leader. Only a few commentators had spotted what was coming. In romantic vein the former Labour MP and now television interviewer Brian Walden was telling people that the country needed someone like Margaret Thatcher: 'In years to come great novels and poems will be written about her.'[3] But this was not the general view. During the 1979 election, using all the skills of her new image-makers and advertising agency, and with a shrewd understanding of the importance of television, she was still trailing Callaghan in the personal popularity stakes, by six points at the beginning of the campaign and a whopping nineteen points by the end. It was Labour unpopularity that cost the party power, not Mrs Thatcher's allure.

The quotation chosen for her to say as she stood for the first time as prime minister on the steps of Number Ten was popularly but wrongly attributed to St Francis of Assisi. It was in fact Victorian. It was also endlessly used to show what a hypocrite she was. Taking what she said as a whole, this is not fair. It read: 'Where there is discord, may we bring harmony. Where there is error, may we bring truth. Where there is doubt, may we bring faith. Where

9

there is despair, may we bring hope.' The harmony, it is fair to say, she rather fell down on. As for truth, in politics it is in the eye of the observer. But for the people she had determined to govern for, the inflation-ravaged and despairing middle classes who doubted whether Britain had a future and believed the unions could never be tamed by the State, she brought both faith and hope. And more than any Prime Minister since the war, she made the difference herself. Without her the Tory government of 1979–83 would have been entirely different. Without that confrontational self-certainty and determination not to be bested, Britain would have been back with a pay policy, Keynesian public spending policies and a business-as-usual deal with the European Community within eighteen months. Only a few had the chance to see the real Thatcher before she won power. The British ambassador in Iran was one. In 1978 he had been with her on a visit to Tehran, when she suddenly said that there were still people in the Conservative Party who believed in consensus politics. The ambassador, Sir Anthony Parsons, replied that most British people did, including him. 'I regard them as Quislings, as traitors,' she replied. Strong language? 'I know. I mean it.' The 'Assisi' quotation was pious and a hostage to events but it was not cynical. Had people been able to hear her words to Parsons at the time, they would have had the full picture.

The crucial issue was grip, which in 1979 meant gripping inflation, which to the Thatcherites meant monetarism. As we have seen, modern monetarism originated in the fifties but had only really become fashionable by the mid-seventies after Heath and

Barber let the money supply out of control and huge inflation followed. Its most prominent theorist, the American economist Milton Friedman, was awarded the Nobel Prize in 1975. Denis Healey had pursued a policy of restraining public spending through cash limits and tax rises which had the effects monetarism suggested, though never believing in the numbers and targets he was obliged to publish. The basic proposition of monetarism is almost universally accepted, which is that inflation is related to the quantity of money in the economy. Where it diverges from Keynesian economics is in arguing that the sole important job of government in economic management is therefore to control the money supply and that this can be scientifically measured and calibrated. The other issues, unemployment, productivity and so on, will eventually resolve themselves. The intellectual attraction is obvious. Conventional economic management had become a horrendously difficult and uncertain business, juggling uncertain and out-of-date information about output, the balance of payments, unemployment, inflation – a game with one too many rules ever to fully grasp. Monetarism swept away all that. Only hold firm to the principle, get the money supply down, and you will succeed. In 1979 it had not been widely tested outside the military dictatorship of Chile.

In practice Thatcher and her tight circle of economic ministers and advisers, who kept the rest of the cabinet in the dark, did have other objectives. They could have restricted the money supply by raising income tax but she was a tax-cutter. Almost immediately Howe cut the basic rate of income tax from 33 per cent to 30 per cent and the top rate from 83 per cent to 60 per cent. Spending cuts were agreed too but to make up the difference a huge rise in value added tax, doubling to 15 per cent, came in. Money was being redistributed from the masses, paying more for meals, clothes and other items, to higher-rate taxpayers. One of the Tory moderates, Jim Prior, following the manifesto, unveiled a bill for trade union reform that banned the closed shop unless 80 per cent of workers wanted it, provided public money for strike and union ballots, and outlawed secondary picketing of the kind that had been so widely seen during the 'winter of discontent'. It would have been radical under another government. Thatcher expressed bitter disappointment that it did not go further and outlaw all secondary action. She castigated him as a 'false squire', one of a class of Tories who 'have all the outward show of a John Bull – ruddy face, white hair, bluff manner – but inwardly they are political calculators who see the task of Conservatives as retreating gracefully before the Left's inevitable advance.'[4] This was a mean and foolish verdict; Prior was simply a shrewd politician, taking one step at a time. In frustration Thatcher suddenly announced that strikers would now be assumed to be getting union strike pay and so would not qualify for social security. The battle lines were being clearly set.

Howe pursued his strategy through a second Budget in 1980 setting out the scientific sounding Medium-Term Financial Strategy, or MTFS, with detailed predictions about the growth of the chosen measurement of money, sterling M3. But with inflation raging, a recession biting and credit restrictions loosened, it was impossible to enforce, just as Healey had predicted. The money supply was meant to be growing for 1980–1 at around 8 per cent but actually grew at nearly 19 per cent. The monetarists risked looking like fools. Strike-ravaged and low-productivity British Leyland came begging for yet more money but instead of telling the State carmaker to close, or ordering it to be sold off, Thatcher gave way, very much as Heath had when Rolls-Royce had tested his opposition to bail-outs. Rolls-Royce eventually thrived, however, while BL died. There was a steel strike and though the government talked tough and stood firm, the eventual settlement was high and the unions were certainly not humiliated. By the second half of the year unemployment was up by more than 800,000 and hundreds of manufacturing businesses were going bust, throttled by the rising exchange rate. Industrialists, who had looked to the Tories with such delight, were beginning to despair. Prices were up by 22 per cent in a year, wages by a fifth. At the Tory conference of 1980 cabinet dissidents began to make speeches subtly criticizing the whole project. These coded bat-squeaks of alarm, demonstrating early on that the Tory left had little real fight in it, were dismissed by Thatcher in a phrase found for her by the playwright Ronald Millar: 'You turn if you want to. The lady's not for turning.'

The word 'wet' was a public schoolboy term meaning soppy or weak. It was being applied by monetarist Tories to their Heathite opponents by the mid-seventies. In the great Thatcher cabinet battles of the early eighties it was appropriated to refer particularly to the senior ministers who did not agree with her – notably Prior, Francis Pym, Sir Ian Gilmour, Mark Carlisle, Norman St John Stevas, Peter Walker, Christopher Soames and (arguably) Michael Heseltine. All had subtly different analyses but all were panicking about the deflation being visited upon an already weak economy by Howe. She would punish them for their lack of faith. They were in the majority and had they revolted the history of Britain would have been very different. But 'wet' was accurate in a wider sense. They rarely tried to face her down, they did not settle on joint action to make her change course and though there were many threats to resign on points of principle, the cabinet dissidents waited till she fired or demoted them.

The great confrontation would have come in 1981. Howe believed that despite unemployment at 2.7 million and heading towards 3 million, despite the economy continuing to shrivel, with new bankruptcies being reported by the day and the biggest collapse in industrial production in a single year since 1921, and despite the lack of any clear control over the money supply, he must go further still. Swingeing cuts and rises in taxes, this time by freezing tax thresholds, would take a further £4 bn out of the economy. Thatcher told her new economic adviser Alan Walters that 'they may get rid of me for this' but that it would be worth it for doing the right thing. Outside her circle, it seemed anything but right. Famously, 364 economists wrote to the papers denouncing the policies. The Conservatives crashed to third place in the opinion polls behind the SDP and the left-wing Labour Party of Michael Foot. On the streets rioting seemed to be confirming all the worst fears of those who had predicted that monetarism would tear the country apart.

This was the moment when Thatcher's self-certainty would be tested most clearly. Any normal politician would have flinched. Churchill, Macmillan, Heath, Wilson and Callaghan would have ordered in the Chancellor and called quietly for a change in direction, blowing smoke in all directions to hide the retreat. Thatcher egged her Chancellor on. If anything, she thought he had not gone far enough. In ringing terms she told the Tory Party faithful to stay calm and strong: 'This is the road I am resolved to follow. This is the path I must go. I ask all who have spirit – the bold, the steadfast and the young at heart – to stand and join with me.' In early April 1981 riots broke out in Brixton. Shops were burned and looted, streets barricaded and more than 200 people, most of them police, were injured. Mrs Thatcher's response was to pity the shopkeepers. Lord Scarman was asked to hold a public inquiry; but in the first week of July, trouble began again, this time in the heavily Asian west London suburb of Southall, with petrol-bombs, arson attacks and widespread pelting of the police. Then Toxteth in Liverpool erupted, the worst of all, and continued for nearly two weeks. Black youths, then whites, petrol-bombed the police, waved guns and burned both cars and buildings. The police responded with CS gas, the first time it had been used on the streets of mainland Britain, and with baton charges. As in London, hundreds were injured and here one man was killed. Toxteth was followed by outbreaks of looting and arson in Manchester's Moss Side.

With unemployment reaching 60 per cent among

young blacks, and both Liverpool and Manchester having suffered badly from recent factory closures, many saw this as clearly linked to the Thatcher–Howe economics; what Denis Healey, from opposition, was now calling 'sado-monetarism'. (He had called it punk monetarism but his children told him this was unfair to punk rockers.) Michael Heseltine at his own insistence was despatched for a series of extraordinarily frank exchanges with young black men in Toxteth. He took up their frank allegations of racism with the local police and bullied local bankers and industrialists into coming with him to see how bad conditions were at first hand. Back in London he wrote a famous internal memorandum, 'It Took a Riot', calling for a change of industrial and social polices to help places like Toxteth – government money to bring in private investment, job creation schemes and a minister for Liverpool, for the next year at least; Heseltine argued that anything less was not compatible with the best traditions of the Tory Party. He stuck with Liverpool for well over a year, helping bring renovation projects, new money and a morale-boosting garden festival, attended by 3 million people.

Mrs Thatcher knew a rival when she saw one. There was only room in this party for one blonde. She described the Heseltine initiative merely as 'skilful public relations'. She had also visited Liverpool and drew very different conclusions:

> I had been told that some of the young people involved got into trouble through boredom and not having enough to do. But you only had to look at the grounds around

16

these houses with the grass untended, some of it almost waist high, and the litter, to see this was a false analysis. They had plenty of constructive things to do if they wanted. Instead, I asked myself how people could live in such circumstances without trying to clear up the mess.

The problem was lack of initiative and self-reliance created by years of dependency on the State, and compounded by the media. It was nothing whatever to do, she snorted, with sterling M3*. No better expression can be found of the gap between the monetarist true believers and the old Tories.

Her views unaltered, Thatcher then went into full-scale battle with the 'wets'. The provocation on both sides was Howe's discovery that after the ferocious Budget of 1981, he would need to implement yet another tight squeeze in the coming year. Another £5 bn cut was needed for the 1982 Budget. There was something like a full-scale cabinet revolt. Heseltine, fresh from Liverpool, warned of despair and electoral meltdown. Other ministers called for a return to planning, warned wildly of what had happened in Hitler's Germany and, in the case of Gilmour, lethally quoted Churchill too: 'However beautiful the strategy, you should occasionally look at the results.' Even monetarist true believers seemed to be deserting. Thatcher herself called it one of the bitterest arguments in a cabinet in her time. She became extremely angry. She had once said that

* Thatcher's favoured measurement of the money in circulation, and hence shorthand for monetarism.

given six strong men, she could get through what was ahead. Now she was well short. Drawing the meeting to a close, she prepared to counter-attack. St John Stevas had already been sacked. Now Soames, Mark Carlisle and Gilmour went too, while Prior was moved away from the centre, to Northern Ireland. She had realized she could afford to take her internal critics out, department by department, clever riposte by clever riposte.

They might have guessed. It was not just on the economy that she was, by the old standards of the seventies, ferociously determined. In a series of strikes she had intervened to stop ministers settling with public sector workers, even when it would have been cheaper to do so. She had already shown her contempt for the top civil servants. She had kept the trade union leaders locked out. Len Murray, the TUC chairman who had spent half the Wilson and Callaghan years sitting round tables with the two of them, lugubriously grazing on the taxpayers' sandwiches, was allowed into Downing Street just three times in Mrs Thatcher's first five years. But the best evidence of the Thatcher style to date had been the struggle with the other European leaders to reclaim roughly £1 bn a year of net British payment to the Community – or, in Thatcherspeak, to get our money back. Doing so involved an anti-diplomatic brawl that careered from Dublin to Luxembourg and from Luxembourg to Brussels. She would not shut up and she would not back down.

The German Chancellor, Helmut Schmidt, pretended to go to sleep and the French President, Valéry Giscard d'Estaing, began to read a newspaper, then got his cars outside to rev

18

their engines – not a subtle hint. She was entirely unfazed. In an epic four-hour meeting over dinner, she simply refused to shut up. Diplomats from all sides suggested interesting side-deals, trade-offs, honourable compromises. She brushed them all aside. Astonishingly, in the end, she got three-quarters of what she had first demanded. Astonishingly, she then said 'No.' It was only when almost her entire cabinet were in favour of settlement that she grudgingly agreed, like a bloodied prizefighter desperate for just another slug, hauled away by worried friends. She might have had the mother of all makeovers – softer voice, softer hair, better teeth – but she was a raw, double-or-quits killer when she was cornered. The press and the country were beginning to notice it. And she wanted supporters, not colleagues, alongside her. Into the ring came Nigel Lawson, Cecil Parkinson and Norman Tebbit. She would need them. For a while chaos inside the Labour Party had helped protect her from the electoral consequences of her move away from the centre-ground. The Tories might be hated but Labour were unelectable.

The Left at War With Itself

Civil wars tend to start with arguments about constitutions, which are always about raw power. Labour's was no different. In its detail it was mind-dazingly complicated. It involved a host of organizations on the left, an alphabet soup of campaigns, coordinating committees and institutes

19

run by people most of whom then disappeared from public life. It began with arguments which seemed merely about party rules, such as whether or not MPs should be able to be sacked by their local parties, and the exact percentage of votes for a Labour leader held by the unions, the party activists and MPs. It was nasty, personal, occasionally physical, and so disgusted the outside world that Labour very nearly disappeared as an effective organization. Those who mocked the smoothness and blandness of Tony Blair's New Labour rarely remembered the voter-repelling punch-up that preceded it. This fight would be fought far from Westminster, in the bars and halls of Blackpool, Brighton and Wembley at Labour and trade union conferences. The issue was simply control – who ran the Labour Party and where was it going?

There was widespread bitterness about what was considered to be the right-wing politics of the defeated Wilson-Callaghan government, and the paltry number of conference decisions which had actually made it into Labour's election manifesto. For years lobby groups had beavered away to change the party's policy, then finally won some 'historic' conference vote, only to see the Labour leadership ignore it all, and then lose anyway. Callaghan, for instance, had simply vetoed an elaborately prepared pledge to abolish the Lords. At the angry Labour conference of 1979 the party's general secretary, no less, told him he wished 'our prime minister would sometimes act in our interests like a Tory prime minister acts in their interests'. One former Labour MP, Tom Litterick, angrily flung a pile of Labour handbooks whose pledges on Europe, housing, women's rights, the disabled and so on had been ditched by Callaghan from the manifesto: ' "Jim will fix it," they said. Aye, he fixed it. He fixed all of us. He fixed me in particular.'[5]

In this atmosphere, the left wanted to take power away from right-wing MPs and the traditional leaders and carry out a revolution from below. They believed that if they could control the party manifesto, choose the leader and bring the MPs to heel, they could turn Labour into a radical socialist party and then, when Thatcher's economics destroyed her, win a general election. Some idea of their ultimate objective is clear from the agenda voted through at Labour's October 1980 conference at Blackpool, which called for taking Britain out of the EC, unilateral nuclear disarmament, the closing of US bases in Britain, no incomes policy and State control of the whole of British industry, plus the creation of a thousand peers to abolish the House of Lords. Britain would become a North Sea Cuba. The Trotskyite Militant Tendency, which had infiltrated the Labour Party, believed in pushing socialist demands so far that the democratic system would collapse and full class revolution would be provoked. Benn, who thought that 'their arguments are sensible and they make perfectly good radical points', saw Militant as no more of a threat than the old *Tribune* group or the pre-war Independent Labour Party. Always a thoroughly decent man, Benn believed the left would end up with a thoroughly decent socialist victory. In fact thuggish intimidation in many local Labour parties by Militants was driving moderate members away in droves. In alliance with them were many mainstream trade unionists who simply felt let down by the Callaghan and Wilson governments;

21

left-wing activists who were not Marxists, and those who were driven above all by single causes such as nuclear disarmament.

Shrewd tactics and relentless campaigning enabled a small number of people to control enough local parties and union branches to have a disproportionate effect in Labour conference votes, where the big and undemocratic union block votes no longer automatically backed the leadership. At the 1980 conference the left won almost every important vote, utterly undermining Callaghan, who quit as leader two weeks later. Because new leadership rules were not yet in place, awaiting a special conference in January, Labour MPs had one final chance to choose their new leader. Michael Foot, the old radical and intellectual who had begun his time in Opposition, characteristically, by composing a book of essays about Swift, Hazlitt, Paine, Disraeli and other literary-political heroes, was persuaded to stand. Benn would have had no chance among Labour MPs, many of whom now saw him as a menacing figure, allied with the Trotskyist sans-culottes outside who would take away their privileges. But Foot was a great parliamentarian and someone had to be found to beat Denis Healey. The former Chancellor, whose natural pugnacity and abusive wit made him plenty of enemies at party conference, had become the villain of the Labour left.

Early on Healey had pinpointed the fatal flaw in their strategy which was that if they did take over the Labour Party, the country wouldn't vote for it. Activists, he told them, were different from 'the great mass of the British people, for whom politics is something to think about once every year at

22

most'.[6] His robust remarks about what would later be called the loony left were hardly calculated to maximize his chances, despite his popularity in the country at the time. At any rate he was eventually beaten by Foot by 139 votes to 129. There are plenty who believe that Foot, who would endure much mockery as a party leader for his shabby appearance and rambling media performances, was actually the man who saved the Labour Party since he was the only leader remotely acceptable to both the old guard and the Bennite insurgents. It was a job that Foot took on entirely out of a sense of duty. With his old-style platform oratory, his intellectualism and his stick, he was always an unlikely figure to topple Margaret Thatcher. Worzel Gummidge against the Iron Lady; it was the stuff of children's pop-up books. It was also the last blast of a romantic socialist intellectualism against the free market.

The left marched on. At the special party conference Labour's rules were indeed changed to give the unions 40 per cent of the votes for future Labour leaders, the activists in the constituencies 30 per cent and the once-dominant MPs only 30 per cent. Labour's struggle now moved to its next and decisive stage, with the left in exuberant mood. It was decided that Benn must challenge Healey for the deputy leadership the following year. This would signal an irreversible move. A Foot-Benn Labour Party was a very different proposition from one in which Healey had a strong voice. Both sides saw it as the final battle. Around the country Benn went campaigning with verve and relentless energy. At public meetings, Healey was booed and heckled and spat at. The vote was clearly going to be very close though with the complicated new electoral college system, no one knew how close.

At this point, two other characters need to be reintroduced, both miners' sons, both left-wingers, both men who had made their names by attacking Heath, one on picket lines and the other on the floor of the Commons. They were Arthur Scargill, the NUM boss, and Neil Kinnock. The intimidation of anyone who would not back Benn was getting worse though Benn himself sailed imperturbably through all that, apparently not noticing what was being said and done in his name. Scargill was one of the most aggressive, enough to finally provoke Kinnock into deciding that he could not support Benn. Nor could he support Healey, a right-winger. So he would abstain. He announced his decision in the Labour newspaper *Tribune*. Kinnock had been slowly moving away from the hard left, and had taken a position as the party's education spokesman. He had run Foot's campaign. Popular in the party, he was regarded with increasing suspicion by Benn himself. But this open break with the left's champion shocked many of his friends. At the conference in Brighton, Benn was eventually beaten by Healey by a whisker, less than one per cent of the votes. Kinnock and Scargill clashed angrily on television. The seaside town was awash with ugly scenes and talk of betrayal. Kinnock was involved in several scuffles and finally, when attacked by a man in a public toilet, 'beat the shit out of him ... apparently there was blood and vomit all over the floor'. It was the inelegant end to an inelegant revolt; after that the left would be powerful in the party but could never hope to seize it.

The Nice Gang

By then, however, many thought it was already too late. For a breakaway had begun and a new party was being formed. The idea had come first from Roy Jenkins before the Bennite revolt, as he contemplated the state of the British party system from his grand offices in Brussels, where he was President of the Commission. Offered a BBC lecture in 1979 to ruminate about the future, he argued that perhaps the two-party system established since Victorian times had come to the end of its useful life. Coalitions, he said, were not such a bad thing. It was time to strengthen 'the radical centre' and find a way through that accepted the free market economy but which also took unemployment seriously. His lecture was coded, tentative but clear enough. He was no longer a Labour politician and he was looking around. He was in touch with David Steel, the Liberal leader, but felt that although he was close to Liberal thinking, only a new party would give British politics the hard poke it needed. Always a famous host, he began holding lunches for old friends from the right of the Labour party, including Bill Rodgers, who was still in the shadow cabinet, and Shirley Williams, who had lost her seat but was still one of the best-liked politicians in the country. Then Jenkins made a second speech to journalists and their guests, Kinnock among them, in the Commons where he speculated more openly about a new party as 'an experimental plane' which might just take off. At this stage the public reaction from

Labour MPs was discouraging. Williams had said that a new centre party would have 'no roots, no principles, no philosophy and no values'. David Owen, the young doctor who had been a rare glamorous star as Foreign Secretary in the Callaghan government and was now fighting against unilateral nuclear disarmament, said Labour moderates must stay in the party and fight even if it took ten or twenty years.

The Bennite revolt changed many minds. After the Wembley conference, at which Owen was booed for his views on defence, he, Jenkins, Williams and Rodgers issued the Limehouse Declaration, describing Wembley as 'calamitous' and calling for a new start in British politics. That was duly formalized as the Social Democratic Party or SDP two months later, in March 1981. In total thirteen Labour MPs defected to it and many more might have done had not Roy Hattersley and others fought very hard to persuade them not to. Within two weeks 24,000 messages of support had flooded in and a temporary headquarters, manned by volunteers, had been found. Peers, journalists, students, academics and others were keen to join. The nice people's party was on its way. Public meetings were packed from Scotland to the south coast of England. Media coverage was lavish and flattering. In September an electoral pact was agreed with the Liberal Party after delirious scenes at the party's Llandudno conference, and the Alliance was formed. Trains proved an unlikely theme of the new party, with the SDP holding (literally) rolling conferences for their first two years, journalists and politicians crammed together singing their way round provincial Britain. After

26

giving Labour a terrible shock in the Warrington by-election, the SDP won their first seat when Shirley Williams took Crosby from the Conservatives in November, with nearly half the votes cast, followed by Jenkins winning Glasgow Hillhead from the Tories the following year. Some sense of the early excitement can be captured by the thought that had they taken their stratospheric opinion poll ratings seriously (which sensibly they did not) the SDP could have expected to win nearly 600 out of the then 635 parliamentary seats.

His victory allowed Jenkins to become the leader of the party in the Commons. But he had lost his old mastery of the place; or perhaps leading a rump group caught between Thatcher's Conservatives and the baleful Labour ex-comrades was simply impossible. In due course Jenkins would lose his seat at the general election and Owen would take over as leader. The personality problems that would later cause such mayhem were soon unavoidable. David Owen was handsome, romantic, arrogant, dogmatic, Welsh, patriotic and never a team player. He had always believed that leadership was more rightly his and feared that Jenkins was leading the SDP towards a merger with the Liberals. Owen saw himself still as a socialist although of a new kind. Jenkins, for his part, found his old protégé Owen prickly and arrogant. In short, their relationship was every bit as cordial as that between Tony Blair and Gordon Brown in later years. As with that, personal rivalry did hold the party back. The upsurge of the SDP shook even Mrs Thatcher, while it led some in the Labour Party to fear their cause was finished.

It also gave a new lease of life to the Liberals. In

27

the early fifties, the once mighty party of Gladstone and Asquith had been a negligible force, down to half a dozen MPs and 3 per cent of the national vote. Under Jo Grimond it had enjoyed a revival as the party of genuine liberalism and in the sixties it attracted an increasingly radical wing, anti-nuclear, anti-apartheid, in favour of community politics and, in general, amiably stroppy. Liberal conferences were distinguished by stalls of organic apples, large hairy men in sandals and enthusiasts for obscure forms of land taxation, as if a medieval fair had somehow collided with a chartered surveyors' seaside outing. Yet so great was the public disenchantment with conventional politics that this unlikely caravan rumbled ahead, particularly under the flamboyant, dandyish, sharp-witted Jeremy Thorpe. Faced with allegations about a homosexual affair and a murder plot (though only a dog perished, and the prosecution failed), Thorpe resigned. By the early eighties the party was being led by Steel, 'the boy David', looking for a strategy. The SDP provided a route back to the centre ground but Owen was not alone in despising the Liberals and the eventual merger between the parties was bitter and difficult. Nevertheless, by the early spring of 1982 the SDP and Liberals could look forward with some confidence to breaking the mould of British politics. Mrs Thatcher was hugely unpopular. Labour was in uproar. What could possibly go wrong?

The Falklands:
Big Hair and Bald Men

One of the many ironies of the Thatcher story is that she was rescued from the political consequences of her monetarism by the blunders of her hated Foreign Office. In the great economic storms of 1979–81, and on the European budget battle, she had simply charged ahead, ignoring all the flapping around her in pursuit of a single goal. In the South Atlantic she would do exactly the same and with her great luck she was vindicated. A pattern was being established – 'blinkered and proud of it' – and she would move in the space of a couple of months from being one of the least popular prime ministers ever to being an unassailable national heroine. It could all so easily have gone wrong. A few more fuses working on Argentine bombs, another delivery of French-made Exocet missiles, a different point chosen for the attack, and the Falklands War could have been a terrible disaster, confirming an Argentine dictatorship in power and ending Mrs Thatcher's political career. Of all the gambles in modern British public life, sending a task-force of ships from the shrunken and underfunded Royal Navy 8,000 miles away to take back some islands by force was one of the more extreme.

On both sides, the conflict derived from colonial quarrels. The Falkland Islands had been named after a Royal Navy treasurer when English sailors first landed there in 1690 and though there had been Spanish and French settlements, the scattering of islands had been declared a British colony in 1833. Argentina, formed out of old Spanish colonies, had claimed them from the start too on the basis of proximity. By the sixties, the economic future of the 1,800 islanders who depended on sheep-farming and fishing looked bleak and the Foreign Office was clearly keen to somehow dispose of the problem. Labour had sent a submarine at one point to warn off an increasingly menacing Argentina. Under the Conservatives, however, a couple of serious mistakes were made. First there was a proposal to give sovereignty to the Argentines, but to lease back management of the islands for a fixed period, so that their Britishness would remain intact. Margaret Thatcher later distanced herself from the whole idea, but it was seriously entertained at the time and only withdrawn after protests from the islanders and angry backbench criticism. Then came the announced withdrawal of the only British naval vessel in the region, a patrol vessel HMS *Endurance,* while the Falkland islanders were given no special status in new legislation on British nationality. In Buenos Aires a newly installed junta under General Leopoldo Galtieri thought it understood what was going on. Galtieri was heavily dependent on the backing of the Argentine navy, itself passionately keen on taking over the islands, known to Argentina as the Malvinas. The following year would see the 150th anniversary of British ownership which the Argentines feared would somehow be used to reassert the Falklands' British future. The junta misread Whitehall's lack of policy and concluded that an invasion would be easy, popular and never reversed.

In March an Argentine ship tested the waters, or rather the land of South Georgia, a small dependency south of the Falklands, landing scrap-metal dealers there without warning. Then on 1 April the main invasion began, a landing by Argentine troops which had been carefully prepared for by local representatives of the national airline. In three hours it was all over, and the eighty British marines surrendered, having nonetheless killed five Argentine soldiers and injured seventeen with no losses of their own. In London, there was mayhem. Thatcher had had a few hours' warning of what was happening from the Defence Secretary, John Nott. Calling a hurried meeting in her Commons office, she had to wait while the Chief of the Naval Staff, Sir John Leach, was rescued by a Tory whip after being detained by the Commons police, who had not recognized him in his civilian clothes. But Leach made the difference, giving her clarity and hope when her ministers offered confusion. He was her kind of man. He told her he could assemble a task-force of destroyers, frigates and landing craft, led by Britain's two remaining aircraft carriers, *Hermes* and *Invincible*. The task-force would be ready to sail within forty-eight hours and the islands could be retaken by force. She told him to go ahead. She would decide later whether to authorize it to actually try to re-invade the islands. Could some kind of deal be done?

A part of the Falklands story not revealed at the time was the deep involvement, and embarrassment, of the United States. Mrs

31

Thatcher and Ronald Reagan had already begun to develop a personal special relationship. But the Argentine junta was important to the US for its anti-communist stance and as a trading partner. The United States began a desperate search for a compromise while Britain began an equally frantic search for allies at the United Nations. In the end, Britain depended on the Americans not just for the Sidewinder missiles underneath her Harrier jets, without which Thatcher herself said the Falklands could not have been retaken, but for intelligence help and – most of the time – diplomatic support too. These were the last years of the Cold War. Britain mattered more in Washington than any South American country. Still, many attempts were made by the US intermediary, the Secretary of State, Alexander Haig, to find a compromise. They would continue throughout the fighting. Far more of Thatcher's time was spent reading, analysing and batting off possible deals than contemplating the military plans. Among those advising a settlement was the new Foreign Secretary, Francis Pym, appointed after the thoroughly decent Lord Carrington had insisted on resigning to atone for his department's sins. Pym and the Prime Minister were at loggerheads over this and she would punish him in due course. She had furious conversations with Reagan by phone as he tried to persuade her that some outcome short of British sovereignty, probably involving the United States, was acceptable.

But as with the European budget Thatcher broke down the diplomatic deal-making into undiplomatic irreducibles. Would the islanders be allowed full self-determination? Would the Argentine aggression be rewarded? Under pulverizing pressure she refused to budge. She was confronted too by a moral question she did not duck, which was that many healthy young men were likely to die or be horribly injured, to defend a word, sovereignty. In the end, almost a thousand did die, one for every two islanders, and many others were burned, maimed and psychologically wrecked. But she argued that the whole structure of national identity and law were in play. She wrote to President Reagan, who had described the Falklands as 'that little ice-cold bunch of land down there', that if Britain gave way to the various Argentine snares, 'the fundamental principles for which the free world stands would be shattered'. Reagan kept trying. Pym pressed. The Russians harangued. Michael Foot, who had been bellicose at first, now entreated her to find an answer. Later she insisted that she was vividly aware of the blood-price that was waiting and not all consumed by lust for conflict. As it happened, the Argentine junta, divided and belligerent, ensured that a serious deal was never properly put. Their political position was even weaker than hers. Buenos Aires always insisted that the British task-force be withdrawn from the entire area; that Argentine representatives take part in any interim administration and that if talks failed Britain would lose sovereignty.

Politically, Thatcher had believed that from the start that to cave in would finish her. The press and the Conservative Party were seething about the original diplomatic blunders. Pressed to the wall, even Labour seemed to be in favour of force to recapture the islands, with Foot harking back to the appeasement of fascism in the thirties. For the SDP

David Owen was as belligerent as any Tory. Thatcher established a small war cabinet, keeping her Chancellor, and hence mere money, out of it. Nor were the politicians out of touch with the mood of the country. The polls showed anger with the government for allowing the invasion to happen. So the task-force, now up to more than twenty vessels strong, was steadily reinforced. Eventually it would comprise more than a hundred ships and 25,000 men. The world was transfixed, if also bemused. The headline on a New York paper read 'The Empire Strikes Back.'

Well so it did. By the end of the month South Georgia was recaptured and a large number of Argentine prisoners taken: Thatcher urged questioning journalists simply to 'rejoice, rejoice'. Then came one of the most controversial episodes in this short war. A British submarine, the *Conqueror,* was following the ageing but heavily armed Argentine cruiser, the *Belgrano.* The British task-force was exposed and feared a pincer movement, although the *Belgrano* later turned out to be outside an exclusion zone announced in London, and steaming away from the fleet. With her military commanders at Chequers Thatcher authorized a submarine attack. The *Belgrano* was sunk, with the loss of 321 sailors. The *Sun* newspaper cheered: 'Gotcha!' The Labour MP Tam Dalyell, a rare early opponent of the war in the Commons, began a lonely campaign to show that the sinking was politically motivated and immoral, possibly connected to an attempt to scotch the latest peace move. Soon afterwards, a British destroyer, HMS *Sheffield,* was hit by an

Argentine Exocet missile. Forty died and she later sank. The war had started for real.

On 18 May 1982 the war cabinet agreed that landings on the Falklands should go ahead, despite lack of full air cover and worsening weather. By landing at the unexpected bay of San Carlos in low cloud, British troops got ashore in large numbers. Heavy Argentine air attacks, however, took a serious toll. Two frigates were badly damaged, another was sunk, then another, then a destroyer, then a container ship with vital supplies. In London the success of the landing seemed on the edge. The requisitioned liner *Queen Elizabeth 2* was nearby, vulnerable and carrying 3,000 troops. Thatcher called it the worst night. And indeed, had the Argentine air force bombs been properly fused for the attacks, far more would have exploded; had their navy had more Exocets, far more would have been launched. Had British Harrier jets not been equipped with the latest US missiles and helped by the secret provision of American AWACS radar cover, the situation would have been desperate. As it was, 3,000 British troops had a secure beach-head and began to fight their way inland. Over the next few weeks they captured the settlements of Goose Green and Darwin, killing 250 Argentine soldiers and capturing 1,400 for the loss of twenty British lives. Colonel 'H' Jones became the first celebrated hero of the conflict when he died leading 2 Para against heavy Argentine fire along with Sergeant Ian McKay of 3 Para.

The battle then moved to the tiny capital, Port Stanley, or rather to the circling hills above it where the Argentine army was dug in on Mount Tumbledown, Wireless Ridge, Sapper Hill and

Mount William. Before the final assault two British landing ships, the *Sir Tristram* and the *Sir Galahad,* were hit by missiles and the Welsh Guards suffered dreadful losses, many of the survivors being badly burned. Ministers talked of losing a ship a day, while at a summit in Versailles Thatcher was again swatting off attempts to halt the fighting by diplomatic means. By now she was determined that nothing short of Argentine surrender would do. The United States, on the other hand, was still desperately hoping to preserve the junta and avoid its humiliation. The scenes at the United Nations were close to farce. They ended after the final attack on the demoralized and badly led Argentine troops forced their leader, General Menendez, to surrender. The British commander arrived at the door of the West Store in Stanley, where many islanders were taking refuge, with the immortal words, 'Hullo, I'm Jeremy Moore. Sorry it's taken rather a long time to get here.'[7]

Many people thought the war mere butchery for a meaningless prize. The most famous comment came from that mordant South American writer Jorge Luis Borges who said it reminded him of two bald men fighting over a comb. Tam Dalyell hounded the Prime Minister with parliamentary questions as he sought to prove the sailors on the *Belgrano* had been killed to keep the war going, not for reasons of military necessity. He was not alone in his outrage. One of the few genuinely dramatic moments in the 1983 election campaign came when Mrs Thatcher was challenged on television about the *Belgrano* by a woman who seemed a match for her, as few men were. Among the Labour leadership, Denis Healey accused her of glorying in slaughter and the next leader, Neil Kinnock, got into trouble when, responding to a heckler who said that at least Margaret Thatcher had guts, he replied that it was a pity other people had had to leave theirs on Goose Green to prove it.

The Falklands War was both throwback and throw-forward. For millions it seemed utterly out of time, a Victorian gunboat war in a nuclear age. Yet for more millions still (it was a popular war) it was a wholly unexpected and almost mythic symbol of rebirth. Margaret Thatcher herself lost no time in telling the country what she thought the war had meant. Speaking at Cheltenham racecourse in early July, she said: 'We have ceased to be a nation in retreat. We have instead a newfound confidence, born in the economic battles at home and found true 8,000 miles away ... Printing money is no more. Rightly this government has abjured it. Increasingly this nation won't have it ... That too is part of the Falklands factor.' The old country had rekindled her old spirit, she concluded: 'Britain found herself again in the South Atlantic and will not look back from the victory she has won.' The Toxteth riots may not have had anything to do with sterling M3 but apparently the activities of 2 Para did.

The Falklands War changed Margaret Thatcher's personal story and the country's politics. But it merged into a wider sense that confrontation was required in public life. There was a raw and bloody edge to the spirit of the age. In Northern Ireland, from the spring of 1981, a hideous IRA hunger-strike was going on, which would lead to the death of Bobby Sands and nine others. 'A convicted criminal,' Margaret of Lincolnshire briskly called him. 'He chose to take his own life. It was a choice that his organisation did not allow to many of its victims.' As with civil service strikers or the United Nations peace party, Thatcher was utterly determined not to flinch, as rock-hard as her ruthless Irish republican enemies. They had assassinated Lord Mountbatten in 1979 and the mainland bombing campaign went on, with attacks on the Chelsea barracks, then the Hyde Park bombings, when eight people were killed and fifty-three injured. And, indeed, none of them were offered any choice.

Overhanging the violence at home and part of the backdrop of the Falklands War, was the residual fear of global nuclear war. With hindsight the grey old Soviet Union of Brezhnev, Andropov and Chernenko may seem a rusted giant, clanking helplessly towards its collapse. This was not how it seemed in the early eighties. The various phases of strategic arms reduction treaties were under way but to well-informed and intelligent analysts the Soviet empire still seemed mighty, belligerent and unpredictable. New SS20 missiles were being deployed by the Russians, targeted on cities and military bases across Western Europe. In response, Nato was planning a new generation of American Pershing and Cruise missiles to be sited in Europe, including in Britain. In the late winter of 1979 Russian troops had begun arriving in Afghanistan. Mikhail Gorbachev was an obscure candidate member of the Politburo, twenty-eighth in the pecking order, working on agricultural planning, and *glasnost* was a word no one in the West had heard of. Poland's free trade union movement Solidarity was being crushed by a military dictator.

Western politics echoed with arguments over weapons systems, disarmament strategies and the need to stand up to the Soviet threat. Moscow had early and rightly identified Thatcher as one of its most implacable enemies in the West and when, eighteen months after her election victory, she was joined by a new US President, Ronald Reagan, she had a soul-mate in Washington. Reagan may have been many things Thatcher was not – sunny, lazy, uninterested in detail and happy to run huge deficits. But like her he saw the world in black and white terms, a great stage where good and evil, God and Satan, were pitched in endless conflict. Their shared detestation of socialism in general and the Soviet Union in particular underpinned a remarkably close personal relationship; she was his first overseas visitor after his election; for her he was always 'Ronnie'. To young politicians watching from the wings – people such as Tony Blair – lessons about the effect of a popular war and the importance of keeping close the White House were being quietly absorbed.

To the public who had barely focused on Thatcher a few years earlier, she was now becoming a vividly divisive figure. On one side were those who felt they at last had a warrior queen for hard times, a fighter whose convictions were clear and who would never quit, someone who had cut through the endless dispiriting fudging of earlier decades. On the other were those who saw her as a dangerous and bloodthirsty figure, driven by an inhumanly stark world view. To the cartoonists of the *Sun, Daily Mail* and other right-wing papers she was a Joan of Arc, a glorious Boudicca, surrounded by cringeing wets, apelike trade unionists and spitting Irish terrorists. To the cartoonists of the *Guardian, Daily Mirror* and *Spitting Image* she was simply mad, with sharply curved vulture's beak nose, staring eyes and rivets in her hair. Sexual confusion was rife. She was the only real man in her cabinet, or the ultimate housewife who had seized control of the country; or she was the eerie repudiation of femininity, cold, barren and vengeful. France's President Mitterand, who in fact had quite a good relationship with her, summed up the paradox better than any British observer when, after an early meeting he told his Europe minister, 'She has the eyes of Caligula but she has the mouth of Marilyn Monroe.'

The Falklands War confirmed and underlined these opposing views of Thatcher. In a flush of over-confidence she seized her moment so hard she nearly throttled it. She encouraged the government's internal think tank, the Central Policy Review Staff, to come up with a paper about the future of public spending. They came up with a manifesto which can be summed up as Margaret Thatcher unplugged, what she would have liked to do, unconstrained. They suggested ending state funding of higher education; student loans to replace grants; no increases in welfare payments in line with inflation and the entire replacement of the National Health Service with a system of private health insurance, including charges for doctors' visits and medicines – in effect, the end of the Attlee Welfare State. Though some of these ideas would become widely discussed much later and student loans would be brought in by a Labour government, at the time the prospectus was regarded as bonkers by most of those around her. The Prime Minister battled for it but ministers who regarded it as her worst mistake since coming to power leaked the CPRS report to the press in order to kill it off In this they were successful. The episode was an early indication, long before the poll tax, that Thatcher's charge-ahead politics could produce mistakes as well as triumphs.

The electoral consequences of the Falklands War have been argued about ever since. The government had got inflation down and the economy was at last improving but the overall Conservative record in 1983 was not impressive. The most dramatic de-industrialization of modern times, with hundreds of recently profitable businesses disappearing for ever, had been caused in part by a very high pound, boosted by Britain's new status as an oil producer. This, with the Howe squeeze, was deadly. Later Joseph admitted that 'we hadn't appreciated, any of us' that this 'would lead to such rapid and large de-manning'. Unemployment 'had not been considered a huge problem'.[8] Given the shrinking of the country's industrial base and unemployment at 3 million this was a mistake and a half. Further, this pro-tax-cutting government had seen the total tax burden rise from 34 per cent of GDP to nearly 40 per cent. Public spending, intended to be 40 per cent of GDP, was 44 per cent. The apparently crucial measurement of the money supply showed that it had grown at about double the target.

So there were plenty of large and obvious targets for competent Opposition politicians to take aim at. In an ordinary election the state of the economy would have had the governing party rocking back on their heels. But this was no ordinary election. After the war the Conservatives shot into a sudden and dramatic polls lead over the two Opposition groups now ranged against them, finishing the equally sudden and dramatic rise of the SDP. In the 1983 general election the new party and its partners, the Liberals, took nearly a quarter of the popular vote. But the electoral system rewarded them with just twenty-three MPs, only six being from the SDP, a bitter harvest after the iridescent bubble-year of 1981–2. Labour was nearly beaten into third place in the votes cast. And the Conservatives won a huge victory, giving Mrs Thatcher a majority of 144 seats, a Tory buffer which kept them in power until 1997. Though there were other factors at play it seems perverse to deny that the Falklands conflict was crucial. It gave Thatcher a story to tell about herself and the country which was simple and vivid and made sense to millions.

The Plague

On 4 July 1982, a gay man called Terry Higgins died in St Thomas's Hospital in central London. He was thirty-seven and one of the first British victims of AIDS, acquired immune-deficiency syndrome, that weakens the body's natural defences and is passed through a virus, HIV. A group of his friends set up a small charity in a flat, the Terrence Higgins Trust, to spread the word about AIDS among gay men, encouraging the use of condoms – since it is spread by blood and body fluid contact – and offering support for others. Though the disease had undoubtedly been present in the late seventies, it was first identified in California in 1981 when gay men started to turn up in medical centres complaining of a rare lung disease and a form of skin cancer until then confined to the elderly. Within a year hundreds of cases had been found, many deaths were occuring and it was clear that the vast majority were among homosexual men – though other groups began to be affected, including some women, intravenous drug users, Haitians, and in Uganda villagers suffering from a mysterious and deadly ailment they called 'slim'. The first target in America was the gay bath houses and saunas known for promiscuous, wild and unprotected sex. These had grown up in San Francisco and Los Angeles, and in New York too, as gay men migrated across America during the sixties and seventies to find the most liberal and liberated culture available.

A similar shift had happened in Britain after the legalization of homosexual acts by men. As in America, gay liberation was confined to the most liberal areas of the largest cities only, in this case mainly London – the gay scenes of Manchester, Edinburgh and other towns followed slightly later. Gay clubs, gay discos and gay saunas, the latter really places for as much promiscuous sex as possible, flourished. Men came south and made up for lost time. Something close to a climate of sexual frenzy developed – a frenzy which would later be imitated by heterosexual youngsters on foreign holidays and resorts. After the years of rationing, the sweetie shop was open. Through the seventies, amid the political and economic grime, a street culture of excess flourished. The excess in clothing, music and football violence has already been discussed. It was accompanied for many by a breaking of sexual restraint, the arrival of the freely available pill for heterosexuals and the new climate of legality for homosexuals. If there was optimism around in these years, it was personal – new freedoms that allowed respite from the surrounding climate of national failure.

So the arrival of AIDS came at a particularly cruel time. Just when homosexuals felt the centuries of repression and shame were finally over, along came a deadly and mysterious disease to destroy their new way of life. For social conservatives, this was exactly the point. AIDS was the medical and moral consequence of promiscuous and unnatural sexual behaviour. As you sow, so shall you reap – almost literally. And thus the scene was set for a confrontation between contending moral philosophies that had been at war since the sixties. Gay culture was briefly on the retreat, clubs closed, clerics drew conclusions. Though gay men were at the cutting edge of the AIDS crisis, it had wider implications. It was not only among homosexuals that promiscuity had become more common; in many ways, gay culture had drawn straight culture along in its wake. So for traditionalists there was a message to the whole society, the possibility of a turn away from the new liberalism.

Except, in the end, it did not turn out quite as anyone expected. Gay organizations sprung up to spread the safe sex message very quickly – the Terrence Higgins Trust became a national institution and is now one of the biggest sexual health charities in Europe, with a staff of 300, plus 800 volunteers. The establishment turned out to be far more sympathetic than might have been expected, from Princess Diana opening the first AIDS-specific ward at Middlesex hospital in 1987, to Thatcherite ministers talking about condoms. It was a cultural turning point of a kind, and certainly a national education. In the early days, the media fell prone to 'we're all doomed' panics, and the moral condemnation of homosexuals as unnatural creatures, getting what they deserved. James Anderton, the chief constable of police in greater Manchester, talked of homosexuals 'swirling about in a human cesspit of their own making'. His language was widely condemned, but many millions of Britons, mainly but not exclusively older people, are likely to have agreed with his condemnation of buggery and other 'abominable practices'. Dislike of homosexuality was, and still is, strongly rooted. Alongside this was a prudishness about sex generally, which meant early discussion of how AIDS was transmitted was so vague it simply was not understood.

Tabloid newspapers described the 'gay plague' which could, according to rumours passed on by newspapers, be variously caught from lavatory seats, kisses, handshakes, communion wine or sharing a restaurant fork with an infected person. In the early eighties, the BBC was predicting that 70,000 people in England and Wales would die within four years (nearly twenty-five years later the total death toll is 13,000) and that 'by the end of the century there won't be one family that isn't touched in some way by the disease.' The BBC science programme *Horizon* had led public awareness of

AIDS in the early days, but in 1986 its film about gay men's sex lives and how the disease was actually transmitted was considered so close to the bone that it was banned, and the negatives solemnly destroyed. Yet across the media, as throughout the political world, attitudes changed rapidly. The same newspapers that spoke about buggers getting their just desserts, now enthusiastically promoted AIDS awareness. The homophobic jibes continued but with less self-confidence. Campaigns for abstinence or the reclaiming of gays back into heterosexual life, which have been common among church groups in America, barely touched more secular Britain. Gay Pride parades, which began as angry, edgy affairs in the eighties, slowly became mainstream to the point where politicians rushed to be associated with them. None of this was expected when AIDS first arrived.

In retrospect, part of the shift in attitude happened not in spite of AIDS but because of it. The public health crisis jolted the way sexuality was discussed. There needed to be a new frankness. This wounded, if not fatally, the grand British tradition of titter and snigger. As it became clear that AIDS could be caught from infected needles and blood transfusions, and occasionally through heterosexual sex, the gay stigma was diluted. Indeed, by rapidly changing sexual practices, gay men were for a time ahead of the rest of the population. Coping with AIDS was one of the most effective public information and healthcare stories of modern times. The turn came in 1986 when Norman Fowler, the health secretary, and Willie Whitelaw, Mrs Thatcher's deputy prime minister, were told to create a national public awareness campaign that would be properly effective. Two more conventional and straight men it would be hard to imagine; Fowler's main concern was family values and he was quickly lobbied by church groups, MPs and others to send out a traditionalist moral message of abstinence. He did nothing of the kind. The advertising agency TBWA was commissioned to produce a campaign, 'Don't Die of Ignorance', which would shock the country into changing sexual habits. They came up with an iceberg image, and a gravel-voiced commentary by the actor John Hurt, which began with the words, 'There is now a dreadful disease …' Every single household in Britain received a clear and for the time explicit leaflet.

Over the next few years £73 million was allocated to the campaign. Broadly speaking, it worked. New diagnoses of AIDS, running at more than 3,000 in 1985, fell dramatically over the next few years, staying stable until 1999, when they began to rise again, because of heterosexual cases, mostly connected to Africa, which was undergoing a much worse, indeed genuinely catastrophic pandemic. Because of the wider use of condoms, all sexually transmitted infections fell in the same period, so that cases of syphilis were just a tenth of their pre-AIDS level by the end of the decade. Fowler said later that all the research on his campaign showed that 'the public saw it, that they understood it, that they remembered the campaign, and most of all it actually did change habits'. Britain's figures on the fall of new cases were better than almost any other country's.

The Enemy Within

If the first Thatcher government had been dominated by monetarism and the Falklands War, the second would be dominated by the miners' strike. This was the longest such strike in British history, one of the most bloody and tragic industrial disputes of modern times, and resulted in the total defeat of the miners followed by the virtual end of deep coal-mining in Britain. For Thatcher the lessons were even bigger: 'What the strike's defeat established was that Britain could not be made ungovernable by the Fascist Left. Marxists wanted to defy the law of the land in order to defy the laws of economics. They failed and in doing so demonstrated just how mutually dependent the free economy and a free society really are.' It was a confrontation which was peculiarly soaked in history on all sides. For the Tories, it was essential revenge after the miners' humiliation of Heath, a score they had long been waiting to settle; Margaret Thatcher did indeed speak of 'the enemy within', as compared to Galtieri, the enemy without. For thousands of militant members of the National Union of Mine-workers it was their last chance to end decades of pit closures and save communities under mortal threat. For their leader Arthur Scargill it was an attempt to pull down the government itself and win a class war. As we shall see he was not interested in the detail of pay packets, or in a pit-by-pit discussion of which coalmines were economic. He was determined to force the government, in Thatcher's contemptuous but accurate words, to pay for mud to be mined rather than see a single job lost.

The government had prepared more carefully than Scargill. An early dispute with the NUM had been settled quickly because the battlefield was not yet ready. For two years the National Coal Board had been working with the Energy Secretary, Nigel Lawson, to pile up supplies of coal at the power stations; stocks had steadily grown, while consumption and production both fell. After the Toxteth and Brixton riots the police had been retrained and equipped with full riot gear without which, ministers later confessed, they would have been unable to beat the miners' pickets. Meanwhile, Thatcher had appointed a Scottish-born American, Ian MacGregor, to run the NCB. He had a fierce reputation as a union-buster in the United States and had been brought back to Britain to run British Steel where closures and 65,000 job cuts had won him the title 'Mac the Knife'. He was briefly idolized by the Prime Minister, rather as she admired John King, later Lord King, who had turned round British Airways in the same period, sacking 23,000 staff, about 40 per cent of the total, and turning the loss-maker into a hugely profitable business. These were her tough, no-nonsense men, a refreshing change from the cabinet, though later she would turn against MacGregor, appalled by his lack of political nous. MacGregor's plan was to cut the workforce of 202,000 by 44,000 in two years, then take another 20,000 jobs out. Twenty pits would be closed to begin with. Though elderly and rich, he was no suave PR man. When MacGregor turned up to visit mines he was pelted with flour bombs, abused and, on one occasion, knocked to the ground.

Arthur Scargill seemed to be relishing the fight as much as the Prime Minister. We last glimpsed him in the miners' confrontation with Heath, when he had led the flying pickets at Saltley coke depot, and then tangling with Kinnock during Labour's civil war. Some sense of his unique mix of revolutionary simplicity and wit comes from an exchange he had with the Welsh miners' leader Dai Francis, when he called to ask for flying pickets to come to Birmingham and help at the coke depot. Francis asked when they were needed:

'Tomorrow, Saturday.'

Dai paused: 'But Wales are playing Scotland at Cardiff Arms Park.'

There was a silence and Scargill replied, 'But Dai, the working class are playing the ruling class at Saltley.'[9]

Many found Scargill inspiring; many others found him frankly scary. He had been a Communist and retained strong Marxist views and a penchant for denouncing anyone who disagreed with him as a traitor. Some found a megalomaniac atmosphere at his Barnsley headquarters, already known as Arthur's Castle. Kim Howells, then a Communist and later a New Labour minister, visited him there and was taken aback to find him sitting at 'this Mussolini desk with a great space in front of it' and behind him a huge painting of himself on the back of a lorry, posed like Lenin, urging picketing workers in London to overthrow the ruling class. Howells thought anyone who could put up a painting like that was nuts and returned to express his fears to the Welsh miners. 'And of course the South Wales executive almost to a man agreed with me. But then they said, "He's the only one we've got, see, boy. The Left has decided." '[10]

Scargill had indeed been elected by a vast margin and had set about turning the NUM's once moderate executive into a reliably militant group. His vice-president, Mick McGahey, was a veteran Scottish Communist who, though wiser than Scargill, was no moderate; and the union's general secretary, Peter Heathfield, was well to the left in union politics. Scargill had been ramping up the rhetoric for some time. 'Sooner or later our members will have to stand and fight,' he said repeatedly – not on the traditional issue of wages, but on the very future of coalmining in Britain. He told the NUM conference in 1982, 'If we do not save our pits from closure then all our other struggles become meaningless ... Protection of the industry is my first priority because without jobs all our other claims lack substance and become mere shadows. Without jobs, our members are nothing ...' Given what was about to happen to his members' jobs as a result of the strike, there is a black irony in those words. By adopting a position that no pits should be closed on economic grounds, even if the coal was exhausted – more investment would always find more coal, and from his point of view the losses were irrelevant – he made sure confrontation would not be avoided. Exciting, witty Arthur Scargill brought coalmining to a close in Britain far faster than would have happened had the NUM been led by some prevaricating, dreary old-style union hack.

The NUM votes which allowed the strike to start covered both pay and closures. But from the start

51

Scargill emphasized the closures. To strike to protect jobs, particularly other people's jobs, in other people's villages and other counties' pits, gave the confrontation an air of nobility and sacrifice which a mere wages dispute would not have enjoyed. Neil Kinnock, the new Labour leader, the son and grandson of Welsh miners, found it impossible to forthrightly condemn the aims of the dispute despite his growing detestation of Scargill. As we shall see, it cost him dear. With his air-chopping, flaming rhetoric, Scargill was a formidable organizer and a conference-hall speaker on Kinnock's level. Yet not even he would be able to persuade every part of the industry to strike. Earlier ballots had shown consistent majorities against striking. In Nottinghamshire, 72 per cent of the area's 32,000 miners voted against striking. The small coalfields of South Derbyshire and Leicestershire were against, too. Even in South Wales, half the NUM lodges failed to vote for a strike. Overall, of the 70,000 miners who were balloted in the run-up to the dispute 50,000 had voted to keep working. This is crucial to understanding what happened. Scargill felt he could not win a national ballot so he decided on a rolling series of locally called strikes, coalfield by coalfield, Yorkshire then Scotland, Derbyshire and South Wales. These strikes would merely be approved by the national union. It was a domino strategy; the regional strikes would add up to a national strike, without a national vote.

But Scargill needed to be sure the dominos would fall. He used the famous flying pickets from militant areas and pits to shut down less militant ones. Angry miners were sent in coaches and convoys of cars to close working pits and the coke depots, vital hubs of the coal economy. Without the pickets, who to begin with rarely needed to use violence to achieve their end, far fewer pits would have come out. But after scenes of physical confrontation around Britain, by April 1984 four miners in five were on strike. To Scargill's horror, however, other unions refused to come out in sympathy, robbing him of a re-run of the 1929 General Strike. It became clear that the NUM had made other historic errors. Kinnock was not the only one from a mining background baffled as to why Scargill had opted to strike in the spring, when the demand for energy was relatively low. The stocks at the power stations were not running down at anything like the rate the NUM hoped, as confidential briefings from the power workers confirmed. It seemed the government could indeed sit this one out. There were huge set-piece confrontations with riot-equipped police bussed up from London or down from Scotland, Yorkshire to Kent, Wales to Yorkshire, generally used outside their own areas to avoid mixed loyalties. It was as if the country had been taken over by historical re-enactments of civil war battles, the Sealed Knot society run rampant. Aggressive picketing was built into the fabric of the strike. Old county and regional rivalries flared up, Lancashire men against Yorkshire men, South Wales miners in Nottinghamshire.

The Nottinghamshire miners turned out to be critical. Without them the power stations, even with the mix of nuclear and oil and the careful stockpiling, might have begun to run short and the government would have been in deep trouble.

Using horses, baton charges and techniques learned from the street riots of the previous few years, the police defended the working miners with a determination which delighted the government and alarmed many others. A battle at Orgreave in South Yorkshire was particularly brutal. As the strike went on, macho policing was matched by violence from striking miners. Scargill could count on almost fanatical loyalty to the union in towns and villages across the land. Miners gave up their cars, sold their furniture, saw their children suffer and indeed lost materially all they had in the cause of solidarity. Food parcels arrived from other parts of Britain, from France and even from Russia. There was a gritty courage and selflessness in mining communities most of the rest of country could barely understand. The other side of the coin was a desperation to win which turned ugly. A taxi-driver taking a working miner to work in Wales was killed when a block of concrete was dropped on his car. There were murderous threats to 'scabs' and their families. When Norman Willis, the affable general secretary of the TUC spoke at one miners' meeting, a noose was dangled above his head.

Violence relayed to the rest of the country on the nightly news, followed eventually by legal action on the part of Yorkshire miners complaining that they had been denied a ballot, put the NUM on the back foot. Scargill's decision to take money from Libya found him slithering from any moral high ground he had once occupied, though some believe this was part of a Security Service 'sting' operation to discredit the NUM leadership. As with Galtieri, Thatcher was lucky in her enemies. Slowly, month by month, the strike began to crumble and miners began to trail back to work, first in tens and scores, then in their hundreds, then in their thousands. There were many crises on the way – a possible dock strike; a vote to strike by pit safety officers and overseers, which would have shut down the working pits too and was promptly bought off, and problems with local courts too overloaded to prosecute strikers. But by January 1985, ten months after they had first come out, strikers were returning to work at the rate of some 2,500 a week; by the end of February more than half the NUM's membership was back at work. In some cases they marched back behind pipes and drums, weeping.

Scargill's gamble had gone catastrophically wrong. He has been compared to a First World War general, a donkey leading lions to the slaughter. There is something in the comparison. The political force ranged against the miners in 1984 was entirely different from the ill-prepared, Heath administration they had defeated ten years earlier. A shrewder non-revolutionary leader would not have chosen that fight at that time or, having done so, would have found a compromise after the first months of the dispute. Today, there are a handful of thousand miners left of the 200,000 who went on strike. Scargill himself lingers on as an official of an international miners' union because he has run out of miners to lead at home. He might once have dreamed the revolution would raise a statue to him. If anyone does, it should be the green lobby, in a spirit of irony. An industry whose origins went back to the Middle Ages and which made Britain a great industrial power, but which was always dangerous, dirty and polluting, lay down and died. For Conservatives, indeed for the majority of people, Scargill and his lieutenants were fighting parliamentary democracy and were an enemy which had to be defeated. But the miners of Kent, Derbyshire, Fife and Yorkshire, Wales and Lancashire were nobody's enemy, just abnormally hard-working, traditional people worried about losing their jobs and overly loyal to their wild and incompetent leader.

Whirlybird Madness

It is a reasonably safe rule in politics that the big fights are about big issues. The great Westland Helicopter crisis that broke over the Thatcher government in the winter of 1984–5 was on the face of it a barmy thing for ministers to fight about. Should a European consortium of aerospace manufacturers or an American defence company, working with an Italian firm, be favoured to take over a struggling West Country helicopter maker? Who cared? This was a government that boasted about its refusal to micro-manage industry, yet the fight about the future of a Yeovil manufacturer cost two cabinet ministers their jobs and led at one point to Margaret Thatcher herself doubting whether she would last the day as Prime Minister. It pitted her against the only other member of her government with real glamour – and as big a shock of hair as hers – and it dominated political life for months. It produced the only walk-out resignation from a cabinet meeting in modern times, indeed since 1903, and the only spontaneous one ever. So what was it all about?

The small storm of Westland gave early notice of the weaknesses that would eventually destroy the Thatcher government, though not for another five years. One was the divide throughout the Tory Party about Britain's place in the world. Helicopters were by the mid-eighties no longer a marginal defence issue. For projecting Western power in countries as far afield as Somalia, Bosnia and Iraq, they would be crucial – the new army mule hauling cannon over mountains, the new floating gunship. Supply an army's helicopters and you have a big hold over that country. United Technologies, the American company whose Sikorsky subsidiary built the Black Hawk helicopter, wanted control over part of Britain's defence industry. Alexander Haig, the US Secretary of State who had been so helpful during the Falklands War, was now back with his old company, and 'called in his markers' for the American bid. The Prime Minister, adopting a position of outward neutrality, would probably have favoured it anyway as further strengthening of the British-American alliance. But on the other side, supporting the European consortium of companies, were those who felt that the EU had to be able to stand alone in defence technology. Michael Heseltine and his business allies thought this was vital to preserve jobs and the cutting-edge science base. The United States must not be able to dictate prices and terms to Europe. So this was about where Britain stood: first with the US, or first with the EU? It was a question which would grow steadily in importance through the eighties until, in the nineties, it tore the Conservative Party apart.

The second issue thrown up by Westland mattered almost as much. It was the Thatcher style of government, which was more presidential and disdainful of her cabinet than that of any previous Prime Minister. We have already seen how she despatched the 'wets' who challenged her on economic policy. She would rage against, mock and browbeat ministers who were on her side too. Sir Geoffrey Howe in particular had a miserable time from her tongue-lashings. The satirical television puppet show *Spitting Image* began to dress their Thatcher figurine in trousers and summed up the popular perception in a sketch showing her lunching with her ministers. She orders her beef. Asked by the waiter, 'What about the vegetables?' her puppet snarls, 'They'll have the same.' Rather more seriously in the real world, she was conducting more and more business in small committees or bilaterally, with one minister at a time, ensuring her near-absolute dominance. A small clique of advisers assumed more significance than the ministers with their grand offices and titles. Later, just before her fall, Nigel Lawson would conclude that she was taking her personal economic adviser Sir Alan Walters more seriously than she was taking him, her Chancellor of the Exchequer. Throughout it all, she was using her beloved press officer Bernard Ingham to cut down to size any ministers she had taken against, using the then-anonymous lobby system for Westminster journalists to spread the message.

In her memoirs she portrays Heseltine as a vain, ambitious and unprincipled man who flouted cabinet responsibility. The Westland crisis, in her view, was simply about his psychological flaws. Ingham, in his memoirs, angrily defends himself against improper briefing. Yet there are too many other witnesses who found the Thatcher style more like a Renaissance court than a traditional cabinet, a place which demanded absolute loyalty and was infested with favourites. It would destroy her, as it would cripple New Labour, this way of ruling. But in the mid-eighties it was a new phenomenon and to ministers on the receiving end, freshly humiliating. And if there was one minister unlikely to take such treatment for long, it was Michael Heseltine. He was the only serious rival as darling of the party and media star in the glory days of Thatcherism. Handsome, glamorous, rich and an excellent public speaker, he was popularly known as 'Tarzan' The story was told about him by his fellow Tory MP, friend and biographer Julian Critchley, that at Oxford he had mapped out his future career on the back of an envelope, running through the need to make a fortune, marry well, enter Parliament and then, '1990s, Prime Minister'. Though Heseltine said he could not remember doing this it was in character. As a young man he had flung himself into the characteristic sixties businesses of property investment and magazine publishing, coming close to bankruptcy before handing his worldly goods to his bank manager and slowly turning his companies round. A passionate anti-socialist, he had won a reputation for hot-headedness since once picking up the Mace, symbol of parliamentary authority, and waving it at the Labour benches during a Commons row about steel nationalization. His speeches to Tory Party conferences were music-hall extravaganzas, full of blond hair-tossing, hilarious invective and fist-thwacks-palm drama. So macho that he was almost camp, he was known for the swoop on Merseyside already described and for dressing up in army gear while taking on the female CND protesters of Greenham Common. As an experienced businessman with a relish for vehement anti-Labour rhetoric he was hardly a typical 'wet', and indeed agreed with Thatcher about much. But he was a more committed anti-racialist than her and deeply in favour of the EU; she always regarded him as a serious and dangerous rival. The two biggest beasts of the Tory Party in the eighties had been eyeing each other and quietly sharpening their claws under the cabinet table well before Westland.

They went to war on behalf of the two rival bidders for Westland. She was livid that he was using his considerable leverage as Defence Secretary to warn the company's shareholders about the dangers of going with the Americans, potentially shutting out European business. She thought he was tipping the scales against Sikorsky, despite Westland's preference for them. Certainly, Heseltine repeatedly made it clear the Ministry of Defence would not be buying their Black Hawk helicopter and did much to rally the European consortium. Thatcher, meanwhile, was deploying the public line that she was only interested in what was best for the shareholders while trying to make sure the Americans were kept in the race, ahead of the Europeans. Eventually she sought advice from the government law officers about whether Heseltine had been behaving properly. A private reply, meant to weaken his case, was leaked. Furious at this wholly improper act which he suspected was the responsibility of Thatcher and Ingham, Heseltine demanded a full inquiry. During a meeting of cabinet she counter-attacked, trying to rein him in by ordering that all future statements on Westland must be cleared first by Number Ten. Hearing this attempt to gag him, Heseltine calmly got up from the cabinet table, announced that he must leave the government, walked by himself into the street and told a startled solitary reporter that he had just resigned.

The question of exactly who had leaked the Attorney General's legal advice in a misleadingly selective way to scupper Heseltine and the European bid then became critical. The leaking of the private advice broke the rules of Whitehall confidentiality, fairness and collective government. The instrument of the leak was a comparatively junior civil servant, the Trade Secretary Leon Brittan's head of communications, Colette Bowe. But who had told her to do this? Many assumed it was her boss, the Number Ten press chief Bernard Ingham. He denied it. He had known she was going to leak the advice and had not ordered her to stop, which he later said he bitterly regretted. But the initiative, he said, had not come from him or Mrs Thatcher. For her part she said she had not known and would not have approved the leaking of the letter had she been asked. None of this matters, except that it nearly finished off the Lady in her prime. After dramatic Commons exchanges during which she seemed vulnerable to the charge of lying to the House, she pulled through. It was Brittan who went for a comparatively trivial mis-statement about another confidential letter – a scapegoat, said the Opposition, which had singularly failed to get the glossy scalp they had hoped for.

After the political row there was a dirty and in some ways even more dramatic struggle for control of the company conducted in hotels and City boardrooms. Some of Thatcher's greatest business supporters such as Rupert Murdoch weighed in on the side of the American-led bid. Eventually amid accusations of arm-twisting and dirty tricks the Europeans were defeated and the company went to Sikorsky. The storm subsided. But it had revealed the costs of the new Thatcher style. Getting your way at all costs with foreign dictators and militant union leaders was one thing. Behaving similarly with senior politicians in your own party was another. Heseltine later wrote: 'I saw many good people broken by the Downing Street machine. I had observed the techniques of character assassination: the drip, drip, of carefully planted, unattributable stories that were fed into the public domain, as colleagues became marked as somehow "semi-detached" or "not one of us".' The great strength of Thatcher's way of governing was the way her self-certainty gave her administration and the country a surging sense of direction. Its weakness was it cut out so many others, ignored advice and humiliated anyone not seen as an uncritical supporter.

Very Big Bang

The City, with its huge bonuses and salaries, freshly sprouted glass towers, banks and merchants from across the world, is so familiar it can be taken for granted, as naturally British as the Jurassic coast. Yet in the fifties there would be no good reason for an observer to believe that the sleepy world of the

London Stock Exchange, the venerable merchant banks and the rest would become a global success story, while British car-making, for instance, with its splendid variety of models and its famous names, would wither to nothing. The great days of the City had been a lifetime earlier in the heady financial markets before the First World War when sterling was a dominant world currency, loans and bonds sluiced freely round the world, and Britain was a great creditor nation. After the Second World War the pound was under almost constant pressure, the dollar was king, postwar exchange controls hobbled any chance of big overseas deals and Britain was a big global debtor.

The wizened traditions of Money remained – the obscure hierarchies, the bowler hats, the rigid division between brokers and jobbers, the long lunches and coal fires, and the exotic titles of firms that had risen in the days of Queen Victoria, engraved on nameplates between the bombed-out squares. But the City was no longer buccaneering. In the age of Macmillan and Wilson its grandees were forced to concentrate on humble domestic business and the modest trade of the unwinding empire, occasionally pootling along to their masters at the Bank of England to lobby for a loosening of regulations, fruitlessly. Magazines and films still exploited the image of the crisp young banker with a furled brolly and bowler hat. But, in truth, the Square Mile was becoming part of heritage Britain, its declining firms like the cashless Palladian houses of Oxfordshire, in which grumpy men with famous names stamped their feet against the cold and mentally apologized to grandpapa. Perhaps it was inevitable? Historically, financial clout had run alongside commercial and political power. A weak Britain meant a weak pound and a weak City. In the forties, fifties and sixties, the golden age of the great US dollar, it was as obvious that New York would replace the Square Mile, as it was equally obvious that the US fleet would take over from the Royal Navy.

That it did not happen was the result of paranoia and bad judgement far away from London, exploited by bright British financiers. At the height of the Cold War, Moscow and her satrapies declined to let wicked capitalist New York look after their dollars. These dollars ended up instead in (apparently less wicked) London and were used from 1957 by a few far-seeing British banks to finance overseas trade in the capital-hungry post-war world. If you are not allowed to fund the world with home-grown pounds, why not do it with other people's dollars? The boss of the Bank of London and South America, Sir George Bolton, was heard in clubs and boardrooms loudly asking why London, with her expertise, should not jump into a new age of world capitalism? London's second opening came thanks to New York itself. Since the war, American bankers had been enjoying the easy pickings from loans to other countries and overseas investors. They were lazily uninterested in the secondary market in such loans. By the early sixties, the ballooning US balance of payments deficit turned the mood in Washington against loans to overseas customers in general. In 1963 President Kennedy worsened Wall Street's position dramatically with a new tax on Americans buying foreign stocks from foreigners. With New York cut off from a surging new international business, London moved in.

The first such 'Eurodollar' loans were negotiated in 1963 between the British merchant banks Warburgs and Samuel Montagu on the one hand, and an Italian state-owned steelmaker and the Belgian government on the other. To avoid British regulations and taxes, deals were done in Holland's Schiphol airport and Luxembourg. Warburgs dodged and hopped around endless obstacles until at the end they found there was no one to print the new bonds to the high pre-war standards demanded by the London Stock Exchange. At the last moment the playing card manufacturers De La Rue found two very old Czech engravers who were brought out of retirement to do the job.[11] Dollar loans by Hambros for hydroelectric schemes in Norway and by a group of merchant banks for the Austrian government quickly followed. Then a spate of loans for the Japanese ... and a new world suddenly opened up for the beaten-up old City of London. Pipelines across the Alps, American oil refineries and exploratory ventures, Japanese office buildings, early computer factories, all would be financed from London, just as in the days of Edwardian finance. As overseas bankers realized what was happening, they began to converge on London for some of the action. European banks were already present, but the big four finance houses in Tokyo opened London offices and so too did the big names on Wall Street. Citibank, Chase Manhattan, Merrill Lynch and Nomura were all there, taking traditional British business as well as trading in the Eurodollar markets. The influence of the Eurodollar and Eurobond market on the culture

65

of the City and by extension British business life generally can hardly be overstated. From the early sixties, it was internationalizing and shaking up London, introducing more aggression, fatter salaries and less of the old school tie. Harold Wilson might complain about sinister international financiers. The traditionalists of the Stock Exchange and the older banks might hint at sharp practice and unsavoury deals. But the Euro-market thrived and grew, shrugging off the crash of 1974 and the Arab boycott of Jewish businesses alike. Just a whiff of the can-do, devil-may-care Wild West spirit was suddenly felt again in the streets of old London.

Only in the side streets, however. For most investors the world of controls still applied. Sir Nicholas Goodison, later Chairman of the Stock Exchange in the Thatcher years, looked back on the mood by the late seventies: 'We still had exchange controls. We had a Labour government intent on controlling everything, and no freedom of capital movement. British people were not allowed to take capital abroad; British institutions weren't allowed to invest capital abroad except by special Treasury permissions ... we were an insulated market.'[12] It was this world which was swept away on 23 October 1979 when Geoffrey Howe, to general shock, abolished exchange controls. Despite what she later said, Thatcher was wobbly and uncertain about the gamble. Howe himself likened it to walking off a cliff to see what happened. Bankers noted there was no planning for this revolution. Tony Benn said it showed that international capitalism had finally defeated democracy. What is certainly clear is that abolishing exchange controls made it inevitable that the core of the 'old City' would be exposed to the cultural revolution that the Eurodollar market-makers had already enjoyed in the side streets. The smaller merchant banks, Antony Gibbs, Keyser Ullman and others, were already disappearing; even the biggest London merchant banks such as Kleinwort Benson had profits of little more than a tenth of Japan's Nomura and a seventh of Wall Street's Merrill Lynch. For the huddled world of the traditional City, it was suddenly a choice between looking for big protective overseas partners or struggling to survive alone.

In 1982, another slice of American business life came to London in the multi-coloured jackets and raucous bear-pit atmosphere of the new international financial futures market, or LIFFE. Here the high-risk bets were made on the future value of commodities and currencies, in one of the older buildings of the City, the Royal Exchange. Inside its elegant shell roared an atmosphere borrowed straight from Chicago, likened by startled observers at the time to an ill-bred casino. LIFFE would turn out to be very profitable for the traders, the raucous 'barrow boys' pumped up on booze, cocaine and fear of failure who became such an emblem of eighties life, many retiring exhausted and vastly rich by their early thirties. It would also be the scene of broken dreams. It was in the derivatives market that old Barings Bank, one of the grander names of the traditional City, lost its money and died. And so to the next question for the City: for how long could the traditional distinction between brokers, dealing with the public, and the jobbers or wholesalers, dealing only with stockbrokers, be maintained? It had been seen as an essential barrier to protect the public, as important for the City as the division between barrister and solicitor was in English law courts. Yet in these new markets it was barely recognized.

The new Chancellor after the 1983 election, Nigel Lawson, a former financial journalist, and the new Trade Secretary, Cecil Parkinson, decided to do a deal with the increasingly archaic looking Stock Exchange. It was struggling with a long and wearisome court case brought by the Office of Fair Trading. The ministers promised the legal action would be dropped if the Stock Exchange reformed itself. This was the final piece of action which led to the 'Big Bang' of City deregulation, something which has a claim to be the single most significant change of the whole Thatcher era, on a par with confronting the unions or privatization. The situation in 1983–4 could be compared to an old market town high street, with its long-established specialist shops, the fishmonger and the drapers, old Mr Bunn at the bakery and Miss Manila the trusted postmistress, at just the moment when a huge new retail park opens on the outskirts. The supermarkets in it are the international financial service companies and the global-trading banks offering every financial service under one roof. Chase Manhattan and Merrill Lynch here play the role of Tesco and Walmart. The high street shops are the City firms, small and specialized but without the financial clout and scale to compete. What do they do? Some doggedly hang on, hoping their name, expertise and traditional customer base will see them through. Others negotiate with the supermarkets, trying to find a space under the roof to carry on trading. Others frantically merge, creating newer, bigger high street retailers.

This is what happened in the City when it became clear that the old rules were about to be abolished. During the winter of 1983–4 jobbers, brokers and bankers began to merge in an unprecedented explosion of defensive alliances. Old merchant banks opened talks with the US mega-banks. Scores of ancient names disappeared or were compressed into new assemblages of initials. In family firms such as N. M. Rothschild and Barings, there were family fights, with sons and brothers going different ways. The streets echoed to the sound of cultures clashing. Cricket and baseball were at war on the same pitch. With a new market for shares in smaller, riskier companies (the Unlisted Securities Market) and the creation of a new joint index of the shares of the hundred biggest companies on the Stock Exchange, the FTSE 100, or 'Footsie', there was a revolutionary mood in the air, a frenzy of optimism and activity which roared through 1984. Many noted the contrast with the devastation of Britain's coal-mining industry as the strike dragged on during just the same time. Across the City big gleaming new dealing rooms were unveiled, filled with computers, edged with glass and marble. Paintings of venerable Jewish patriarchs from Edwardian days were rehung in bland new surroundings. Minimum commissions, bedrock of the old cartel, went overnight. Outsiders were at last ushered into the temple of temples, the Stock Exchange itself.

And then on 27 October 1986, this London Stock Exchange ceased to exist as the institution it had formerly been. Its makeover made it all but unrecognizable. The new screen-quoted system SEAQ finally came on stream, the moment remembered as the 'Big Bang' itself. A few months later the physical floor of the Stock Exchange, once heaving with life, was almost desolate as the deals were made by computer screen and phone. Scandals, shocks, crashes would follow but as the spring and summer of 1987 arrived, it was clear there would never be any way back to the cosy, particular, tradition-hallowed old high street of London's City a few years before. Twenty years on, share deals which had taken quarter of an hour or longer to process were completed in a few seconds. The markets were opening two and a half hours earlier each morning, and closing a couple of hours later. The volume of trading was fifteen times higher than it had been in the early eighties. A country which had exported £2 billion of financial services a year before the Big Bang was exporting twelve times that amount. With only 330,000 people working there in City jobs, it was supporting the entire country's overseas account.[13] Though the City brought a super-rich class to Britain, whose vast salaries and staggering annual bonuses made a good swathe of the middle class feel ill over their breakfast newspapers when they were reported each year, and which pushed the more beautiful, well-placed and prestigious homes out of reach of hospital consultants, criminal lawyers, head-teachers and diplomats, the truth is that without the Big Bang, Britain's books would be in much worse condition.

For millions of ordinary Britons who had only the haziest idea about the world of finance, the revolution in lending to buy their houses was as

70

big a shock. Until the early eighties, most people's experience of getting a mortgage involved a barrage of suspicious questions from a building society manager, followed by a long wait (for the loans were rationed) and eventually followed by a mortgage whose cost was fixed by the Building Societies' Association. Generally speaking, the size of the low-cost loan, funded by deposits from building society members, would be limited to two and a half times the would-be homeowner's annual salary. But by 1983 the ordinary clearing banks were muscling in on the business and this cartel began to go too. American and other mortgage lenders offered better deals. As Nigel Lawson later wrote, this happened in the new deregulated world 'in which direct credit controls were out of the question; and the only checks on excess were the price of credit, which the Government remained able to control [it cannot do so now] and prudence, which it cannot.' Three years later he responded to the clamour of building societies who felt unfairly hampered by their old status. He freed them to raise money in the capital markets, issue chequebooks and cheque guarantee cards, make other loans and indeed behave almost like banks. He also allowed them to convert themselves into banks if they got a sufficiently large majority of their members to agree. This duly happened, beginning with the Abbey National.

The effect of this was to suddenly take the brake off mortgage lending and to upend the old power relationship. Before, would-be borrowers limped along to the local building society and patiently endured many obstacles before they were allowed a mortgage. Now the building societies and banks

71

started to ingratiate themselves with the public, thrusting credit at them. It became a good thing, a virtuous thing, to be a big-time borrower. People found themselves harangued in advertisements and junk mail to borrow more, to defect from one bank to another, to extend the mortgage rather than paying it off. The old rules about the maximum proportion of income began to dissolve – four times income began to be acceptable in some cases. House prices began to rise accordingly. (Today the average cost of a house in Britain is rising towards five times average income.)

In many cases banks and building societies began to lend people more than the total value of the house they were buying. The extra helped fuel a more general high-street splurge. The old system of checking people's real financial status went out of the window. During 1986–8 a borrowing frenzy gripped the country, egged on by swaggering speeches about Britain's economic miracle from the Chancellor and Prime Minister. The abolition of mortgage tax relief saw a rush of borrowing to meet the deadline. Lawson, not a man to underrate his achievements, acknowledged a critic who said 'my real mistake as Chancellor was to create a climate of optimism that, in the end, encouraged borrowers to borrow more than they should and lenders to lend more than they should.' All this would end in tears with the bust that followed and would be used for many years afterwards by Labour's Gordon Brown as evidence of the Tory 'boom-and-bust' policies. But it was the consequence of a decisive break in the financial regulations governing City and everyday life, which changed Britain, probably for ever. It felt heady and exhilarating to millions. It was like getting properly drunk for the first time.

The Big Bang itself was thus only a moment in a longer process, rooted in the Eurodollar market of the sixties and given its most dramatic kick by Geoffrey Howe's abolition of exchange controls, followed by the deregulation of lending. It meant that Britain for the first time in her history, and entirely willingly, gave up control over financial dealings done from her soil except as a neutral regulator. The State lost control over credit. In return the City gained a huge quantity of international financial business, the profits dripping down from some of the biggest deals in the world which might otherwise have gone to Berlin, Tokyo or (more likely) New York. The end of the age of controls and nationalistic finance meant also that British manufacturing lost any hope of the kind of long-term banking arrangements that German and French rivals had enjoyed. The asset-stripping habit, buying companies, dismantling them into component parts and selling them on, had become a controversial part of British business life in the seventies. The eighties' financial revolution ensured it would remain so. There would be no room for old connections or long-term thinking in the new world.

For politics, the freeing of the City gave Margaret Thatcher and her ministers an entirely loyal and secure base of rich, articulate supporters who helped see her through some rough times. Rothschilds and other banks would spread the get-rich-quick prospect to millions of people in Britain through the privatization issues and the country would, for a time, come closer to the share-

73

owning democracy Thatcher dreamed of. But all this came at a price – the crude and swaggering 'loadsamoney' years satirized by the comedian Harry Enfield and the culture of excess and conspicuous display that would percolate from the City through London, then the Home Counties, then much of southern England. For one generally sympathetic observer of the City in the mid-eighties it was worryingly infected with hype: 'Febrile, driven by greed, pushing back the boundaries of acceptable behaviour, this was a brief, intense phase that in some ways was a rerun of the late 1920s, this time with added attitude.'[14]

Sid Gets Lucky:
the Privatization Years

There is a popular belief that the Thatcher governments never really intended to privatize very much, and that they stumbled upon an easy way of raising cash by selling off assets almost by accident. If so, it was one heck of a stumble. During the decade £29 bn was raised in sales of land and businesses and £18 bn from the sale to their tenants of 1.24 million council homes. The gas that cooked meals and warmed houses, oil coming ashore, aircraft taking businessmen and holiday-makers, and the airports they flew from, the phones and phone-lines used to communicate, cars, engines, steel and the water pipes and filtration systems bringing the British their baths and tea – all would be affected by the greatest shift of assets from the State to private companies and individuals in the history of this country. By the 1992 election, forty-six businesses had left the public sector, carrying with them 900,000 people. The notion that this was accidental is wrong. The Conservatives had promised to sell off council houses to their tenants from the mid-seventies. Privatization of state corporations had not featured much in the 1979 manifesto only because the party's plans were still sketchy and partly because its leader did not want to scare off the voters. But privatization had been long discussed on the right. In his first Budget speech Howe said he wanted to reduce the size of the public sector, that 'the scope for the sale of assets is substantial' and that this was 'an essential part of our long-term programme'.

So it would prove. One of the influential economic writers about the Thatcher years said that coining the word privatization was 'a master-stroke of public relations' by the government, which put it into worldwide circulation. Privatization would become the major idea exported from Britain in modern times, though as it happens the word was not one Mrs Thatcher liked or much used. ('De-nationalization' was even uglier, however, and inaccurate, since some of the corporations and assets sold had never been nationalized in the first place.) It started tentatively, with small steps in 1981–2 including shares in BP, the scientific corporation Amersham, half of Cable & Wireless and then the British National Oil Corporation, discussed elsewhere. The motives were mixed. Early on, with a horrendous public sector borrowing requirement to fund, simply raising cash was important. Yet this was neither the origin of the idea, nor its real point. Howe and Lawson were making clear from 1980 onwards that creating a large bulwark of new shareholders was essential to the Tories' political vision. Lawson would cite the fears of extending voting in the nineteenth century, allowing political power to people who had no stake in the country: 'But the remedy is not to restrict the franchise to those who own property: it is to extend the ownership of property to the largest possible majority of those who have the vote. The widespread ownership of private property is crucial to the survival of freedom and democracy.'

Another way of putting it was that this was one part of the oneway ratchet, pulling Britain away from socialism. If Labour had been accused of creating a giant state sector whose employees depended on high public spending and could therefore be expected to become loyal Labour voting-fodder, then the Tories were intent on creating a 'property-owning democracy' of voters whose interests were entirely different. The despair of Labour politicians as they watched it working was obvious. There was now to be a large and immovably pro-private sector Britain of share-owners and home-owners, probably working in private companies and increasingly un-unionized. The cost of renationalizing the industries made Labour pledges about it increasingly hollow. Twenty years later the idea of reversing privatization is something discussed only on the very margins of politics. The proportion of adults holding shares rose from 7 per cent when Labour left office, to 25 per cent when Thatcher did. Thanks to the 'right to buy' policy, more than a million families purchased their council houses, repainting and refurbishing them and watching their value shoot up, particularly since they had been sold them at a discount of between 33 and 50 per cent. The proportion of owner-occupied homes rose from 55 per cent of the total in 1979 to 67 per cent a decade later. And people did indeed become much wealthier, overall, during the Tory years. In real terms, total personal wealth rose by 80 per cent in the eighties, entirely changing the terms of trade of ordinary politics. Old Labour was killed off not in the Commons but in the shopping centre and the estate agents' office.

Yet if we look a little below the surface, the story is more blurred. Of that huge rise in wealth, relatively little was accounted for by shares. An increase in earnings and the first house-price boom were much more important. And the boom in shareholding was fuelled more by the prospect of a bargain than by any deep change in culture. Clearly, there was always a potential conflict between the government's need to raise money quickly, and its hopes of spreading share ownership – both of them intensely political, since the former affected tax levels and the latter the size of the property-holding electorate. Again and again, from the grossly undervalued Amersham sale, to the later and greater privatizations, ministers erred on the side of getting the maximum spread of ownership, rather than the maximum price. The breakthrough privatization was that of 52 per cent of British Telecom in November 1984, which raised an unheard-of £3.9 bn. It was the first to be accompanied by a ballyhoo of television and press advertising. It was easily oversubscribed.

In the event 2 million people, or 5 per cent of the adult population, bought BT shares, almost doubling the number of people who owned shares in a single day. After this came British Gas. Natural gas fields had been supplying Britain from the North Sea since the late sixties, pumping ashore at Yarmouth and Hull, and replacing the old 'town gas' system of coal-produced gas, which had long given so many neighbourhoods their distinctive architecture and smell. With its national pipe network and showrooms it had become the country's favourite source of domestic energy and was, in most respects, a straightforwardly monopolistic business. Its chairman Sir Dennis Rooke fought a riotously aggressive private campaign to avoid British Gas being broken up before the sale, and was successful. Again, the government and its advisers prepared for the sale with a TV campaign featuring an anonymous neighbour who had to be kept away from a good thing – 'Don't Tell Sid' – and then, when the issue details were finally announced, 'Tell Sid'. This raised £5.4bn, the biggest single privatization of all.

Yet there was something about the very name that fell oddly on the ear. Does 'Sid' perhaps have a half-echo of 'spiv'? Was someone in the advertising team subconsciously sending a message? For the truth was that the huge oversubscribing of shares reflected a general and accurate belief that something was being given away for nothing, that this was a one-way bet. Sid knew which side his bread was buttered on, but this did not necessarily make him a kitchen capitalist. With the equally bargain-price shares offered to members of building societies, such as Abbey National, when they demutualized and turned themselves into banks, Britain developed a 'thank you very much' class of one-off shareholders. In the early years of the twenty-first century, the Office of National Statistics looked back at the privatization story and found that the proportion of stockmarket wealth held by private shareholders had fallen from 20 per cent in 1994 to 14 per cent. 'Many shareholders', they said, 'have clearly subsequently disposed of their holdings rather than become long-term stockmarket investors as was once hoped.' Of the 22 per cent of adults holding stocks or shares, more than half only had their old privatization or building society ones. The UK Shareholders' Association concluded that 'there are enormous number of shareholders in the UK (about 10m perhaps) but the vast majority hold only a few shares, and many of those will have come from privatisations, demutualisations or former employments. Such shares are rarely traded.'

The failure to get a shareholding democracy properly rooted, despite endless Treasury initiatives to nurture it, is a more telling criticism of privatization than the one most commonly heard at the time, which was that the assets were being sold off too cheaply. They were – to the tune in total of some £2.5 bn, according to the National Audit Office. But in part this was deliberate – 'wider share ownership was an important policy objective and we were prepared to pay a price for it,' said Lawson. Second, as the government and its advisers learned from each privatization, the pricing grew shrewder. Third, the price critics would not have sold the companies anyway. What the stultified share ownership pattern showed was that, below the level of political rhetoric, there were limits to the Thatcher revolution.

The other great question is whether privatization increased the efficiency and responsiveness of the corporations being sold. This was supposed to happen not because public sector managers were inherently lazy but because they lacked the spur and whip of a stockmarket price and the possibility of going out of business. Yet the impetus of being in the private sector would be much less if the business was still a monopoly. The most successful privatizations in that sense were the ones where the company was pushed instantly into full competition, as British Airways was, or Rolls-Royce, or British Aerospace. But the utilities – gas, electricity, water – were always different. It was hard to envisage rival North Sea natural gas companies competing in every part of the country with their own system of pipes and storage. It was hard to imagine many different energy companies with their own grids. Yet without competition, where would the efficiency gains come from? The technical and political argument behind these privatizations was how to break up the state monopolies to create competition, without infuriating and discommoding the consumer.

In the heyday of the Thatcher privatizations, it was more common for public corporations to be sold as single entities than broken up. British Telecom made the case that to compete in international markets, it must stay as a single unit, able to make the big investments needed for the telecommunications revolution. British Gas, under its pugnacious boss, managed to play the Whitehall power game sufficiently well to stay single. The water and electricity industries were split up, but to create local monopolies, with power generation being split into just two mega-companies, National Power and Powergen. (The railway industry would prove one of the most intellectually demanding and least successful of all, though this story comes later.) In essence, what ministers did was to replace competition by regulation and the growth of new public bodies, such as the National Rivers Authority. Oftel, Ofcom, Ofgas, Ofwat were all given detailed targets and penalty systems to oversee the newly privatized utilities. Only much later would some of them, such as British Gas, be further broken up in the private sector, generally by government diktat through new competition policies, and exposed to more realistic market pressures. Soon, foreign firms would begin to move in and buy up the fragmented privatized utilities, causing remarkably little public protest, except when years of poor investment or management meant a service was patently failing, such as the leaking pipe systems of German-owned Thames Water.

Politicians learned two things. The first was that outside the Westminster village, few British people seemed to care at all who owned the companies and services they depended upon, so long as the service was acceptable. This was becoming a much less ideological country. The second thing they learned was that politics could not step back and wash its hands of what the privatized companies then did. Ministers, not simply chief executives, would still be the target of public anger and held responsible for any failings. This was becoming a more aggressively consumerist country. The result was that, while hundreds of thousands of employees left the public sector to work for newly private corporations, the

State grew in other ways, through the quangos, regulatory bodies and bureaucrats now found necessary to regulate and oversee the privatized services.

Rainbows and Pots of Black Gold

Jim Callaghan was brought up piously, so when he told an audience in 1977 that God had given Britain her best opportunity for a hundred years in the shape of North Sea oil, there is a chance that he meant it. The Foreign Office, in a memo a little earlier, had called it 'a rainbow spanning the sombre horizon'. These had been terrible days for Britain, with 25 per cent inflation and the stockmarket plunging. The oil seemed like a fairytale intervention, for whichever group of politicians found themselves in power when the pot of gold could finally be yanked open. The story of what happened to the Almighty's handout, a ripple of organic residue left 9,000 feet below the seabed from dinosaur-haunted landscapes and warm seas of 200 million years earlier, is one of the most remarkable and under-discussed in modern British history. The discovery and exploitation of huge oil and gas fields far out under cold, stormy and turbulent waters – so far out that the biggest fields were roughly equidistant between Scotland and Norway – is a modern epic of technical skill, bold finance, endurance and individual courage. Hundreds would die, few fortunes would be made. By the boom year before prices suddenly fell, 1985, Britain was producing

127 million tonnes and was responsible for nearly a tenth of world exports. She had broken free from the old shackles of oil dependency, at least for a while. Official figures suggest Britain will be importing oil again by 2010 though many economists think it will be sooner. So we are talking about a span of between thirty and forty years. Was it well managed, that great gift?

This story is, to begin with, technically awe-inspiring. The oil in most of the rest of the world was ridiculously easy to win compared to the job of finding and pumping out very deep deposits a long way from dry land in very stormy seas. In civil engineering terms, from the steel and concrete jackets as tall as the Post Office Tower that had to be built in specially chosen havens and floated hundreds of miles out, to the huge undersea pipelines dropped from boats, this was a project unlike any other in peacetime since the Victorians' creation of the railways in the 1840s.[15] Its impact on the politics and public finances of Britain, first in the dying days of old Labour and then during the crucial years of the early Thatcherite experiment in monetarism, can hardly be exaggerated. It helped bankroll Thatcherism, for Britain was self-sufficient in oil by 1980. As the future Chancellor, Nigel Lawson, noted, revenues for the government 'soared from zero in 1975 to nearly £8 billion in 1982–3, at which point they accounted for almost 8.5 per cent of all tax revenues.' Some economists, though certainly not Lawson, have argued that without it the Thatcher experiment would have collapsed during 1981–2. One observer says: 'The industrial shake-out of the early eighties, of which unemployment above three million was the consequence, was indeed financed with the considerable help of the oil revenues.'[16] So there, to start with, is an irony. A great new source of national wealth helped to produce mass unemployment, or at least make it politically possible.

The possibilities of the oil boom were not underestimated at the time. Thanks to the oil price shocks of earlier years, the power and wealth of the Sheikhs, epitomized by the ebullient Saudi oil minister Yamani, was well understood. Could Britain have a little of that? In the seventies, in clubs of St James's and the City offices of the *Financial Times,* or the new little tower-block where *The Economist* was edited, they argued about whether oil would so boost the pound that manufacturing industry would be destroyed; or alternatively whether it would mean a golden age for Britain, when vast fortunes could be reinvested in wonderful schools and cutting-edge high-tech industries.

Whitehall's defence experts worried about how to defend the hundreds of miles of pipes against Irish terrorists, and the rigs against the Soviet navy. In those parts of the Commons tea-room and bars colonized by Labour MPs, there was a vigorous argument between those who wanted to see oil nationalized and kept under direct government control and those who felt this was impracticable. For by the time the big strikes had been made, the great American 'oil majors' were the people who had actually invested in the risky and technically difficult business of finding the stuff and preparing to bring it ashore. In the first few years, official Britain was hugely excited by the whole thing.

84

When the first oil arrived ashore in November 1975 at Cruden Bay in Aberdeenshire, the Queen was present with the Prime Minister, assorted other ministers, pipers, a huge tent, red carpets and crowds with Union Jacks. (The oil workers, being in general rather hairy and impolite, were kept well out of the way.)

So it is curious that this great technical, economic and social story features so little afterwards in the memoirs and biographies of the politicians most affected by it. In her autobiography Margaret Thatcher barely touches on North Sea oil, even though her husband Denis was an oilman, involved in the near-collapse of Burmah Oil in 1975, and even though she took a close day-to-day interest in the relevant cabinet committees. About this awesome story she manages just four or five throwaway references, tacked to the end of remarks about exchange controls or tax policy. Geoffrey Howe dismisses the epic tale in a few words, far fewer than he devotes to the mildly amusing theft of his trousers from a train. Neither of them mentions the great tragedy of Piper Alpha, when 185 men were burned or blown to death (two thirds of the British toll in the Falklands War). The great tomes on Wilson and Callaghan, Major and Blair, likewise find nothing much to say about North Sea oil. Nigel Lawson writes lucidly about it, brushing aside the arguments in favour of treating oil as a national resource to be husbanded with his customary panache. In many of the more general histories, economic and political, North Sea oil gets meagre treatment. Its cultural legacy seems slender, too: the occasional agitprop play, a few poems, but no memorable novel, television drama or film,

85

unless one counts *Local Hero,* which is more about a village community. Those wild years, when 80,000 hard-drinking, hard-working, brave and often dysfunctional men turned a corner of Scotland into the Wild East have left few footprints. A rare historian of the industry points out that among Scotland's hundreds of museums there is not one devoted to oil. Compared to the much-discussed miners' strikes, or the IMF crisis, or the City rude-boys of the Big Bang, North Sea oil – which continues to profitably flow – is already forgotten.

Why is this? Those parts of the national story that nobody seems keen to talk about have messages of their own. In the case of oil, embarrassment and confusion are part of the answer. For the truth is that the great adventure was lived at the edge of the British experience. It was not just that the rigs were so far from the coast, halfway to Scandinavia, and that the wild scenes were played out in the bars of Aberdeen and Shetland, both remote from the media in Glasgow, never mind London. It was also that the funding of the exploration and production was so heavily dominated by the United States and that so much of the technology was designed and built outside Britain that it is hard to tell, thirty years after It began to flow, quite what message God was really sending with the oil. The number of British refineries actually fell during the great oil decade of 1980–90, from twenty-one to thirteen, and 40 per cent of that was American-owned. Government advisers had prepared detailed plans about how to grab a great industrial bonanza on the back of the oil boom but by 1974, when the rigs were desperately needed to cope with the huge discoveries out at sea, only three rigs out of 119 were being built in Britain. The ageing, underfinanced yards of the Clyde, Tyneside and Belfast, which in the forties had still produced nearly 40 per cent of the world's ships, were now down to 4 per cent. Cheaper, better-equipped deep-water yards overseas had taken over. So when it came to the rigs, Norway, Finland even France were getting more of the business. Scotland's specialist yards for the huge 'jackets', like the Meccano sets of giants, at Nigg, Ardersier and Methil, lurched, it has been well said, 'between clamour and closure'. It was the same story with the all-important service boats bringing vital drilling supplies alongside. The technical breakthrough of positioning propellers at the bow as well as the stern, so they could keep position in heavy waters beside the platforms was made by Norwegian yards. It was their boats, not British ones, which were then sold around the world. Even when it came to oil supply services, which more or less had to come locally, British companies were slow to catch up and won little extra business overseas.[17]

Finance was a similar story. In the early days of exploration, the US giants were able to fund their work in the North Sea themselves, developing rigs from their earlier experiences in the Gulf of Mexico. The opaque nature of their internal accounting, and the much higher cost of getting any oil out, meant they were appallingly hard for British ministers and the Treasury to deal with. The government's handling of early leases for exploration, blocks of a hundred square miles each, was criticized by the Commons public accounts committee in 1972 as far too generous, 'as though Britain were a gullible Sheikhdom'. In the Middle East, they thought so too. Among the odder political vignettes of the seventies was an interview between Britain's energy minister Tony Benn and the Shah of Iran, at the latter's palace in Tehran. There, after noting the signed photographs of Brezhnev, Mao and the Queen, Benn was informed that North Sea oil could transform Britain's prospects 'if we were not imprudent'.[18] The Shah warned Benn to stand up to the American giants of the oil business. Benn went back and did his best which in the case of Amoco left him 'boiling with rage – I felt like the president of a banana republic negotiating with a multinational'. Labour's answer was to set up the British National Oil Corporation, BNOC, in 1976, which was meant to be both the government's eyes and ears in the industry, to buy 51 per cent of the oil landed, and then to sell it on. It gave the government some grip on the developing industry and built up formidable expertise at its Scottish headquarters. Yet it was essentially a bystander with modest powers, compared to the great oil companies. Its oil-producing business was in any case privatized by Nigel Lawson in 1982, the largest privatization the world had then seen; and the subsequent company Britoil was taken over by BP six years later.

British business as well as British manufacturing was slow to seize the possibilities of the oil boom, though the Scottish banks and the merchant banks clustered round Edinburgh's genteel Charlotte Square began forming oil subsidiaries and hiring expert economists by the end of the seventies. Among the partnerships was one between Thomson Scottish Petroleum, part of the group which also owned the *Scotsman* newspaper; and Armand Hammer, the one-time business ally of Lenin, with Occidental. They found the Piper field, one of the big ones following the huge Forties find by BP and Brent by Shell and Exxon. There were many smaller oil-investing companies, some of them successful. Onshore, some Aberdeenshire companies did well in building the offices and prefabricated living quarters, servicing the endless helicopter flights, developing expertise in valves and electronic equipment. Yet the grand hopes of ministers back in the mid-seventies that the oil discoveries would kick-start a great renaissance in banking, engineering, shipbuilding and new service industry, was very wide of the mark.

Why was this? It was partly that the boom came just when British industry was at its lowest ebb, strike-prone, short of money, short of good management. It was partly that the oil-boosted pound did indeed make the recession of the early eighties even worse, rising faster and further than ministers expected. The petro-currency helped squeeze the economy and improved efficiency, at: the inevitable cost of widespread closures, sufficient to enrage many naturally pro-Conservative business people. Michael Edwardes, Chairman of the State-owned carmaker British Leyland, said at the time that if the government could not find a way to deal 'with North Sea oil, then I say: leave the bloody stuff in the ground'.[19]

Before 1979 Labour was struggling to rein in the American companies that had arrived early and eager. But after 1979 the Conservatives were determined to use the oil revenues quickly, to pay debt and cut taxes, rather than to invest it in some long-term plan for industry. This was the key 'rate of depletion' argument played out across Whitehall, which was really about how best Britain should use its bonus. The Norwegians, with a much smaller population and their industry run by the State, invested the proceeds in a great Nordic piggy-bank. When the Scottish Nationalists seized the oil issue in the early seventies they came up with a similar plan for a Scottish oil fund, paying out a permanent dividend to benefit the Scots henceforth. The argument between 'extract as much as possible now, and spend the proceeds' and 'extract slowly, and invest' was, however, a complicated one, since nobody knew what would happen to the oil price. With North Sea oil so expensive to produce, leaving the stuff under the seabed might mean that if the world price fell it became uneconomic.

Nor was it clear that money invested elsewhere by British ministers would turn out to be money well invested – particularly if it was also meant to kick-start industries. Under Labour, the so-called Varley assurances had been given to the oil industry, a promise that the government would not impose cutbacks beyond a certain level but allow the oil companies to take out most of what they could. According to Professor Alex Kemp of Aberdeen University, who has been writing the official history of North Sea oil, the argument in the early Tory years was between David Howell at the Department of Energy, who believed in slower extraction, and Howe at the Treasury, who needed the revenue as quickly as possible. Howe won the day, with Margaret Thatcher's consent, imposing a punitive 90 per cent marginal tax rate and treating oil taxes just like income tax or VAT even though oil revenue was finite, a one-off. Professor Kemp concludes that 'oil revenues were used as part of macro-economic management rather than energy policy, looking thirty years ahead.'

Good thing, or bad thing? This can be seen as a one-off waste, funding the squeeze of the early Thatcher years but leaving little for future generations left in the pot of gold at the end of the North Sea rainbow. Yet for those who saw that drastic economic squeeze as essential, it was money well spent. Lawson said the oil taxes gave 'a healthy kick-start' to the process of cutting the government deficit, though he always argued that the overall impact of North Sea oil was exaggerated. As to the profits from oil, they would be better invested privately. Lawson made his point by comparison: 'A peasant finds gold in his garden. Should he be allowed to mine it at his own speed and be left to allocate the proceeds between extra spending and saving for the day when the gold has been exhausted? Or should some authority force him to leave some of the gold in the ground to guard against profligacy?'[20] So in his view, the transfer of oil profits into investments overseas, as happened after the abolition of exchange controls, rather than in (say) British manufacturing, was a good bargain for the country as a whole.

British manufacturing continued to slither downhill, falling from 34 to 30 per cent of national output in 1970–7, before oil properly came on stream, and then from 30 per cent to 23 per cent in the great oil decade. (By 2006 it accounted for less than 15 per cent.) According to the government's own figures, 2 million manufacturing jobs were lost at this time.

Productivity inevitably rose in consequence and the economy would recover very strongly, though this does finally answer the question about whether too much expertise and chains of supply were lost, putting Britain permanently out of markets she could otherwise have retained. Whichever view you take, this 'British revolution' could not have been sustained without the pipes and the rigs. Why did Margaret Thatcher say so little about North Sea oil? Or Geoffrey Howe? Could it be simply that in the heroic story of their remaking of the British economy, the Almighty's underwater gift was an embarrassingly vital support mechanism, for which they could take absolutely no credit? And that therefore they were as unlikely to draw attention to it, as actors apparently leaping through the air would be to the wires supporting them? Still, it was unfortunate. The roughnecks and roustabouts, the shuttle helicopter pilots landing in gale-force winds on postage-stamp-like platforms, and the divers taking horrible risks on the ocean bed, deserve a larger role in modern history. Un-unionized, risk-taking, freebooting, they were after all, model Thatcherites, every one.

Let us return to Lawson's metaphor of the peasant with gold in his garden. The question is, whose garden? Had Scotland been an independent country and had the lines of national territorial waters been drawn at an appropriate angle (the legal arguments about this were dense), then Scotland would undoubtedly have been a rich country. Like Biafra in Nigeria, it could have funded a breakaway on the basis of oil – though hopefully with less tragic effects. As we have seen, the Scottish National Party had spotted the possible consequences of oil early on. They had begun to worry Labour in the sixties with a series of stunning by-election successes. Whitehall had hit back; the Treasury produced a notional Scottish budget for 1967–8 showing Scotland deeply in the red. Given that Scotland had a relatively poor and relatively scattered population, and a shrinking economic base, this was hardly surprising. But what difference would the oil revenues make? Suddenly, Whitehall came over all coy. Oil money was expertly mixed into national revenues. Jim Sillars, the MP who moved from Labour to the SNP via the briefly fashionable Scottish Labour Party, protested: 'The potential embarrassment of each drop of the magic oil was dealt with by the simple, crooked device of removing oil revenues from any purely Scottish statistics ... The fish caught and landed from Scottish waters are allowed to remain in Scotland's accounts, but the oil over which those fish swim – well, that's different!'

The SNP was not waiting for official confirmation of what it suspected, however. It had strong covert support in the Edinburgh banking world and could draw on some of the brightest economists north of the border. Within months of the first big BP oil strike its chairman Billy Wolfe was declaring that oil should be a dominant part of its propaganda. In 1972 it launched its most famous slogan, 'It's Scotland's Oil' followed a year later by the still more aggressive, 'Rich Scots or Poor Britons?' Thanks to the recent release of government documents we now know just how jumpy this made Whitehall. Civil servants told Labour ministers after the second 1974 election they should delay Harold Wilson's promised Scottish assembly ('Powerhouse Scotland') to stop the British economy being destabilized. By then the SNP was claiming the support of a third of voters and had won eleven seats in the Commons. 'Progress toward devolution should be delayed for as long as possible ...' said one mandarin: 'The longer this can be played, the better.' The problem was that the civil service thought the SNP's calculations on the huge wealth that could come Scotland's way with oil were, if anything, an underestimate. One Treasury official wrote: 'It is conceivable that income per head in Scotland could be 25 per cent or 30 per cent higher than that prevailing in England during the 1980s, given independence.' Another wrote bluntly: 'The Scots have really got us over a barrel here.'[21] But the Scots, whatever their suspicions and however vigorous the campaigning of the SNP, never knew quite how large that oily barrel was. Had they done so, it is likely that the politics of the later seventies and eighties would have been very different.

The Scots and the Welsh Leave Us Close to Tears

Scotland and Wales had very different political cultures but by the sixties they shared the sense of being parts of the UK in decline, whose old Labour elites no longer delivered the goods. Scotland's industrial heartland was dominated by coal, steel, shipbuilding and engineering. South Wales, built on coal and steel, was also culturally besieged, as people migrated to the richer new towns of southern England, and the Welsh language declined. Both these smaller countries asked themselves whether, if they cut free from the United Kingdom, they might somehow achieve a new beginning. The European Common Market showed that it was possible for small countries to thrive perfectly well. Even outside it, the Norwegians, Icelanders and Swiss seemed to be managing. No Western country seriously felt threatened by her neighbours any more. Living through the political traumas of the seventies, almost everyone in England was to an extent trapped inside the nightmare. For Scots and the Welsh there was the possibility at least of simply closing the door and walking away.

Yet in neither country did the secessionists ever have majority support. In both countries, their base tended to be among small business people, academics and public servants, the kind who in England were at the same time joining the Liberals. But the Scottish National Party and Plaid Cymru had clear objectives, effective political organizations, a certain fashionable rebel quality; and they scared the wits out of the established parties. These would be years when the breakup of Britain haunted many politicians and when nightmares of IRA-style violence being copied elsewhere fuelled best-selling books and television dramas. Once it had been easy to satirize Druidical Welshmen capering about and plunking their harps, or collections of wild-eyed, bushy-haired Scottish poets in kilts and jerseys. But by the seventies, it was not funny any longer.

The Scottish story can be traced back to the beginning of this postwar story. On 29 October 1949, a raw day in Edinburgh, a solemn faced, dark suited crowd walked into the gloomy headquarters of the Church of Scotland, a parade of landowners and miners, aristocrats and shipyard workers, fat businessmen and lean clerics. They had come to sign a Scottish Covenant, a practice last heard of in the bloody seventeenth century, when fanatic Presbyterians were taking on London and the losers had their heads lopped off in public. But this lot were hardly a revolutionary sight, and their document was full of sonorous assertions about their loyalty to the Crown. There was an impromptu prayer. The Duke of Montrose signed his name. There would be another 2 million signatures in due course, nearly half of Scotland's adult population, politely requesting a Scottish Parliament again.

Fast forward a few months, and move to Westminster Abbey at dead of night. A handful of dark-coated Scottish students were busily jemmying loose a lump of stone allegedly carried by a Greek prince and Pharaoh's daughter in the time of Moses to Scotland, via Ireland. This is the 'Stone of Destiny' on which Scotland's ancient kings sat to be crowned. It had been swiped by the wicked English and was being smuggled back to Scotland where it would be hidden as an inanimate hostage. (The Stone was eventually returned to the police, draped in Scottish flags, and was finally returned to Scotland again in the nineties by the Conservatives.) Soon afterwards brand-new postboxes with the symbol QEII for the new Queen, were being defaced or blown up across Scotland, where there had been no QEI. These are parts of the history of post-war Britain which hardly anyone in England has heard about, or understands. Yet at a time when Scotland is becoming ever more politically disassociated from London, it is a story which deserves to be remembered.

Having abolished their own parliament in the 1707 Act of Union, the Scots had become steadily keener on getting it back again, ever since Victorian times. The first National Party of Scotland was formed in 1928, merging with the Scottish Party to become the Scottish National Party or SNP in 1934. By the end of the Second World War Labour was committed to some kind of Scottish Parliament. Yet home rule disappeared as an issue again for most people during the forties and fifties, and indeed into the sixties. This was partly the binding-together effect of the war, which increased pride in being British. It was also because both Labour and the Conservatives (called Unionists in Scotland) had pursued policies of granting the Scots factories, agencies and jobs. In the age of centralism and planning, Scotland seemed to be getting quite a good deal.

During the war, Churchill had appointed a visionary socialist called Tom Johnston, who had once been considered an excellent alternative to Attlee as the next Labour leader, as his Secretary of State for Scotland. Johnson was soon dubbed 'the uncrowned King of Scotland' and set about scattering hydroelectric schemes through the Highlands, bringing electricity and work; ordering great commercial forests to be planted; reforming education, and generally carrying on like a progressive dictator. After the war, he continued running the hydro schemes, forestry and Scottish tourism outside party politics, a one-man socialist planning bureaucracy. He even tried to get fish farming started, half a century before the technology was ready, though it would eventually employ tens of thousands. The Tories, then quite popular in Scotland, pursued similar policies, doling out industrial plants such as the Ravenscraig steelworks and obliging the British Motor Corporation to build cars in Bathgate, and the Hillman Imp to be constructed at Linwood. During the Wilson years, Scotland was run by Willie Ross, a Scottish Secretary as authoritarian, self-certain and skilled as Johnston himself, a veritable second uncrowned king. His gifts included a nuclear reactor at Dounreay, the Invergordon aluminium smelter and rescuing a Clyde shipyard. He set up the Highlands and Islands Development Board and the Scottish Development Agency. If planning could make a country rich, Scotland would be paradise. In the sixties, public spending per head there was a fifth above the English average.

Through most of this time Scottish Nationalism was a mere midge of a movement, producing intense but veiy local irritation. That grand Scottish Covenant signed in 1949 had simply been ignored. Labour dropped its old commitment to a Scottish Parliament in 1956. Nationalism was associated with poets, dreaming students and the odd eccentric aristocrat, a tartan irrelevance to the modern world. The man who did most to change that is almost forgotten now, including in his own party. He was not Billy Wolfe, the SNP's first charismatic post-war leader, but a farmer from Ayrshire called Ian Macdonald who left his farm to organize the 'Nats' full-time. Before 1962 when he took over, the SNP had fewer than twenty active branches and a membership of around two

98

thousand. Three years later under Macdonalds organizing, there were 140 branches and six years on, in 1968, the SNP had 484 branches across Scotland and 120,000 members. It is hard to think of a similar rate of growth in any British political party. With the distinctive CND logo everywhere at the time, the SNP came up with its own modernistic thistle loop, and that was soon glinting from lapels and jerseys across Scotland.

It was at this stage a classic protest party, whose members tended to be prominent in anti-Vietnam and anti-nuclear protests. As disillusion grew, both with the post-Profumo Tories and with Harold Wilson, the SNP began to win first local council seats and then parliamentary by-elections. The first breakthrough came in Hamilton, a small industrial town outside Glasgow where one of the SNP's new generation, Winnie Ewing, won a safe Labour seat in 1967 and was driven in triumph in a scarlet Scottish-made Hillman Imp to Westminster. Though she lost the seat in the general election she was followed by Margo MacDonald, the 'blonde bombshell' of Govan on the Clyde, and by rising success in local elections. In 1970 Donald Stewart became the first SNP victor in a general election contest, winning the Western Isles. In the first 1974 election, the party won a further six Commons seats, and four more in the October election, taking its total to an all-time record of eleven, and the support of just over 30 per cent of Scottish voters. This would give them a crucial power-broking role in the politics of the late seventies which, as we shall see, they badly mishandled. Scotland's economy was doing badly in profound ways. Apart from the short-term boost of oil-related jobs, mainly in the north-east, industry was old-fashioned, riven by strife, badly managed and losing ground in every direction. There was a feeling that the country could not be run worse by its own parliament; that the days of London planning and the gifts of uncrowned kings had not, in fact, produced the modern country everyone hoped for.

Labour became increasingly panicky. Harold Wilson deployed a favourite device, the setting up of a Royal Commission ('takes minutes and wastes years' in his own formulation) which duly suggested devolution for Scotland and Wales. After plots and counter-plots Wilson finally imposed this on a reluctant Scottish party. It was a form of devolution strong enough to outrage many Labour left-wingers at Westminster, including the young Neil Kinnock, yet too weak to please the out-and-out home rulers in Scotland. A handful of politicians, officials and journalists left the Labour Party in the winter of 1975 to form the breakaway Scottish Labour Party under the charismatic Jim Sillars. It briefly captured the headlines before being infiltrated by Trotskyists who, like crocheted bedspreads and lava lamps, seemed to turn up everywhere in the Seventies. The SLP duly split and then collapsed. Some of its members returned to Labour. Others, including Sillars, eventually ended up in the SNP.

Back at Westminster the new Labour leader Jim Callaghan began a long and weary battle to deliver home rule. Leading the fight was Michael Foot, a romantic enthusiast for devolution, despite the fact that his great hero Nye Bevan had been wholly opposed to such 'chauvinism'. Yet the most single-minded and influential MP in the devolution

100

debates of the seventies was probably the anti-devolution backbencher Tam Dalyell who later led the *Belgrano* inquisition. An Old Etonian left-winger, he fuelled himself late into the night with pockets full of hard-boiled eggs prepared by his housekeeper and a head full of hard-boiled arguments about the breakup of Britain, prepared entirely by himself. His 'West Lothian question' asked how Parliament could tolerate having Scottish and Welsh members who could vote on matters affecting the English, while not having any authority over the same issues in their own constituencies (because they would be handled by a devolved parliament). It has never been satisfactorily answered. Many believe it will one day end the Union of Scotland and England. A bill for Home Rule was eventually enacted on 31 July 1978 after an exhausting parliamentary battle in which the government's fate hung in the balance night after night. But a key concession would end up scuppering the bill and Callaghan and the SNP too.

The government had accepted that the Scottish Parliament would only be set up after a referendum in Scotland in which a simple majority would not be enough; at least 40 per cent of the Scottish electorate must vote 'Yes'. Would this be so hard to achieve? When the referendum was finally held, the 'Yes' and 'No' campaigns were both rather ragged. Most of the Scottish media were in favour of devolution revolution and a 'Yes' vote was generally thought to be inevitable. The timing, however, was pitch-perfect terrible. The campaign ran in February 1979 against a backdrop of the 'winter of discontent', terrible weather and a

101

collapse in government prestige. Voting against devolution was for some a way of registering contempt for Labour. Others simply could not be bothered. In the end, though most of Scotland voted in favour of home rule, turnout was low and only 32.9 per cent voted 'Yes', far below the 40 per cent hurdle.

Devolution was dead for twenty years to come. Callaghan, Foot and John Smith did everything they could to find some way of reviving the bill or postponing it but by now the majority of the SNP had had enough. They issued ultimatums to the government and eventually put down a motion of censure, though not all of them voted. Mrs Thatcher saw her chance. Labour lost the vote by a whisker and the general election of 1979 was duly triggered. This would bring about the election of a now implacable opponent of home rule. It would plunge Labour into chaos in Scotland as well as elsewhere. The SNP group was cut from eleven MPs to just two, and never regained the initiative. Earlier in this section we noted that Mrs Thatcher was lucky in her enemies and the Scottish Nationalists were yet another good example.

Wales's part in the story runs parallel to Scotland's in many ways. Like Scotland, Wales had become a post-war Labour stronghold in her industrial heartland, with a Liberal tradition in the rural areas. Like Scotland, Wales had experienced a rise of interest in the national question between the wars – Plaid Cymru, the party of Wales, had been founded in 1925, nine years before the SNP. Like the Scottish nationalists, the Welsh nationalists were dominated in the early years by literary men, poets and lecturers, and had little working-class support. In the post-war years Wales, like Scotland, had benefited from the scattering of regional policy initiatives, above all the great steel rolling-mill at Llanwern in 1962 but also the Shotton blast furnace, the Licensing Centre at Swansea, the Passport Office at Newport, two nuclear power stations, and factories run by Rover, Ford, Hoover, Hotpoint and others – the equivalent to the car-making plants and aluminium smelters of the Scots. Just as in the Scottish Highlands, vast acreages of conifers were planted by the Forestry Commission, so too it happened across the hillsides of rural Wales. The Scots got a development agency. So did the Welsh. If the Scots popularly expressed their national pride through the up-and-down fortunes of their football team, and the occasional even dodgier pop phenomenon like the Bay City Rollers, the Welsh had rugby. At Cardiff Arms Park, renamed the Welsh National Stadium in 1970, England failed to win a single game between 1964 and 1979.

Politically, however, Wales was in a weaker position. She had been incorporated by England too early in her history to have developed separate institutions of modern statehood. Her 'Act of Union' came in 1536, not 1707, and it was a crucial difference. Wales had no single powerful national church, no parliament to look back on, no Enlightenment universities or modern legal code of her own. Indeed she had no official capital until Cardiff was recognized as such as late as 1955; no minister or administrative offices until the fifties and no Secretary of State for Wales until 1964. Welshness was celebrated more as a linguistic and religious quality, though the decline in religious attendance hit the nonconformist chapel tradition

103

almost as hard as it hit the Church of England. Politically, the Welsh had looked to Westminster men as their heroes, David Lloyd George most obviously, but Nye Bevan too. The decline of Liberalism had left Wales dominated by Labour and with all the drawbacks of the one-party statelet – internal backbiting, political stagnation and an unbalanced attitude to London, which was simultaneously the remote and alien capital and the source of power, money and jobs. Clever Welshmen from Raymond Williams to Dylan Thomas often emigrated, becoming exiled professors and writers, endlessly harking back to the romantic day-before-yesterday.

In the Fifties Welsh nationalists began to find cultural and political issues which spurred them on. Instead of attacking post-boxes and stealing the Stone of Destiny, Welsh nationalism was inspired to fight for the survival of the Welsh language. English road-signs would be painted out, people refused to fill in forms written in English and there were successful campaigns for more Welsh broadcasting. But the biggest early spur was water. Indeed it could almost be said that water was the Welsh oil, particularly after the drowning of the Tryweryn valley in north-west Wales to create a reservoir for the people of Liverpool. This was done by Act of Parliament in 1957, despite almost all Welsh MPs voting against it. As one historian put it: 'Liverpool's ability to ignore the virtually unanimous opinion of the representatives of the Welsh people, confirmed one of the central tenets of Plaid Cymru – that the national Welsh community, under the existing order, was wholly powerless.'[22] Attacks on the Tryweryn reservoir followed and the Free Wales Army was formed in 1963. Violent Welsh nationalism was, thankfully, almost as unpopular and badly organized as violent Scottish nationalism, but there were explosions in the sixties and two men died in 1969 trying to blow up the Royal train during the Prince of Wales's Investiture. There would also be a more widespread and persistent campaign of burning out holiday homes and full-time homes owned by English incomers to Welsh-speaking areas.

Plaid Cymru's first breakthrough came at the Carmarthen by-election of 1966, a year before the SNP won Hamilton. Gwynfor Evans, a nationalist campaigner since the thirties and Plaid Cymru's leader since 1945, would lose the seat in the 1970 general election but two striking Plaid Cymru by-election performances in Rhondda West and Caerphilly in 1967 and 1968 suggested it was no flash in the pan. At last complacent Welsh Labour was being challenged. In the first 1974 election, Plaid Cymru would win two seats, and take a third in the second election of that year. Just as in Scotland, this produced a divided response among Labour in Wales. Should the nationalists be fought, as Neil Kinnock believed, or should they be paid to go away, with offers of devolution, as Michael Foot thought?

By then, like Scotland, the client economy of Wales was in very deep trouble. Yet despite the success of Plaid Cymru in local elections during the final years of 'old Labour' rule, they did not seem to pose quite the threat of the SNP. And of course, there was no oil boom in Welsh waters. So the proposed Welsh assembly was to have fewer powers than the Scottish one. It was to oversee a large

105

chunk of public expenditure but would not be able to make laws. This was hardly likely to make anyone's blood pound. When the matter was put to a referendum the Welsh voted overwhelmingly against the planned assembly, by 956,000 votes to 243,000. Every one of the new Welsh counties voted 'No' Plaid Cymru, unlike the SNP, did not vote for the end of the Labour government but in the Thatcher years Wales, like Scotland, was dominated by the politics of resistance to Conservatism. It would be a long wait.

The Boyo and the Bolsheviks

Michael Foot's leadership saved the Labour Party from splitting into two but was in all other respects a disaster. He was too old, too decent, too gentle, to take on the hard left or to modernize his party. Foot's politics were those of a would-be parliamentary revolutionary detained in a second-hand bookshop. When roused (which was often), his hair would flap, his face contort with passion, his hands would whip around excitedly and denunciations would pour from him with a fluency Martin Luther would envy. He was in his late sixties during his time as leader – he would be seventy just after the 1983 election – and he looked his age. Contemptuous of the shallow presentational tricks of television, he could look dishevelled and was famously denounced for wearing a 'donkey jacket' (it was actually, he insisted, rather a smart green woollen coat) at the Cenotaph. His skills were for whipping up the socialist faithful in meetings or for finger-stabbing attacks on the Tory enemy in House of Commons debates. He seemed to live in an earlier century, though it was never clear which one, communing with heroes such as Swift, Byron or Hazlitt, rather than in a political system which depended on television performance, ruthless organization and managerial discipline. He was a political poet in a prose age.

Perhaps nobody in the early eighties could have disciplined the Labour Party or reined in its wilder members. Foot did his best yet he led Labour to the party's worst defeat in modern times, on the basis of a hard-left, anti-Europe, anti-nuclear, if-it-moves-nationalize-it manifesto aptly described by Gerald Kaufman as 'the longest suicide note in history'. Kaufman had also bravely but fruitlessly urged him to stand down before the election. The campaign which followed has gone down in history as one of the least competent, most disorganized few weeks of chaos ever arranged by a modern political party. Foot impersonated a late nineteenth-century radical, touring open meetings and making long semi-literary effusions from crowded platforms to gatherings of the faithful. It was as if he had not condescended to notice the radio age, never mind the television one. He appeared with the very Trotskyists he had earlier denounced and was clearly at odds with his deputy, Denis Healey, over such minor matters as the defence of the country. Labour's two former prime ministers, Wilson and Callaghan, both publicly attacked Foot's principled unilateralism. After all this, it was surprising that the party scraped into second place and held off the SDP-Liberal Alliance. It is a measure of the affection felt for Michael Foot that his swift retirement after that defeat was greeted with little recrimination.

Yet it also meant that when Neil Kinnock won the subsequent leadership election he had a mandate for change no previous Labour leader had enjoyed. 'Enjoyed' is perhaps not the word. Kinnock had won by a huge majority. He had 71 per cent of the electoral college votes, against 19 per cent for his nearest rival Roy Hattersley, while Tony Benn, the obvious left-wing challenger, was out of Parliament briefly, having lost his Bristol seat. Kinnock had been elected after a series of blistering campaign speeches, a left-winger by the standards of anyone who wasn't actually a revolutionary. He wanted the swift abandonment of all Britain's nuclear weapons. He believed in nationalization and planning. He wanted Britain to withdraw from Europe. He wanted to abolish private medicine and to repeal the Tory laws on trade union reform. And to start with, the only fights he picked with his party were over organizational matters, such as the campaign to force Labour MPs to submit to reselection, which handed a noose to militant local activists. Yet after the chaos of the 1983 campaign, he was also sure that the party needed radical reform.

Though the modern age of attempted ruthless control over the media is popularly believed to have begun with Peter Mandelson's arrival as Labour's director of communications, it actually began when Patricia Hewitt, a radical Australian known for her campaigning on civil liberties, joined Kinnock's new office. It was she who began keeping the leader away from journalists, trying to control interviews and placing him like a precious stone only in flattering settings. Kinnock, for his part, knew how unsightly old Labour looked to the rest of the country and was prepared, if not happy, to be groomed. He gathered round him a rugby scrum of tough and aggressive aides, many of whom went on to become ministers in the Blair years – Charles Clarke, the burly son of a powerful Whitehall mandarin; John Reid, a wild former Communist Labour backbencher; Hewitt; and Peter Mandelson. Kinnock was the first to flirt, indeed to enter into full physical relations, with the once-abhorred world of advertising, and to seek out the support of pro-Labour pop singers such as Tracey Ullmann and Billy Bragg, long before 'Cool Britannia' was thought of in the Blair years. He smartened up his own style, ending the informal mateyness which had made him popular among colleagues, and introduced a new code of discipline in the shadow cabinet, a code which would have had him thrown out a few years earlier.

In the Commons he tried hard to discomfit Thatcher at her awesome best, which was not easy and rarely successful. The two of them loathed each other with a chemical passion. Labour's dreadful poll ratings very slowly began to improve. There was talk of 'the Kinnock factor'. But there were awesome problems for Labour which could not be dealt with by pop stars, friends in the advertising world or well-educated Australian ladies barking at journalists. The first of these was that the party harboured a substantial and vocal minority of people who were not really parliamentary politicians at all, but revolutionaries of one kind or another. They included Arthur Scargill and his brand of insurrectionary trade unionism; the

Trotskyist Militant Tendency, which had been busy infiltrating the party since the sixties; and assorted hard-left councils, determined to defy 'Thatcher' (also known as the democratically elected government) by various illegal stratagems.

Kinnock dealt with them all. Had he not done so New Labour would never have happened and Tony Blair would have enjoyed a well-remunerated and obscure career as a genial barrister specializing in employment law. Yet Kinnock himself was a passionate man whose own politics were to the left of the new mood of the country. He was beginning an agonizing journey which meant confronting and defeating people who sounded not so different from his younger self; while moving steadily, but never quite far enough, towards the centre. On this journey much of his natural wit, his balls-of-the-feet, exuberant, extempore rhetoric and convivial bounce would be silenced, sellotaped and sedated (as he might well have alliterated). He had come into politics as if it was rugby, us against them, a violent contact sport much enjoyed by all participants. He found that in leadership it was more serious, drearier and nastier than rugby. The game was changing. Week after week, he was confronting in Thatcher someone whose principles had set firm long before and whose politics, love them or hate them, seemed to express those principles. Yet he was by necessity changing, a man on the move, who could not renounce his former beliefs nor yet quite stand by them. He was always having to shade, to hedge and to qualify, to dodge the ball, not kick it. The press soon dubbed him 'the Welsh windbag'.

The first and hardest example of what he was up

against came with the miners' strike. As we have seen, Kinnock and Scargill loathed each other – indeed, the NUM president may have been the only human being on the planet that Kinnock disliked more than Margaret Thatcher. He distrusted Scargill's aims, despised his tactics and realized early on that he was certain to fail. As the spawn of socialist Welsh miners, Kinnock could not demonize the strike without demonizing his own upbringing and origins, yet he knew it was a disaster. As the violence spread, the Conservatives and the press were waiting for him to denounce the pickets and to praise the police. He simply could not. Too many of his own side thought the violence was the fault of the police. As the strike hardened, one obvious tactic was to attack Scargill's failure to hold a national ballot. Yet acutely conscious of the feelings of striking miners, he could not bring himself to attack the embattled trade union. So he was caught, volubly, even eloquently inarticulate, between the rock of Thatcher and the hard place of Scargill. In the Commons, white-faced, week by week, he was taunted by the Tories for his weakness. In the coalfields he was denounced as the miner's son too frightened to come to the support of the miners. So he made lengthy arguments about the case for coal and the harshness of the Tories which were, as he knew full well, only adjacent to the row consuming the nation. These were impossible circumstances. In them, Kinnock at least managed to avoid fusing Labour and the NUM in the mind of floating voters, ensuring that Scargill's utter political defeat was his alone. But this lost year destroyed his early momentum and damped down his old blazing

111

certainty. It stole his hwyl – and a Welsh politician without hwyl is like a Jewish agent without chutzpah.

It is said that the difference between being an Opposition politician and a Government one is that in Government you get up each morning and decide what to do while in Opposition you get up and decide what you are going to say. It is hardly Kinnock's fault that in British politics he is remembered for talking. His critics recall his imprecise long-windedness, the product of self-critical and painful political readjustment. His admirers recall his great platform speeches, the saw-edged wit and air-punching passion. There was one time, however, lasting for just a few minutes, when Kinnock spoke so well he united most of the political world in admiration.

This happened on 1 October 1985 at the main auditorium in Bournemouth, the well-off Dorset coastal resort where Labour conferences never seem entirely at home. A few days earlier Liverpool City Council, formally Labour-run but in fact controlled by the Revolutionary Socialist League, had sent out redundancy notices to its 31,000 staff. The revolutionaries, known by the name of their newspaper *Militant,* were a party-within-a-party, a parasitic body nuzzled inside Labour and chewing its guts. They had some five thousand members who paid a proportion of their incomes to the RSL, so that the Militant Tendency had 140 full-time workers, more than the staff of the Social Democrats and Liberals combined.[23] They were present all round the country but Liverpool was their great stronghold. There they practised Trotsky's politics of 'the transitional demand' – the habit of making impractical demands for more spending, higher wages and so on, so that when the capitalist lackeys refuse them, you can push on to the next stage, leading to collapse and then revolution. In Liverpool where they were building thousands of new council houses, this meant setting an illegal council budget and cheerfully bankrupting the city. Sending out the redundancy notices to the council's entire staff was supposed to show Thatcher they would not back down, or shrink from the chaos ahead. Like Scargill, Militant's leaders thought they could destroy the Tories on the streets.

Kinnock had thought of taking them on a year earlier but had decided the miners' strike made that politically impossible. The Liverpool mayhem gave him his chance. So in the middle of his speech at Bournemouth, up to then a fairly conventional Labour leader's address, attacking the other parties and cheering up the hall, Kinnock struck. It was time, he suddenly said, for Labour to show the public that it was serious. Implausible promises would not win political victory.

> I'll tell you what happens with impossible promises. You start with far-fetched resolutions. They are then pickled into a rigid dogma, a code, and you go through the years sticking to that, outdated, misplaced, irrelevant to the real needs, and you end in the grotesque chaos of a Labour council – a *Labour* council – hiring taxis to scuttle round a city handing out redundancy notices to its own workers.

113

By now he had whipped himself into real anger, shouting yet also – just – in control. The best speeches are made on the lip of the curve of the track, an inch away from crashing into incoherence. Kinnock's enemies were in front of him. All the pent-up frustrations of the past year were being released. The hall came alive. Militant leaders like Derek Hatton, a man with the looks of a recently retired footballer, stood up and yelled back. Boos came from left-wingers. Uncertain applause came from the loyalists. The pompous left-wing MP Eric Heffer (who had once begun a speech in the Commons with the immortal words, 'I, like Jesus Christ, am the son of a carpenter') stood up and stomped from the hall, followed by camera crews and journalists. This was drama of a kind even Labour conferences were unused to. Kinnock went on:

'I'm telling you, and you'll listen, you can't play politics with people's jobs and with people's services, or with their homes.'

There was another huge outburst, now both of cheers and of boos. Kinnock insisted that the voice of people with real needs was louder than all the booing that could be assembled: 'The people will not, cannot, abide posturing. They cannot respect the gesture-generals or the tendency tacticians.'

Alliteration, then eruption. Most of those interviewed said it was one of the most important and courageous speeches they had ever heard, though the hard left was venomously hostile. The newspapers, used to kicking Kinnock, were almost delirious with praise. David Blunkett, the blind socialist leader of Sheffield city council, who would later serve in the Blair cabinets, organized a climbdown on a Militant-sponsored motion, much to Kinnock's annoyance. But the speech was a genuine turning point. By the end of the following month Liverpool District Labour Party, from which Militant drew its power, was suspended and an inquiry had been set up. By the spring of 1986 leaders of Militant had been identified and charged with behaving in a way incompatible with Labour membership. The process of expelling them was noisy, legally fraught and time-consuming, though more than a hundred were eventually expelled. As important, there was a strong tide towards Kinnock across the rest of the party, with many left-wingers cutting their ties to the revolutionaries. There were many battles with the hard left to come, and several pro-Militant MPs were elected to the Commons. Newspaper stories about 'loony left' councils allegedly banning black bin bags on the grounds of racism and ordering teachers to stop using nursery rhymes for the same reason, would continue to be used to taunt Labour. Yet by standing up openly to the Trotskyist menace, as Wilson, Callaghan and Foot had not, Kinnock gave his party a new start. It began to draw away from the SDP-Liberal Alliance in the polls and do much better in local elections too. It was the moment when New Labour became possible.

Yet neither this, nor the new fashion for better-controlled, slicker and sharper management that Kinnock brought it, would do the party much good against Thatcher in the election that followed. Whatever glossy pamphlets, well-made adulatory films and carefully planned photo-opportunities could do, was done. Mandelson, a former student leader and television producer whose grandfather had been Herbert Morrison, became the best-known of the modernizers. Prince Charles greeted him as 'the red rose man' for his role in ditching the old red banner as Labour's symbol and substituting a long-stemmed rose. Mandelson was certainly a single-minded and devoted reformer, cajoling and bullying a generally anti-Labour press. But he was not the only one. The red rose had been suggested by others, a copy of European socialist party imagery. Yet symbolism could not mask the fact that in its policies, Labour was still behind the public mood. Despite mass unemployment Thatcher's market optimism was filtering through. Labour might have ditched the red flag but it was still committed to renationalization, planning, a National Investment Bank and unilateral nuclear disarmament, a personal cause for both Kinnock and his wife Glenys over the previous twenty years.

The mid-eighties were a time when, after ferocious arguments about disarmament and the Russian invasion of Afghanistan, then a spate of espionage cases, the Cold War was finally thawing. In the White House President Reagan, scourge of the 'evil empire', was set on creating 'Star Wars', the orbiting satellite and anti-missile system intended to make the United States invulnerable to Russian attack. Yet he was ready to talk too, as the famous summit with Gorbachev at Reykjavik showed. There the Russians agreed to big missile reductions and the Americans declined to scrap 'Star Wars'. It was not a time for the old certainties. Yet for Kinnock, support for unilateral nuclear disarmament was fundamental to his political personality. It was the reflex response to those who accused him of selling out his socialism. It was

116

a source of some of his best rhetoric. He therefore stuck with the policy, even as he came to realize just how damaging it was to Labour's image among swing voters.

He was clear about it. Under Labour all the British and American nuclear bases would be closed, the Trident nuclear submarine force cancelled, all existing missiles scrapped and Britain would no longer expect any nuclear protection from the United States in time of war. Instead more money would be spent on tanks and conventional warships. Kinnock was forceful and detailed about all this, and the more he spoke, the more Labour's ratings went down. He set off gamely trying to sell the CND line as no kind of surrender when in Russia; and something wholly compatible with Nato membership while in Washington, where on his third visit Reagan's team humiliated him with a twenty-minute meeting, followed by a coldly hostile briefing. All of this did him a lot of good among many traditional Labour supporters; Glenys turned up at the women's protest camp at Greenham Common. But it was derided in the press, helped the SDP and was unpopular with just the floating-voter, middle England people Labour desperately needed to win back. In the 1987 general election campaign Kinnock's explanation about why Britain would not simply have to surrender if threatened by a Soviet nuclear attack sounded as if he was advocating some kind of *Dad's Army* guerrilla campaign once the Russians had got here. With policies like these, he was not putting Thatcher under the kind of pressure which, perhaps, she needed.

A Revolution's Mid-Life Crisis

There had been some bad moments for the second Thatcher government. Most obviously, she had nearly been assassinated. The IRA bomb which demolished a chunk of the Grand Hotel at Brighton during the 1984 Conservative conference was intended as a response to Mrs Thatcher's hard line at the time of the 1981 hunger strike. The plot had been to murder the British cabinet and Prime Minister and plunge the country into political chaos, resulting in withdrawal from all Ireland. As for her, when it went off at 2.50 she was still working on an official paper about Liverpool's garden festival, having finished writing her speech ten minutes earlier so she was not even woken up. The blast scattered broken glass on her bedroom carpet and filled her mouth with dust. She then decamped to lie fully clothed in the bedroom of a nearby police college, pausing only to kneel and pray with her personal assistant Cynthia Crawford, or 'Crawfie', when they heard that the bomb had killed the wife of the cabinet minister John Wakeham and nearly killed him; killed the Tory MP Anthony Berry; had badly injured Norman Tebbit, and paralysed his wife.

After less than an hour's fitful sleep and with her cabinet hurriedly dressed in clothes from a nearby branch of Marks & Spencer, their dresses and suits still being in the half-wrecked hotel, she rewrote her speech and told the still stunned conference that they had witnessed an attempt to cripple the government. 'And the fact that we are gathered here now, shocked but composed and determined, is a sign not only that this attack has failed, but that all attempts to destroy democracy by terrorism will fail.' The final death toll from Brighton was five dead and several more seriously injured but its consequences for British politics, which could have been momentous, turned out to be minimal.

If the IRA could not shake her, could anything else? There had been internal rows, not only over Westland but more ominously for the future, about economic policy. Her Chancellor, Nigel Lawson, had wanted to replace the old and rather wobbly system of controlling the money supply through targets, the Medium Term Financial Strategy, with a new stratagem – tying the pound to the German mark in the European Exchange Rate system, or ERM. This was an admission of failure; the older system of measuring money was useless in the world of global fast money described earlier. Using Germanic bondage was an alternative. In effect, Britain would have subcontracted her anti-inflationary policy to the more successful and harder-faced disciplinarians of the West German Central Bank. Lawson was keen. She was not; if anyone was to play dominatrix round here, it would be her. At the time, little of this debate bubbled from the specialist financial world into general political life.

Other rows did. There was the Westland affair itself but also a botched sale of British Leyland and the highly unpopular use of British airbases for President Reagan's attack on Libya in 1986. After her hugely successful fight to claw back some of Britain's overpayment to the European Community budget in her first term, these were years of

Thatcherite drift over Europe, which would so fatally damage her at the end. Jacques Delors, later her great enemy, had been appointed President of the European Commission and begun his grand plan for the next stages of union. The Single European Act, which smashed down thousands of national laws preventing free trade inside the EC, promising free movement of goods, capital, services and people, and presaging the single currency, was passed with her urgent approval. She pooh-poohed the idea that when the continentals talked of economic and political union, they really meant it. She would regret all this later.

At home a wider dilemma was emerging right across domestic policy, from the inner cities to hospitals, schools to police forces. It was one which would puzzle both her successor governments, John Major's and Tony Blair's. It was simply this: how does a modern government get things done? In the economy, she had an answer. Government sets the rules, delivers sound money and then stands back letting other people get on with it. In practice she often behaved differently, always more pragmatic and interventionist than her image suggested. At least, however, the principle was clear. But when it came to the public services there was no similar principle. Where were the staunch, independent-spirited movers and shakers in the hospitals, town halls or the school system, the equivalent for public life of the entrepreneurs and risk takers she admired in business? If government stood back and just let go of schools, hospitals, inner cities, who would be waiting to catch them?

Before the Thatcher revolution the Conservatives had been seen as, on balance, defenders of local democracy. They were very strongly represented in councils across the country and had been on the receiving end of some of the most thuggish threats from Labour governments intent, for instance, on abolishing grammar schools. Conservatives had seen local representatives on hospital boards and education authorities as bulwarks against socialist Whitehall. Margaret Thatcher herself had good reason to recall the days of sturdy local independents, doing the public's work on unpaid committees for her father, Alderman Roberts, had been one of them. In the seventies, Tory think tanks regularly produced reports calling for stronger localism, the building of a rich 'civil society' in which independent institutions – churches, schools, charities, clubs and the rest – would spread autonomy and freedom. It was the theme of the most influential conservative philosopher of post-war Britain, Michael Oakeshott. The Tory vision emphatically included elected local government. In 1978, two right-wing Conservative politicians, for instance, wrote a passionate pamphlet complaining that 'local government is being deprived of more and more of the functions it used to be thought capable of fulfilling.'[24]

Yet in power, Thatcher and her ministers could not trust local government, or any elected and therefore independent bodies at all. Between 1979 and 1994, an astonishing 150 Acts of Parliament were passed removing powers from local authorities, and £24 billion a year, at 1994 prices, had been switched from them to unelected and mostly secretive gatherings. The first two Thatcher governments transferred power and discretion away from people who had stood openly for election, and towards the subservient agents of Whitehall, often paid-up party members and well-meaning stooges. Ministers, whether 'wet' or 'dry', competed to show her their zeal by taking the initiative away from organizations on the ground. Michael Heseltine attacked local government with new auditing arrangements, curbs on how much tax they could raise, and then spending caps as well. Nicholas Ridley, an Environment Secretary, forced them to put out a wide range of services to tender for private companies, telling local councils in the harshest terms that no dissent was permissable: 'we might have to force them to expose their activities to competition if they did not choose to do that themselves.'[25]

So there was no public service equivalent of privatization. In hospitals and schools Thatcher had eventually rejected the radical alternatives of fees, private management, selection and independence when offered them by the CPRS (Central Policy Review Staff). Stirred by the idea, she was too cautious to follow where it led. If neither new private nor old public, then what? The answer turned out to be expensive bureaucratic central activity which made ministers feel important. In the health service, early attempts to decentralize were rapidly reversed and a vast top-down system of targets and measurements was put in place, driven by a new planning organization. It cost more and the service seemed to get worse. Similar centralist power-grabs took place in urban regeneration, one of the most visible and immediate areas of government action, where unelected corporations, UDCs, rather than elected councils, got the money to pour into rundown cities. The biggest city councils, notably the Greater London Council, were simply abolished. Its powers were distributed, including to an unelected organization controlled by Whitehall. As one critic, Simon Jenkins, pointed out, by 1990 'there were some 12,000 laymen and women running London on an appointed basis against just 1,900 elected borough councillors.' Even in housing, the gap left by the sale of council homes was met by the rise of the Housing Corporation, disbursing 90 per cent of the money used by housing associations to build new cheap homes. In the Thatcher years its staff grew sevenfold and its budget, twentyfold.

Back in the mid-eighties she did, to be fair, have other things on her mind. Personal relationships matter as much in modern diplomacy as they did in the Renaissance, and the Thatcher–Gorbachev courtship engaged her imagination and human interest. She was becoming the closest ally Ronald Reagan had, in another international relationship which was of huge emotional and political significance to her. In these years she had become an international diva of conservative politics, feted by crowds from Russia and China to New York. Her wardrobe, coded depending on where an outfit had first been worn, told its own story: 'Paris Opera, Washington Pink, Reagan Navy, Toronto Turquoise, Tokyo Blue, Kremlin Silver, Peking Black'.[26] Meanwhile she was negotiating the hard detail of Hong Kong's transitional status before it was handed over to Communist China in 1997. She got a torrid time at Commonwealth conferences for her opposition to sanctions against the apartheid regime in South Africa – and where she gave as good as she got. At home, the problem of persistently high unemployment was nagging away, though it started to fall from the summer of 1986, while Tory strategists still seemed to lack a clear idea about how to deal with the unfamiliar threat of the 'two Davids' and the Liberal-SDP Alliance. And electorally, the multiple failures and political threats turned out to matter not at all.

1987: The Revolution Confirmed

When the 1987 election campaign began, Thatcher had a clear idea about what her third administration would do. Just like Tony Blair later, she wanted more choice for the users of state services. There would be independent state schools outside the control of local councillors, called grant-maintained schools. In the health service, though it was barely mentioned in the manifesto, she wanted money to follow the patient. Tenants would be given more rights. The basic rate of income tax would be cut. She would finally sort out local government, ending the rates and bringing in a tax with bite. On paper the programme seemed coherent, which was more than could be said for the management of the Tory campaign itself. Just as Kinnock's Labour team had achieved a rare harmony and discipline, Conservative Central Office was racked by hissy fits and screaming cat-fights between politicians and ad-men. The Leaderene began to snap at her former favourite, the carnivorous 'Chingford Skinhead', Norman Tebbit, now party chairman.

At one point in the campaign when the Labour leader seemed to have closed the gap to just four points and when Mrs Thatcher herself was performing badly, hit by agonizing toothache, the Tories had a real panic, 'Wobbly Thursday'. That dreadful Kinnock, it seemed, was having a better campaign than she was. He sailed around, surrounded by admiring crowds, young people, nurses, waving and smiling and little worried by the press while she was having a horrid time. What was going on? In the event, the Conservatives need not have worried at all. Despite a last-minute BBC prediction of a hung Parliament, and a late surge of Labour self-belief, they romped home. The Tories had an overall majority of 101 seats, almost exactly the share of the vote (42 per cent) they had enjoyed after the Labour catastrophe of 1983. Labour had made just twenty net gains. At home in his Welsh constituency, despairing, Kinnock punched the wall. His police protection officer, who had been much moved by some of the great Kinnock speeches he had witnessed in the past three weeks, offered words of comfort. 'Don't worry, sir, it could have been worse.' Kinnock is said to have swivelled round towards him, eyes narrowed, looking suddenly dangerous. 'Worse? Could have been worse? Just tell me, how could it have been worse?' The police officer blandly replied: 'Well sir, in the old days, they'd have chopped your head off.'

Afterwards, surveying the wreckage of their hopes, Kinnock and his team won plaudits from the press for the brilliance, verve and professionalism of their campaign. It had been transformed from the shambles of only four years earlier. At the same time the Conservatives had been flat-footed and unsure of themselves compared to their previous two elections, which only goes to show that the detail of electioneering, which obsesses Westminster politicians, is perhaps less important than they think. And what of the SDP-Liberal Alliance, the big new idea of eighties politics? They were out of puff. They had been floundering in the polls for some time, caught between Kinnock's modest Labour revival and Thatcher's continuing popularity with a large and solid minority of voters. Their gamble was that Labour was dying, and it had failed. The public had enjoyed robust media mockery of the competing David Steel/David Owen dual leadership as much as the leadership itself. Though Owen was popularly seen as the dominant partner his Social Democrats had a woeful election, seeing their eight MPs reduced to five and losing Roy Jenkins in the process, a tribulation Owen bore with fortitude. The SDP would soon begin to fall apart, though an Owenite rump party limped on for a while after the rest merged with the Liberals. Good PR, good labelling, goodwill; none of it had been good enough. In 1987 Thatcher had not created the country she dreamed of, but she could argue that she had won a third consecutive victory on the back of ideas, not on the back of envelopes.

The Year of Hubris, 1988 – and Why We Still Live There

For true believers the story of Margaret Thatcher's third and last administration can be summed up in the single word, betrayal. Her hopes of a free-market Europe were betrayed by the continentals, abetted by her own treacherous Foreign Office. Her achievements in bringing down inflation were betrayed by her Chancellor, Nigel Lawson. Finally she was betrayed directly – 'treachery with a smile on its face' – when her cabinet ministers turned on her and forced her to resign on 20 November 1990. The British revolution was sold out by faint-hearts, its great leader exiled to an executive home in south London, and glory departed from the earth. But there is another word that sums up the story better – not betrayal, but hubris. In the late eighties the Thatcher revolution overreached itself. The inflationary boom happened because of the expansion of credit and a belief among ministers that, somehow, the old laws of economics had been abolished; Britain was now in a virtuous, endless upward spiral of increasing prosperity. Across the Welfare State swaggering, highhanded centralism continued on steroids, ever grander. Near the end, Thatcher's fall was triggered by a disastrous policy for local taxation whose blatant unfairness was never properly considered by ministers, as if it did not really matter. And by the end, her own brutal rudeness to those around her left her almost friendless. She had been in power too long.

The year after the election, 1988, was the real year of hubris. The Thatcher government began laying about it with a frenzy unmatched before or since, flaying independent institutions and bullying the professions as if it was a short-tempered teacher and they were uppity children. England's senior judges came under tighter new political control. They would hit back. University lecturers lost the academic tenure they had enjoyed since the days

127

when students arrived by ox-cart, making jokes in Latin. In Kenneth Baker's Great Education Reform Bill, or 'Gerbil' of that year, Whitehall grabbed direct control over the running of school curriculums, creating a vast new state bureaucracy to dictate what should be taught, when and how, and then to monitor the results. Teachers could do nothing. The cabinet debated the detail of maths courses; Mrs Thatcher spent much of her own time worrying about the teaching of history. It happened at a time when education ministers were complaining bitterly in private about the appalling quality of talent, not among teachers, but civil servants, the very people they were handing more power to.

A former and penitent Education Secretary from the age of comprehensives, Thatcher believed schooling was now a national disgrace. She wanted to scupper trendy-lefty teachers by giving parents, generally traditionalist, more choice about which school to choose. That meant establishing Whitehall-controlled independent state schools specializing in technical subjects, City Technology Colleges. It also meant persuading other schools to opt out of local authority control to become grant-maintained, rewarded with a small bribe. Neither idea worked. Only a small number of highly costly CTCs ever opened and the few schools who opted out found they had opted in – to tight Treasury and Department of Education control. Later under John Major's government, the inevitable extension of central financial control would produce yet another Whitehall-style organization (though, in fact, based in York), the Funding Agency for Schools. It was meant to be able to close schools, open schools, expand them, change their character and cut their scale, all without reference to local wishes. It was described by a right-wing think tank as having 'an extraordinary range of dictatorial powers' giving the Education Secretary 'authority similar to Henry VIII's dissolution commissioners'.[27]

It was the same pattern in health. In 1988 too, the new Health Secretary, Kenneth Clarke, pressed ahead with the system of 'money following the patient', a Monopoly-board version of the market in which hospitals 'sold' their services, and local doctors, on behalf of the ill, 'bought' them. The market was not real, of course, because the hospitals could not go out of business and the doctors, with a limited range of hospitals to choose from, could hardly withhold their money and refuse to buy their patients a heart bypass or hip replacement. The initial theory was perfectly intelligent. It was an attempt to bring private sector-like behaviour into the health service, a new regime of efficiency and tight budgeting. It looked enough like a real market to cause a huge and lengthy revolt by doctors and patients' groups. They were worrying about the wrong problem.

Because the government did not really trust local people to work together to improve the health service, the Treasury seized control of budgets and contracts. And to administer the system nearly 500 National Health Service trusts were formed, apparently autonomous but staffed by failed party candidates, ex-councillors and party donors. Any involvement by elected local representatives was brutally terminated. Mrs Thatcher later wrote: 'As with our education reforms, we wanted all hospitals

129

to have greater responsibility for their affairs ... [and] the self-governing hospitals to be virtually independent.' But as with her education reforms, the real effect was to create a new bureaucracy overseeing a regiment of quangos. Every detail of the 'internal market' contracts was set down from the centre, from pay to borrowing to staffing. The rhetoric of choice in practice, meant an incompetent dictatorship of bills, contracts and instructions. Those who could voted with their chequebooks. Between 1980 and 1990, the number of people covered by the private health insurance company Bupa nearly doubled, from 3.5 million to a little under 7 million. It wasn't only salaried, professional people with health insurance written into their contracts who paid for private medicine: by the late eighties private hospitals had queues of tattooed men in jeans waiting to be seen, cash in hand.

Hubris about what the State can and cannot do was found everywhere. Training may be unglamorous but it is crucial to any modern economy. Here too a web of unelected bodies was spun, disbursing Treasury money according to Whitehall rules. The same happened in housing, which Thatcher said was more serious a matter even than health and education at the time, and which in 1988 saw the establishment of unelected Housing Action Trusts to take over the old responsibility of local authorities for providing cheap homes. Nearly twenty years after most of these bodies began work, there is still a puzzle here.

Mrs Thatcher said she was trying to pull the State off people's backs. In the end, that was the point of her. She thought so, too. In her memoirs she wrote

130

of her third government, 'the root cause of our contemporary social problems ... was that the state had been doing too much.' So why did she let it bustle around doing more and more? Simon Jenkins concluded that 'Her most potent legacy was potency itself.'[28] The more a leader is self-certain, the more there is in the world around her that she wants to change and the fewer other people she can trust. That means taking more powers. Letting other institutions and smaller-scale leaders find their own way through a busy world goes for a Burton. The institutions most hurt were local councils. Under our constitution, local government is defenceless against a Prime Minister with a secure parliamentary majority and a loyal cabinet. So it has been hacked away. It is time to address the moment when this programme of crushing alternative centres of power came so badly unstuck it destroyed the Lady Lenin of the free market herself.

Enter the Peasants, with Billhooks

Margaret Thatcher would say the poll tax was actually an attempt to save local government. Like schools, hospitals and housing, councils had been subject to a grisly torture chamber full of pincers, bits, whips and flails as ministers tried to stop them spending money, or raising it, except as Whitehall wished. Since the war local government had been spending more but the amount of money it raised independently came from a relatively narrow base of people, some 14 million property-owners.

Thatcher had been prodded by Edward Heath into promising to replace this tax, the 'rates', as early as 1974 but nobody had come up with a plausible and popular-sounding alternative. She intensely disliked rates, regarding them as a tax on self-improvement and inherently un-Conservative. Yet in government, the problem nagged away at her.

There was a malign dynamic at work. The more powers government took away from local councils, the less councils mattered and the more local elections were used merely as giant referendums on central government, a cost-free protest vote. Once, local elections were not national news; they were about who was best to run towns and counties. In the late sixties and seventies they became national news, a regular referendum in which the Prime Minister was applauded or slapped. It was generally the latter. Under Margaret Thatcher the Tories lost swathes of local councils in bloody electoral defeats, again and again. The result was more socialist councils, mistrusted even more by central government, which therefore, as we have seen, took still more powers away from them, which made the elections even less relevant, and fuelled more protest voting and so on. If this was not bad enough, then it was clear to Thatcher and her ministers that socialist councils were pursuing expensive hard-left policies partly because so few of the local voters were ratepayers. Too many could vote for high-spending councils without feeling any personal pinch.

One way of cutting the knot would to be to make all those who voted for local councils pay towards their cost. This was the origin of the poll tax, or community charge as it was officially known, a single flat tax for everyone. It would mean lower bills for many homeowners and it would make local councils more responsive to their voters. On the other hand, it would mean a new tax for approximately 20 million people which would be regressive. The poorest in the land would pay as much as the richest. This broke a principle which stretched much further back that the 'post-war consensus'. The idea had been knocking around for some years before it was picked up by the government and subjected to a long and intense internal debate, which we will skip, except to note that not everyone thought it was a good idea. The poll tax was sold to Mrs Thatcher by her Environment Secretary, Kenneth Baker, at a seminar at Chequers in 1985, along with the nationalization of the business rate. Nigel Lawson tried very hard to argue the Prime Minister out of it, telling her it would be 'completely unworkable and politically catastrophic'.

He was outgunned by a stream of lady pleasers keen to prove him wrong, and indeed the tax was being discussed at the very same cabinet meeting Heseltine stalked out of during the Westland affair. It might have been less of a disaster – it might even have been successful – had it been brought in very slowly, over ten years as first mooted, or four as was then planned. But at the 1987 Tory conference there was a collective rush of blood to the head. Intoxicated by the bold simplicity of the thing, party members urged Thatcher to bring it in at once. Idiotically, she agreed. There was, to be fair, a reason for hurry. Rates, like the modern council tax, depended on the relative value of houses across Britain, which changed with fashion and home improvement. Every so often, therefore, there had to be a general revaluation to keep the tax working. Yet each revaluation meant higher rates bills for millions of homeowners and businesses, and governments tended to try to put them off. In Scotland a crisper law did not allow this. There, a rates revaluation had finally happened and caused political mayhem. It gave English ministers a nasty glimpse of what was in store for them too eventually. Scottish ministers begged Thatcher to be allowed the poll tax first. They were given their head.

Exemptions were to be made for the unemployed and low paid but an attempt by wisely nervous Tory MPs to divide the tax into three bands so that it bore some relation to people's ability to pay, was brushed aside despite a huge parliamentary rebellion. When the tax was duly introduced in Scotland, as we shall see later, it caused chaos and widespread protest. In England, the likely price of the average poll tax kept rising. Panicking ministers produced expensive schemes to cap it, and to create more generous exemptions, undermining the whole point. Capping the tax would remove local accountability; and the more exemptions, the less pressure on councils from their voters. Yet even Thatcher began to grow alarmed, as she was told that well over 80 per cent of people would be paying more. On 31 March 1990, the day before the poll tax was due to take effect in England and Wales, there was a massive demonstration against it which ended with a riot in Trafalgar Square. Scaffolding was ripped apart and used to throw at mounted police, cars were set on fire, shops smashed. More than 300 people were arrested and 400 policemen hurt. Thatcher dismissed it as mere wickedness. More than a riot, though, it was the growing swell of protest by middle-class, normally law-abiding voters who insisted they simply would not pay it, that shook her cabinet. As the Conservatives' ratings slumped in the country, Tory MPs who had opposed the tax, including Michael Heseltine's key organizer, Michael Mates, began to ask their colleagues whether it was not now time that she was removed from power.

The Final Curtain

The killing of Margaret Thatcher's political career has a dark lustre about it, like something from a book of old stories. She had conducted her premiership with a sense of vivid and immediate self-dramatization, the heroine of peace and war, fighting pitched battles in coalfields and on the streets, word-punching her way through triumphal conferences, haranguing rival leaders, always with a sense that history was being freshly minted, day by day. This is why so many insults levelled at her tended to twist into unintended compliments – the Iron Lady, La Pasionara of Privilege, She Who Must Be Obeyed, the Leaderene, the Blessed Margaret, even the Great She-Elephant. Reflected in her bloodied breastplate the eighties glowed more luridly than any other modern decade, flashing gold with the City's new wealth, sunny as the Soviets collapsed, livid in its confrontations and cruelty nearer to home. She had no sense of her own limits. The world was made anew. Her fall lived

135

up in every way to her record. When a great leader topples, poetry requires that her personal failings bring her down. The story insists it must be more than a trip on the carpet, weariness or age. And this story's ending lives up to its earlier scenes.

There were several powder-trails that led towards the final explosion. One was the poll tax. Another was economic policy, and Europe, which had become almost the same thing. We have seen how Lawson wanted to tie the pound to the anti-inflationary expertise and reputation of the West German Central Bank, 'shadowing' the Deutschmark in the European exchange rate mechanism. In effect, he was looking for somewhere firm to plant down policy in the queasy morass of the new global financial free-for-all. Thatcher disagreed. She thought currencies should float freely, Ariel to his Caliban. She also knew that the ERM was intended one day to lead to a single European currency, part of the European Commission President Jacques Delors's plan for a freshly buttressed European federal state. Lawson, dogged, bull-like, ignored her and shadowed the German currency anyway, a fact somehow both denied yet generally known. Thatcher read about it in the newspapers. When the cost of Lawson's policy became excessive she finally ordered him to stop. He grumpily agreed but the two of them stopped talking.

Bruges in Belgium is a pretty town. Thanks to the channel tunnel and cheap flights, British people flock there for romance, beer, art and chocolate. When Margaret Thatcher rode into town in 1988, year of hubris, none of these things was on her agenda. She had come to make her definitive speech against the federalism now openly advancing towards her. The Foreign Office had tried to soften her message. She had promptly pulled out her pen and written the barbs and thorns back in again. She had not, she informed her audience, 'successfully rolled back the frontiers of the state in Britain' (a claim already anatomized) 'only to see them reimposed at a European level, with a European super-state exercising a new level of dominance from Brussels.' There was much else besides. Her bluntness much offended continental politicians and the Foreign Secretary, Sir Geoffrey Howe. Next, she reappointed as her economic adviser a lugubrious and outspoken monetarist academic, Sir Alan Walters, who was contemptuous of Lawson's exchange rate policy and said so, repeatedly. Thus she was taking on Howe and Lawson, the two Chancellors of her revolutionary years, together. A dangerous split was becoming evident at the top of government. She seemed not to care, biffing Howe about as carelessly as she always had. Nor was anyone much convinced when she told the world she 'fully, gladly, joyfully, unequivocally, generously … fully, fully, fully, fully' supported Lawson as her Chancellor. People said she had no sense of humour. They were wrong. It was just a slightly strange one.

Then Jacques Delors, the wry and determined French socialist, re-entered the story, with his fleshed-out plan for economic and monetary union, which would end with the single currency, the euro. To get there, all EU members would start by putting their national currencies into the ERM, which would draw them increasingly tightly together – just what Lawson and Howe wanted and just what Thatcher did not. Howe and Lawson, Pinky and Perky, ganged up. They told her she must announce that Britain would soon join the ERM, even if she left the single currency itself to one side, for the time. She wriggled, then fought back. On the eve of a summit in Madrid where Britain had to announce her view the two of them visited her in private, had a blazing row and threatened to resign together if she did not give way. Truculently she did, and the crisis passed. But she was merely waiting. Four weeks after the summit, in July 1989, Thatcher hit back. She unleashed a major cabinet reshuffle, compared at the time to Macmillan's 'night of the long knives' in 1962. Howe was demoted to being Leader of the Commons. She reluctantly allowed him the face-saving title of Deputy Prime Minister, a concession rather diminished when her press officer, Bernard Ingham, instantly told journalists it was a bit of a non-job. Howe was replaced by the relatively unknown John Major, the former chief secretary. Lawson survived only because the economy was weakening and to lose him was thought too dangerous just then.

So the drama advanced. The atmosphere in the Commons was a combustible mix of sulphur and adrenalin. Lawson was having a bad time on all sides, including from the Labour shadow chancellor John Smith. When Thatcher's adviser Walters had another pop at his ERM policy, he decided enough was enough and resigned on 26 October, telling the Prime Minister she should treat her ministers better. She pretended to have no idea what he was on about. Lawson was replaced by the still relatively unknown John Major, who was having an interesting autumn. Around them all, the world was changing. A few days after these events, East Germany announced the opening of the border to the West and joyous Berliners began hacking their wall to pieces. Then the communists fell in Czechoslovakia. Then the Romanian dictator Ceauşescu was dragged from power. A few weeks after that, in February 1990, Nelson Mandela, a man she had once denounced as a terrorist, was released to global acclaim. In the middle of all this the Commons had witnessed an event which seemed the opposite of historic. Thatcher had been challenged as leader of the Conservative Party by Sir Anthony Meyer, an obscure, elderly pro-European backbencher much mocked as 'the stalking donkey'. It was a little like Ronnie Corbett challenging Mike Tyson to a punch-up. Yet, ominously for Thatcher, when the vote was held sixty Tory MPs either voted donkey or abstained. In the shadows, prowling through Conservative associations and the corridors of Westminster was a more dangerous creature. Michael Heseltine, no donkey, self-expelled from the Thatcher cabinet four years earlier, was looking uncommonly chipper. Tory MPs whimpered to him about the trouble they were in with the poll tax. He sympathized, trying neither to lick his lips nor sharpen his claws too obviously.

One by one, the inner core of true Thatcherites fell back. Her bone-dry Environment Secretary, Nicholas Ridley, had to resign after being rude about the Germans in a magazine interview – given, piquantly, to Lawson's son Dominic. John Major turned out to be worryingly pro-European after all.

139

Ian Gow, one of her closest associates, though no longer in the government, was murdered by an IRA bomb at his home. Abroad, great world events continued to stalk the last days of Margaret Thatcher's premiership. Saddam Hussein invaded Kuwait and she urged President George Bush the elder towards what would become the first Gulf War – 'Don't wobble, George.' There was another summit in Rome and further pressure on the Delors plan. Again, Thatcher felt herself being pushed and dragged towards a federal scheme. She vented her contempt and anger in the Commons, shredding the proposals with the words, 'No ... No ... No!' And at this point the one person who could never have been expected to finish her off, did so.

For years Geoffrey Howe had absorbed her slights, her impatience, her mockery, her snarls. He had taken it all, with the rubbery fatalism of the battered husband who will never leave. Now, observing her flaming anti-Brussels crusade, he decided he had had enough. She probably tipped him over the edge by turning on him savagely and unfairly over some legislation that was not ready, but he had decided to go. On 13 November 1990 he stood up rather lugubriously in the House of Commons and did her in. His resignation statement was designed to answer the story put around by Number Ten that he had gone over nothing much at all. To a packed chamber he revealed that Lawson and he had threatened to resign together the previous year and accused her of sending her ministers to negotiate in Brussels like a cricket team going to the crease, having first broken their bats in the changing room. She was wrong over Europe, he insisted; and then threw the door open to the further leadership challenge that was now inevitable: 'The time has come for others to consider their own response to the tragic conflict of loyalties with which I myself have wrestled for perhaps too long.' Television cameras had just been allowed into the Commons. Across the country people could watch Howe, with Nigel Lawson nodding behind him, could see Heseltine's studied, icy calm, and observe the white-faced reaction of the Prime Minister herself. The next day Heseltine announced he would stand against her as leader. She told *The Times* that he was a socialist at heart, someone whose philosophy at its extreme end had just been defeated in the Soviet Union. She would see him off, of course.

The balloting system for Tory MPs required her to beat Heseltine by winning both a clear majority of the parliamentary party and being 15 per cent ahead of him in votes cast. At a summit in Paris, surrounded by many old enemies, she heard that she had missed the second hurdle by four votes. There would be a second ballot. As one of the few people in public life who could swarm all by herself, she swarmed out of the summit, somehow found a BBC microphone and announced that though disappointed, she would fight on. Then she returned with heroic sangfroid to sit through a ballet with the other leaders, who were pleasant enough to her face. While she watched the ballet, Tory MPs were dancing through Westminster in anger or delight. It was a night of softening support and hardening hearts. Many key Thatcherites believed she was finished and feared that if she fought again, Heseltine would beat her. This would tear the party in two. It would be better for her to withdraw and let someone else assassinate the assassin.

Even then, had she been in London throughout the crisis and summoned her cabinet together to back her, she might have pulled it off. But by the time she was back and taking advice from her whips the news was bleak. In what was probably a tactical mistake, she decided to see her cabinet one by one in her Commons office. Douglas Hurd and John Major had already given her their reluctant agreement to nominate her for the next round of voting but the message from most of the rest of her ministers was strangely uniform. They would personally back her if she was determined to fight but, frankly, she would lose. That would mean Heseltine. Better, Prime Minister, to stand aside and free Major and Hurd from their promises of support. Later, she was wryly amusing about the process. It looked very much as if most of them had agreed the line beforehand. The whips concurred. The cabinet were going through the motions of supporting her if she insisted, but they did not mean it, or mean her to believe it. She had lost them. Only a few ultras, mostly outside the cabinet, were sincerely urging her to continue the struggle. One was that wicked diarist and right-wing maverick Alan Clark, who told her to fight on at all costs: 'Unfortunately he went on to argue that I should fight on even though I was bound to lose because it was better to go down in a blaze of glorious defeat than to go gentle into that good night. Since I had no particular fondness for Wagnerian endings, this lifted my spirits only briefly.'[29]

So it was over. In their various ways, her cabinet were too tired to support her any longer and her

MPs were too scared of the electoral vengeance to be wreaked after the poll tax. She returned to Downing Street, conferred with Denis, slept on it, and then announced to her cabinet secretary at 7.30 the next morning that she had decided to resign. She held an uncomfortable cabinet meeting with those she believed had betrayed her, saw the Queen, phoned other world leaders and then finished with one final splendid Commons performance – 'I'm enjoying this!' – vigorously defending her record. Come back, cried one emotional Tory MP. When Margaret Thatcher left Downing Street for the last time in tears, she already knew that she had successfully completed a final political campaign, which was to ensure that she was replaced as Prime Minister by John Major, rather than Michael Heseltine. She had rallied support for him by phone among her closest supporters. They felt he had not been quite supportive enough. She also harboured private doubts. So ended the most extraordinary and nation-changing premiership of modern British history.

PART 5

NIPPY METRO PEOPLE:
BRITAIN FROM 1990

Thatcher's children? By the time she left office, only a minority were true believers. Most would have voted her out had her cabinet ministers not beaten them to it. History is harshest to a leader just as they fall. She had been such a strident presence for so long that many who had first welcomed her as a gust of fresh air now felt harried. Those who wanted a quieter leader were about to get one. Yet most people had in the end done well under her, not just the Yuppies and Essex boys, but also her snidest middle-class critics. Britons were on average much wealthier than they had been at the end of seventies. The country was enjoying bigger cars, a far wider range of holidays, better food, a wider choice of television channels, home videos, and the first slew of gadgets from the computer age. Yet this was not quite the Britain of today.

More people smoked. The idea of smoke-free public areas, or smoking bans in offices and restaurants, was lampooned as a weird Californian innovation that would never come here. People seen talking to themselves with a wire dangling from one ear would have been considered worryingly disturbed. There were no Starbucks: coffee shops were still mainly locally owned places selling instant coffee, tea, fried food or cakes. Lunch had been under threat for some years in the City and the days of midday drinking were beginning to die in other professions too. The chic sandwich bar had begun to spread since the early eighties, when BLTs, avocado and blue cheese began to be regularly offered, alongside the traditional fillings of cheese, ham and egg. At a by-election outside Liverpool in 1986 a Labour activist had allegedly pointed to the mushy peas in a local chip-shop and asked for some of the 'avocado dip' too: it was a story, perhaps an urban myth, much re-told as symbolizing the gap between real Britain and the new metropolitan Britain of the south. The habit of urbanites carrying bottled water wherever they went had not yet taken off, though meaningless corporate language was already sullying business life. The ubiquitous PowerPoint presentation was in its infancy. Passengers, rather than 'customers', travelled on British Rail trains, with the double-arrow symbol which had been familiar since 1965. On the roads were plenty of flashy Ford Sierras, Austin Montegos and nippy Metros.

For a wealthy country, the mood was uneasy. An old jibe, 'public affluence, public squalor', was much heard. The most immediate worry was economic as the hangover effects of the Lawson boom began to throb. Inflation was rising towards double figures, interest rates were at 14 per cent and unemployment was heading towards two million. Over the next four years a serious white-collar recession was to hit Britain, particularly in the south, where house prices would fall by a quarter. An estimated 1.8 million people found that their homes were worth less than the money they had borrowed to buy them in the heady easy-credit eighties. During 1991 alone, more than 75,000 families would have their homes repossessed. With hindsight it is generally accepted that the Thatcher revolution reshaped the country's economy and prepared Britain well for the new age of globalization waiting in the wings, but in 1990 it did not feel quite like that.

There were other changes too. The British were fewer than they are today. The population was smaller by at least three million souls. Also, the ethnic mix of the country was simpler. Of the roughly three million non-white British, the largest groups were Indian (840,000), black Caribbean (500,000) and Pakistani (476,000), pretty much what an extrapolation from the seventies would have predicted. No serious concern was expressed politically about whether Muslims could fully integrate. In the interests of keeping an eye on troublemakers, and maintaining Britain's traditions of tolerance, a number of the most radical Islamic militants, on the run from their own countries, had been given safe haven in London. The largest white migrant group was from Ireland, which was still relatively poor. Any Poles or Russians in Britain were diplomats or refugees from communism. The term 'bogus asylum seeker' would have met with a puzzled frown. Looking to east or west, Britain was far less penetrated by overseas culture and people than she would soon become.

Britain was also about to go to war again as the junior partner to the Americans in the first Gulf conflict, which freed Kuwait from Saddam Hussein's invasion and immolated the Iraqi army's Republican Guard. Despite British forces losing lives and the use by Saddam of human shields, the war generated nothing like the controversy of the later Iraq war. It was widely seen as a necessary act of international retribution against a particularly horrible dictator. After the controversies and

149

alarms of the Thatcher years, foreign affairs generated less heat, except for the great issue of European federalism. There was a real sense of optimism caused by the end of the Cold War, which had resulted in the deaths of up to 40 million people around the world, and involved no fewer than 150 smaller conflicts. At last, perhaps, the West could relax. Politicians and journalists talked excitedly of the coming 'peace dividend' and the end of the surveillance and espionage secret state that had been needed for so long. The only present threat to British security was the Provisional IRA, which would continue its attacks with ferocity and cunning for some years to come. They would hit Downing Street with a triple mortar attack on a snowy day in February 1991, coming close to killing the Prime Minister and the top team of ministers and officials directing the Gulf War.

Environmental worries were present too, though a bat-squeak compared to today's panic. British scientists played a big role in alerting the world. Among the handful of Britons in the second half of the twentieth century who may be remembered centuries hence is James Lovelock. He is the scientist who in 1965 after studying the long-term chemical composition of the planet's systems, and their interaction with living organisms, developed the 'Gaia' theory. The name, from a Greek goddess, came from the British Nobel Prize-winning novelist William Golding, a neighbour of Lovelock's in Devon, during a country walk. 'Gaia' demonstrated how fragile the life-supporting atmosphere and chemistry of the planet is, an immensely complex self-regulating system keeping temperatures fit for life. Some hippies and 'New Age' mystics mistakenly thought Lovelock was saying the Earth was herself alive. He was using a metaphor but one with powerful implications for man-made climate change. At the same time as Lovelock was writing his most influential book, in the late seventies, far south the British Antarctic Survey was just beginning to notice a thinning of the ozone layer. It is said that when the first measurements were taken later in 1985 the readings were so low the scientists assumed their instruments were faulty and sent home for replacements. This led to an important treaty cutting ozone-depleting CFCs. British influence was important at the first world climate conference in Geneva in 1979, which had appealed to nations to do more research.

By 1990, a follow-up conference attended by 130 countries focused on the growing evidence that global warming was a real threat, but no agreement was reached about what should be done. Were any senior politicians worried? One was. Two years earlier Margaret Thatcher, science-trained, had made a speech about global warming. She had been persuaded that it was a profound issue by Britain's outgoing ambassador to the United Nations, Sir Crispin Tickell, who had ironically enough got at her with worrying data during a long international plane flight. So in September 1988 she had told the Royal Society that she believed it possible that 'we have unwittingly begun a massive experiment with the system of the earth itself.' Such was the interest that no television cameras were sent to record her speech and the prime minister had to read it by the light of wax candles held over her head in an ancient hall. For most people in 1990 'the environment' or green issues meant containable local problems such as the use of chemical pesticides or the problems of disposing of nuclear waste. Books about the fate of the earth concerned themselves with nuclear weapons.

Culturally, the country was as fixated by imported American television as it would continue to be: *Baywatch* and *The Simpsons* were popular new imports. And the national self-mocking strand of comedy which would be such a mark of the next fifteen years was well established, with Harry Enfield's Wayne and Waynetta Slob joining his 'Loadsamoney' attacks on the big-bucks Thatcher years, *Spitting Image* puppetry at its most gleefully venomous, and the arrival of a new quiz show, *Have I Got News For You*. This heralded a time when interest in ideology and serious policy issues was being replaced by politics as entertainment, a stage on which humorists and hacks could prove themselves wittier than elected parliamentarians. Unsurprisingly, this would not result in a better-run country.

After a spate of transport disasters there was a widespread feeling that large investment was needed in the country's infrastructure. French and British engineers celebrated in 1990 when they met under the Channel. Mobile phone use was tiny by modern standards, mainly confined to commercial business travellers' cars and a few much-mocked City slickers carrying objects the size of a brick. The computer age was further advanced. The Thatcher years had seen a glittering waterfall of new products and applications, most of them generated in California's new 'silicon valley', a hotbed of computer inventiveness recognized by name as early as 1971. The revolutionary Apple II

152

computer had been launched in 1977, followed by Tandys, Commodores and Ataris with their floppy disks and basic games. The first IBM personal computer had arrived in 1981, using the unfamiliar MS-DOS operating system by a little known company called Microsoft. The Commodore 64 of the following year would become the best-selling computer of all time, though there were British computers: here, Sir Clive Sinclair's ZX Spectrum computer caught most of the headlines. Then in 1983 an IBM clone arrived, the Compaq, first of countless many, and the unveiling of Microsoft Word and Windows. A year later came the first Amstrad personal computer from the British entrepreneur Alan Sugar's electronics company and, from the US, the Apple Macintosh. A cult novelist called William Gibson introduced a new word, cyberspace.

By the end of the eighties the hot new topics were virtual reality, computer gaming – Sim City was launched in 1989 – and the exponentially increasing power of microprocessors. Computer graphics were becoming common in films, even though they were clunky and basic by modern standards. But the biggest about-to-happen event was the internet itself. The single most significant achievement by a British person in the early nineties had nothing to do with politics. Sir Tim Berners-Lee, inventor of the World-Wide-Web, stands alongside James Lovelock for influence above that of any politician. Today's internet is a combination of technologies, from the satellites developing from the Soviet Sputnik success of 1957, to the US military programs to link computers, leading to the early 'net' systems developed by American universities, and the personal computer revolution itself. But Berners-Lee's idea was for a worldwide hypertext – the computer-aided reading of electronic documents – to allow people to work together remotely, sharing their knowledge in a 'web' of documents. His creation of it would give the internet's hardware its global voice.

Berners-Lee was an Oxford graduate who had made his first computer with a soldering iron and cut his teeth with British firms in Dorset, before moving to the European particle physics laboratory (CERN) in Switzerland in 1980. This is the world's largest research laboratory where scientists were constantly evolving ways of communicating with one other by computer, so it is no coincidence that it was in Switzerland that Berners-Lee wrote his first program. In 1989 he proposed his hypertext revolution which arrived as 'World-Wide Web' inside CERN in December 1990, and on the internet at large the following summer.

An admirably unflashy, decent man, Berners-Lee chose not to patent his creation, so that it would be free to everyone. He could have been fabulously wealthy but preferred to live the life of a moderately salaried academic, latterly in Boston, driving a second-hand car and living quietly. He was knighted in 2004 and, two years later, warned that misinformation and undemocratic forces were spreading through the web, calling for more research on its social consequences. In the immediate aftermath of the fall of Margaret Thatcher, all this was still to come. There were articles proclaiming some kind of new computer world community taking shape, but they were confusing to most people. Would this internet be basically for scientists? Was it a new kind of telephone-cum-typewriter, or an automated library system? Nobody knew for sure. In 1990 there were no 'www' prefixes, no dotcoms.

John Ball, More Interesting than He Looks

To guide this confusing new Britain, teetering on the edge of a new spate of globalism arrived an unlikely and very English figure, a Prime Minister whose seven years in office make him one of the longer-serving of modern times but who already gets half-overlooked. John Major was not what he seemed. He appeared to be a bland, friendly loyal Thatcherite. She thought so. So did Tory MPs, who elected him their leader because of who he was not. He was not the urbane, posh, old-school Tory Douglas Hurd and he was not the floppy-haired enchanter and lady-killer, Michael Heseltine. So who was he? Major had none of Thatcher's certainty or harshness. It is a reasonable principle that when you probe the history of a normal, middle-of-the-road English person, you find it surprisingly exotic. That is the case with Major. He was a sensitive boy from the wrong part of town, from a mixed-up, rather rum family. His father was one of the music-hall artistes described much earlier in this book, a remarkable man who had been partly brought up in the United States, returning to Britain in Edwardian times to pursue a long stage career, then rampaging cheerfully round South America, marrying twice and

155

producing two illegitimate children. His name was Tom Ball. The 'Major' was a stage name. As John Major said later he might more properly have been named John Ball, like the leader of the peasants' revolt against the original poll tax.

Major was born late. His father was already an old man, now pursuing yet another career making garden ornaments. When an informal business deal went wrong he lost almost everything and the family moved from their comfortable suburban house to a crowded flat in Brixton, which they shared with a cat-burglar, a Jamaican later arrested for stabbing a policeman, and a trio of cheery Irish tax-dodgers. The flat turned out to be owned by Major's (much older) secret half brother, though he never knew this at the time. Methodist Grantham this was not. Major, infuriated at being saddled with the name Major-Ball when he was sent to grammar school, was a poor pupil and left at sixteen. His early life was ragged and formless in shape. He worked as a clerk, made garden gnomes with his brother, looked after his mother and endured a 'degrading' time of unemployment, before eventually pursuing a career as a banker and becoming a Conservative councillor. Unlike Margaret Thatcher, his politics were formed by the inner city and he was on the anti-Powellite, moderate wing of the party. After a long search, he was finally selected as Tory candidate for the rural seat of Huntingdon and entered Parliament in 1979 as the Thatcher age began.

There he rose almost without trace, through a minor job with the Home Office, to the whips' office which, as the internal security machine of a parliamentary party, can be a useful training ground for the ambitious, to two years at Social Security. After the 1987 election Thatcher promoted him to the cabinet as Chief Secretary to the Treasury, when he haggled with ministers about their spending plans. She liked him because he had stood up to her in argument, not because he was a stooge. There followed the abrupt further promotions to the Foreign Office where he served as Foreign Secretary for all of ninety-four days, and Treasury. As Chancellor he had promoted a short-lived alternative to monetary union, the 'hard ecu', which would have been a kind of voluntary euro, running alongside the old currencies. He had then won Thatcher round to membership of the ERM, though entering as it turned out at too high a rate. By the time he suddenly emerged as a possible candidate to replace her as Prime Minister, Major was known by those who knew him for being affable, reliable, hardworking, self-deprecating and, it was assumed, as her protégé, a model Thatcherite. But to everyone outside Tory politics, he was a blank canvas. He was the least known new Prime Minister in post-war Britain as well as the youngest of the century so far. At forty-seven, he was barely a public figure.

Most Conservatives had grown sick and tired of dramatics. Here was a bloke from next door with an easy smile leading them to easier times. Chris Patten, then the brightest man in the cabinet, acted as its spokesmen when he recalled the prisoners' chorus to freedom in Beethoven's opera *Fidelio*. If only they knew what was coming. Thatcher, belatedly slightly wary, promised to be a good 'back-seat driver'. Major wanted none of her advice. He considered offering her a job, either in the cabinet or as ambassador to Washington. He decided not to. He talked of building a 'society of opportunity' and compassion, and for privileges once available to 'the few' to be spread 'to the many'. This sounds like an early try-out for the language of New Labour: Major came to believe Blair had simply swiped many of his ideas and presented them as his own, with more verve. As we shall see there is some truth in this. But Major had little time to plan his own agenda. There were immediate crises. He was quick to kill off the poll tax and replace it with a new council tax bearing an uncommon resemblance to the old rating system. He was equally quick to meet the elder President Bush and support him through the Gulf War. Above all, he had to turn straight away to confront the great hydra-headed monster that was devouring his party, the federal agenda of Jacques Delors.

If ever a place was well chosen for debating the end of a Europe of independent nation states, it was Maastricht in Holland, an attractive cobbled town nestled so close to the German and Belgian borders it is almost nationless. Here the great showdown of winter 1991 took place. A new treaty was to be agreed and it was one which made the federal project ever more explicit. There was to be fast progress to a single currency. Much of foreign policy, defence policy and home affairs were to come under the ultimate authority of the EU. A 'social chapter' would oblige Britain to accept the more expensive work guarantees of the continent and surrender some of the trade union reforms brought in under Thatcher. For a country with a weak industrial base whose economy partly depended on undercutting her continental rivals,

158

all this would be grave. For a Conservative Party which had applauded Lady Thatcher's defiant Bruges speech, it was almost a declaration of war, in which Europe's 'federal' destiny had become made explicit and imminent. Fretting and moody in exile Thatcher saw Maastricht as a recipe for national suicide. She now believed she had been removed from Downing Street because of her stand over Europe. Hearing Major declare he wanted Britain to be 'at the heart of Europe', a mere bromide of a phrase, she added him to the long list of traitors. Her admirers hissed. He refused to rule out a single currency for all time. They became angrier still. So did she.

Major was trying to be practical, not exciting. He decided that he had no absolutist views on the single currency. One day it would happen. It had obvious business and trading advantages. But now was too soon, partly because it would make life harder for the central European countries being freed from communism to join the EU. So he was neither a 'never' nor a 'now'. Most people assumed he was glibly steering between two whirlpools, trying to keep his party united. In his memoirs, a great deal better written than most such books, he protested that he was accused of dithering, procrastination, lacking leadership and conviction. As to his true and subtle position, 'I have given up hope that this will ever be understood.' Yet at Maastricht he managed against all the odds during genuinely tense negotiations to slip Britain out of paying fealty to the EU on most of what was demanded. He and his Chancellor, Norman Lamont, negotiated a special British opt-out from monetary union and managed to have the social

159

chapter excluded from the treaty altogether. Major kept haggling late and on every detail, wearing out his fellow leaders with more politeness but as much determination as Thatcher ever had. For a man with a weak hand, under fire from his own side at home, it was quite a feat. Major returned to hosannas in the newspapers and the widely reported remark of an aide that it was 'game, set and match' to Britain. He was briefly a hero. He described his reception by the Tory Party in the Commons as the modern equivalent of a Roman triumph, quite something for the boy from Brixton.

Soon after this, flushed with confidence, Major called the election most observers thought he must lose. The economy was so badly awry, the pain of the poll tax so fresh, the Labour Party of Neil Kinnock now so efficiently and ruthlessly organized, that the Tory years were surely ending. Things turned out differently. Lamont's preelection budget had helped a lot. It proposed cutting the bottom rate of income tax by five pence in the pound, which would help people on lower incomes, and badly wrong-footed Labour. Under a pugnacious Patten, now the party chairman, the Tories targeted Labour's enthusiasm for higher taxes. It was tough stuff. Patten called himself 'the liberal thug'. During the campaign itself, Major found himself returning to his roots in Brixton and mounting a soap-box – in fact, a plastic container – from which he addressed raucous crowds through a megaphone. This stark contrast to the careful control of the Labour campaign struck a chord with the media and he kept it up, playing the underdog to the Kinnock's 'government in waiting'. Right at the end, at an eve of the poll rally in Sheffield, Kinnock's self-control finally gave way and he began punching the air with delight, crying 'y'aw'right!' This is often said to have finally turned middle England against him. That seems a bit neat.

On 9 April 1992 Major's Conservatives won 14 million votes, more than any party in British political history. It was a great personal achievement, also based on people's fear of higher Labour taxes. It was also one of the biggest percentage leads since 1945, though the vagaries of the electoral system gave Major a majority of just twenty-one seats. Kinnock was devastated and quickly left front-line politics. But never has such a famous victory produced such a rotten result for the winners. Patten lost his seat in Bath and went off to become the final governor of Hong Kong, tussling with the Chinese ahead of the long-agreed handover of Britain's last proper colony. Despite the popular vote, the smallness of the majority meant Major's authority was now steadily eaten away. He has not gone down in history as a great leader of this country, but under a parliamentary system greatness is generally related to parliamentary arithmetic. What kind of revolutionary would Margaret Thatcher have been had she had a majority of twenty-one in 1979 or 1983? Nor were the economics propitious. Had Labour won in 1992 it would have been quickly tarnished too. The choice of governing in that year was what rugby players call a hospital pass. For now John Major, the delighted and much-relieved victor, had the slippery ball in his hands and was acknowledging the cheers of the crowds. Meanwhile a platoon of nasty looking, bone-crushing, twenty-stone forwards were just about to jump him.

Old Labour's Lost King

The story of modern British political life has, so far, thrown up a high proportion of nuts, or at least of unsettled people with something to prove. John Smith was not a nut. After Neil Kinnock gave up in despair following Major's victory in 1992, he was replaced by a placid, secure, self-certain Scottish lawyer with a very boring name. Today almost everyone has an interest in writing John Smith out of the history books. For the Blairites, he was the timid, grey background for the heroic drama of modernization about to unfold. For those who loved Kinnock, he was the election-losing Shadow Chancellor. For the Tories, he was an embarrassingly good parliamentary inquisitor. In politics, predictions about what will happen a month ahead are dangerous but though Smith died of a heart attack in 1994, three years ahead of an election, it is fairly safe to suggest that, after the tarnishing years of the mid-nineties, he would have become Prime Minister. Had he done so, Britain would have had a traditionalist social democratic government, much closer to those of continental Europe, and our history would have been different.

Smith came from a family of herring fishermen on the West Coast of Scotland and, though bald as a coot himself, was the son of a bristly small town headmaster known as Hairy Smith. Labour-supporting from his earliest days, bright and self-assured, he got his real political education at Glasgow University, part of a generation of brilliant student debaters from all parties who would go on to dominate Scottish politics. Back in the early sixties, Glasgow University Labour Club was a hotbed not of radicals, but of Gaitskell-supporting moderates. It was a position Smith never wavered from, as he rose through politics as one of the brightest stars of the Scottish party, and then through government under Wilson and Callaghan as a junior minister dealing with the oil industry and devolution before entering the cabinet just in time as President of the Board of Trade, its youngest member at forty.

In Opposition, he managed to keep at arm's length from the worst of the in-fighting (he and Tony Benn liked one another, despite their very different views, after working together at the Energy Department) and eventually became Kinnock's shadow chancellor. He was a good lawyer and a brilliantly forensic parliamentary operator. This won him acclaim in the Westminster village even if, in Thatcher's England, he was spotted as a tax-raising corporatist socialist of the old school. One letter he got briskly informed him: 'You'll not get my BT shares yet, you bald, owl-looking Scottish bastard. Go back to Scotland and let that other twit Kinnock go back to Wales.'[1] Smith came from a somewhat old-fashioned Christian egalitarian background which put him naturally out of sympathy with the materialist, pleasure-orientated and aspirational culture that had grown so vigorously in Thatcherite England. Just before he became leader he told a newspaper he believed above all in education because 'it opens the doors of the imagination, breaks down class barriers and frees people. In our family ... money was looked down

163

on and education was revered. I am still slightly contemptuous of money.'[2] This could not in all honesty be said of the man who replaced him.

Smith was never personally close to Kinnock, but scrupulously loyal. A convivial (not drunken) workaholic who ate too much, he nevertheless succeeded him by an overwhelming vote in 1992. By then he had with great good luck survived a major heart attack and taken up hill walking. The *Sun,* not always a good guide to the future, greeted his triumph with the eerily accurate and predictive headline: 'He's fat, he's fifty-three, he's had a heart attack and he's taking on a stress-loaded job.'

Though Smith swiftly advanced the careers of the brightest younger stars, Tony Blair and Gordon Brown, they swiftly became depressed by his style of leadership. He did not believe Labour needed to be transformed, merely improved. He was reluctant at first to take on the party over issues such as one-person, one-vote internal democracy. He had an instantaneous dislike of the Mephistopheles of the modernizers, Peter Mandelson, which may have been tinged with Scottish Presbyterian homophobia. Blair, Brown and Mandelson thought Smith was smug and idle. He on the other hand was equally sure they were making too much fuss and that Labour could regain power with something of its traditional spirit. A little-known newspaper journalist called Alastair Campbell divided the party into two camps, the 'frantics', led by Brown, Blair and Jack Straw, and the 'long-gamers', led by Smith. At one point Blair was contemplating leaving politics, so despairing was he of Smith's leadership. He should, he reflected, have stuck to the law, where his elder brother was doing so well. What was there in politics for him?

Smith died of a second heart attack on 12 May 1994. After the initial shock and grieving had finished, Labour moved rapidly away from his legacy. There is, however, one part of the Smith agenda which survived intact and is a big influence on the shape of Britain today. As the minister who had struggled to achieve devolution for Scotland in the dark years of 1978–9 he remained a passionate supporter of the 'unfinished business' of establishing a Scottish Parliament and Welsh Assembly. With his friend Donald Dewar he had committed Labour so utterly to the idea in Opposition that Blair, no particular fan of devolution, found this one part of old Labour's agenda that stuck and had to be implemented later.

Black Wednesday and Party Suicide

The crisis that now engulfed the Conservative government was a complicated, devilish interaction of themes but in other ways very simple. The first thing that happened was that they lost their economic policy in a single day when the pound fell out of the European exchange rate mechanism. Major's opening words in the chapter of his book that deals with this are a fair summary: 'Black Wednesday – 16 September 1992, the day the pound toppled out of the ERM – was a political and economic calamity. It unleashed havoc in the Conservative Party and it changed the political landscape of Britain.'[3] It is worth recalling just what the ERM was and why it mattered so much in the early nineties.

Europe's old currencies, the marks, francs, lira, crowns and the rest, were supposed to move in close alignment, like a flight of mismatched aircraft in tight formation. They would stick together against outsider currencies, notably the US dollar, behaving almost as if they were one currency. Speculators would not be able to drive them apart. Eventually, they would fuse and become one, which is where the aircraft analogy falls down, because so would the aircraft. The strongest currency by far was the German Deutschmark, so the rest followed it up and down.

Like the others the pound had a narrow band of values against the mark – its own airspace, as it were – which it had to keep to, as it swept through the turbulence and storms caused by the international money markets. Once it had chosen its entry rate, the value in marks that sterling would try to maintain, the government's only steering mechanism was interest rates – plus, at the margin, protestation. What was the point of this? Dangerously, that depended on your vantage point. For Major and his government, the point was that because the German central bank had a deserved and ferocious reputation for anti-inflationary rigour, having to follow or 'shadow' the mark meant Britain had purchased a respected off-the-shelf policy. Sticking to the mighty mark was a useful signal to the rest of the world that this government, after all the inflationary booms of the past, was serious about inflation. On the continent the point of the ERM, however, was entirely different. It would lead to a strong new single currency. So a policy which Mrs Thatcher had earlier agreed to, in order to bring down British inflation, became a policy Lady Thatcher abhorred, because it drew Britain towards a European superstate. Confused? So was most of the Conservative Party.

Thus the bomb was prepared. What happened to set it off was that the US dollar began to fall because interest rates there were being cut, and pulled the pound down with it. Worse, the money flowed into Deutschmarks which duly rose; so the lead aircraft was gaining altitude, just as the pound was plunging. The government raised interest rates, up to an eye-watering 10 per cent, to try to lift the pound. But this did not work. The obvious next move was for the Germans to cut their interest rates, lowering the altitude of the mark, and keeping the ERM formation intact. This would have helped not just the pound but other weak currencies such as the Italian lira. But Germany had just reunited after the downfall of communism. The huge costs of bringing the poorer East Germans into West Germany's embrace meant a real fear of renewed inflation and all those Weimar memories. So the Germans, heedless of the pain of Britain, Italy and the rest, wanted their interest rates high. Major begged, cajoled, warned and wrote stiff letters of protest to Chancellor Kohl who would not move. He warned of the danger of the new Maastricht Treaty failing completely, for the Danes had just rejected it in a referendum and the French were now having a plebiscite of their own. None of that cut any ice either.

In public, the British government insisted the pound would stay in the ERM at all costs. The

167

mechanism was no mere technicality. It was Major's anti-inflation strategy. Ever since as Chancellor he had told the unemployment-hit and house-repossessed British that 'if it isn't hurting, it isn't working', his credibility had been tied to the ERM. But it was his foreign policy too. British membership of the ERM showed the country was serious about being 'at the heart of Europe'. It was Major's big idea for Britain's economic and diplomatic survival. Norman Lamont, who as Chancellor was as apparently committed as Major himself, told the markets Britain would neither leave the ERM nor devalue. It was 'at the centre of our policy' and there should not be a 'scintilla of doubt'. Major then went further, telling an audience in Scotland that with inflation down to 3.7 per cent and falling, it would be madness to leave the ERM. 'The soft option, the devaluer's option, the inflationary option, would be a betrayal of our future.'

But he could hold out for not much longer. The lira crashed out of the ERM formation. The international money traders turned their attention to the weak pound and carried on selling. They were betting Major and Lamont would not keep interest rates so high the pound could remain up there with the mark – an easy, one-way bet. For in the real world, British interest rates at 10 per cent were already painfully high. On the morning of Black Wednesday, at 11 a.m., the Bank of England raised them by another two points. This would be agonizing for home-owners and business alike. But Lamont said he would take 'whatever measures are necessary' to keep the pound in the system. The sense of panic mounted. The selling went on. A shaken Lamont rushed round to tell Major the interest rate rise had not worked. But sitting in Admiralty House – Number Ten was being refurbished after the IRA mortar attack – Major and his key ministers decided to stay in the poker game. The Bank announced that interest rates would go up again, by three points, to 15 per cent, which if sustained would have caused multiple bankruptcies across the country. This made no difference either. Eventually, at 4 p.m., Major phoned the Queen to tell her he was recalling Parliament. The government cracked. At 7.30 p.m., Lamont left the Treasury with his closest advisers, including David Cameron, to announce to a throng of cameramen and bystanders in Whitehall that he was 'suspending' the pound's membership of the ERM and was reversing the first of the day's interest rate rises. Major wrote out his resignation statement for broadcast. It was the most humiliating moment for British politics since the IMF crisis of September 1976, sixteen years earlier.

If Major had actually resigned Lamont would have had to go as well. The country would have lost the two senior ministers in the middle of a terrible crisis. So Major decided to stay on, though he was forever diminished by what had happened. Lamont, always a bubblier and more resilient figure, better suited perhaps to the Regency than the fag-end of the twentieth century, announced that he had been singing in the bath after the ERM debacle, and later added to the insouciant impression by quoting Edith Piaf s song 'Je ne regrette rien'. He decided that he was delighted as the economy began to react to lower interest rates, and the slow recovery began. While others could see only endless sleet and

169

frozen mud of unemployment, repossession and bankruptcy, he was forever spotting the 'green shoots' of economic rebirth. Perhaps it was the twitcher in him; keen bird-watchers are alert to nature.

In the following months Lamont created a new unified budget system and took tough decisions to repair the public finances but as the country wearied of recession, he became an increasingly easy butt of media derision. A few trivial incidents combined to make him something of a laughing-stock. To Lamont's complete surprise and utter shock, Major sacked him as Chancellor a little over six months after Black Wednesday. Lamont retaliated later in a Commons statement. The government listened too much to pollsters and party managers, he said: 'We give the impression of being in office, but not in power.' It was a well-aimed and painful blow. Major appointed Kenneth Clarke, one of the great characters of modern Toryism, a pugnacious, pro-European, beer-drinking, jazz-loving One Nation brawler, to replace Lamont. Though Lamont then moved increasingly towards full-on Euro-scepticism and never forgave Major, these three unlikely musketeers were jointly responsible for the strong economy inherited by New Labour four years later.

As to Major himself, his stony road just got flintier and steeper. In the Commons the struggle to ratify the Maastricht Treaty, hailed as such a success before the election, became a long and bloody one, conducted in late-night cabals, parliamentary bars and close votes night after night. Major's small majority was more than wiped out by the number of anti-Maastricht rebels, egged on by Lady Thatcher and her former party chairman, Norman Tebbit, now also in the Lords. Black Wednesday emboldened those who saw the ERM and every aspect of European federalism as disastrous for Britain. As John Major later wrote, it turned 'a quarter century of unease into a flat rejection of any wider involvement in Europe … emotional rivers burst their banks.' Had not the Germans let us down again? And had lower interest rates and 'green shoots' of recovery not followed Britain's self-expulsion? If the ERM had been bad, so surely was the whole federal project? Most of the newspapers which had welcomed Maastricht were now as vehemently against it. The most powerful Conservative voices in the media were hostile both to the treaty and to Major. Lady Thatcher's new oppositionism echoed loudly through Westminster. Principle, pique and snobbery swirled together. Major's often leaden use of English, his resolute lack of panache or cool, led many of England's High Tories to brand him shockingly ill-educated and third-rate for a national leader. His own sensitivity to criticism and occasional exhibitions of self-pity simply made things worse. He lacked that layer of nerveless flesh leaders today require.

The story of the long progress through Parliament of the Maastricht bill during the autumn, winter and spring of 1992–3 is too convoluted to be recorded here. Suffice it to say that a constantly shifting group of around forty to sixty Tory MPs regularly worked with the Labour opposition to defeat key parts of their government's main piece of legislation, and that Major's day-to-day survival was always in doubt. Whenever he called a vote of confidence and threatened his rebellious MPs with an election, he won. Wherever John Smith's Labour Party and the anti-Maastricht rebels could find some common cause, however thin, he was in danger of losing. The rebels ranged from the most fastidious and high-minded MPs who were profoundly worried about the constitutional damage European Union would do an ancient parliamentary democracy, to the mischievous and the embittered. Some backbench rebels found that they were interviewed constantly on television. Their views were sought by the papers and they became very minor national characters. This can be, as the current author witnesses, dangerously intoxicating. In the end Major got his legislation and Britain signed the Maastricht Treaty but it came at appalling personal and political cost. Talking in the general direction of an eavesdropping microphone, he spoke of three anti-European 'bastards' in his cabinet – a reference to Michael Portillo, Peter Lilley and John Redwood. The country watched a divided party tearing at itself and the country was unimpressed.

By the autumn of 1993 Norman Lamont was speculating aloud that Britain might have to leave the European Union altogether, and the financier Sir James Goldsmith was preparing to launch his Referendum Party to force a national plebiscite. The next row to break was over the voting system to be used when the EU expanded, a murky matter of realpolitik which directly affected each country's leverage. Forced to choose between a deal which weakened Britain's hand and stopping the enlargement from happening at all by vetoing it, the new Foreign Secretary, Douglas Hurd, went for a compromise. In Parliament, once again, all hell broke loose. Tory rebels began talking of a challenge to Major as leader. This subsided briefly but battle began again over the European budget, and fisheries policy. Formal membership of the Tory Party was withdrawn from eight rebels. By now Smith, who had given Major some of the worst parliamentary moments of his life, had suddenly died, and had been replaced by Tony Blair. When Major readmitted the rebels, the young Opposition leader told him: 'I lead my party, you follow yours' As with Lamont's 'in office but not in power' this caricatured the dreadful dilemma Major was in. But like Lamont's remark, Blair's struck a chord with the country.

The Age of Major

While the central story of British politics in the seven years between the fall of Thatcher and the arrival of Blair was taken up by Europe, at home the government tried to continue the British revolution. After many years of dithering, British Rail was broken up and privatized, as was the remaining coal industry. After the 1992 election it was decided that over half of the remaining coalmining jobs must go, in a closure programme of thirty-one pits to prepare the industry for privatization. This depressed or angered many Tory MPs who felt the strike-breaking effect of the Nottinghamshire-dominated Union of Democratic Mine-workers deserved a better reward, and it roused much public protest. Nevertheless, with power companies moving towards gas and oil, and the union muscle of the miners broken long since, the sale went ahead two years later. Faced with a plan by Michael Heseltine to sell off the Post Office too, Major baulked. It was a service with the stamp of Royalty on it and a long tradition. His refusal was probably good for the country. Why? Because the privatization of the railways was a catastrophe.

There has long been a problem with some politicians and railways. Perhaps it was all those Hornby models in boys' bedrooms or attics. Perhaps it was the simple romance of an industry which has beauty and complexity, which appeals to the mathematically minded in the structuring of its timetables, and to romantics in its engineering. At any rate, fiddling with the railway system became a dangerous obsession of governments of different colours. Thatcher, not being a boy, knew that railways were also too much part of the working life of millions to be lightly broken up or sold. She is said to have told Nicholas Ridley when he was Transport Secretary, 'Railway privatization will be the Waterloo of this government. Please never mention the railways to me again.'[4] Yet just before she resigned, under pressure from a Treasury privatization unit with too little left to do, she began to soften, and rail privatization was taken up by John Major with gusto. Trains! What could be more fun? Was not old-fashioned, curled-sandwich-serving, rail accident prone British Rail a national joke? Could not any reforming government worth its salt, brimming with nostalgia for the old days of

174

brightly painted trains run by private companies, do better than that?

The problems with selling off an elderly, loss-making railway system on which millions of people depend, are obvious. If your first aim is to raise money, then you have to accept that fares will rise briskly, and services may be cut, as the new owners try to make a profit. This will make you less popular. If, however, your aim is to increase competition, just how do you do that? Each route has only one railway line. Different train companies can hardly compete directly, racing each other up and down the same track. Do you give up on competition and sell off all of British Rail as a single unit? The Conservatives decided against that which left them essentially with two options. They could cut up BR geographically, selling off both trains and track for each region, together, so that the railway system would end up looking much as it had in the thirties. Competition would not be direct, but it would become clear that, say, the Great North Eastern operator was offering a pleasanter and more efficient service than the company running trains to Cornwall and Devon, and in due course one might lose, and the other gain, market power. Licences could be revoked, or there might be takeovers. Alternatively, the railway could be split vertically, so that the State owned the track, some companies owned the stations, and others the trains. This could be called the Complete Horlicks option.

Under Treasury pressure to produce the maximum competition and revenue, the new Transport Secretary, John MacGregor, chose it. A vastly complicated new system of subsidies, contracts, bids, pricing (of almost everything), cross-ticketing and regulation was created, topped off when late in the day, it was decided to sell off the nation's railway tracks separately to a single private monopoly to be called Railtrack. Suddenly to get across the country could become a complicated transaction, involving two or three separate train companies. They would not, however, be left to get on with it in a new market. Trains were too important for that. A Franchise Director would be given powers over the profits and pricing, including ticket prices, of the new companies and a Rail Regulator would deal with the track. Both would end up reporting directly to the Secretary of State so that any public dissatisfaction, commercial problem, safety issue – indeed, almost everything – would be back in the lap of the politicians. If this was privatization, it was a strange and possibly pointless one, which would end up costing the taxpayer far more than old-fashioned, much-mocked British Rail. The historian of this curious tale, Christian Wolmar, dubbed it 'the poll tax on wheels'. The writer Simon Jenkins, who had sat on the British Rail board, concluded: 'The Treasury's treatment of the railway in the 1990s was probably the worst instance of Whitehall industrial mismanagement since the Second World War.'[5]

Citizens and Hoop-jumpers

As a Brixton man who had known unemployment, and as a sensitive man quick to feel slights, Major

176

was well prepared by upbringing and temperament to take on the arrogant and inefficient quality of much so-called public service. In his early years he himself had been the plaintive figure who found 'telephones answered grudgingly or not at all. Booths closed while customers were kept waiting ... Remote council offices where, after a long bus journey, there was no one available to see you who really knew about the issue ... Anonymous voices and faces who refused to give you a contact name.'[6] He was making a good point. Why in a country that spent so much on public services were so many of them so bad? The answer of the Thatcher revolution was that in the end only the market is properly responsive. Yet nobody in power during the eighties or nineties, including Margaret Thatcher, was prepared to take this logic to its limit and privatize the health service or schools or road system, compensating the worse off with vouchers or cash help. Nor, under the iron grip of the Treasury, was there any enthusiasm for a revival of local democracy to take charge instead.

This left a fiddly and highly bureaucratic centralism as the only option left, one which we have seen gather momentum in the Thatcher years and which would flourish most extravagantly under Blair. Under Major, the centralized Funding Agency for Schools was formed and schools in England and Wales were ranked by crude league tables, depending on how well their pupils did in exams. The university system was vastly expanded by simply allowing colleges and polytechnics to rename themselves as universities, and a futile search began for ways in which civil servants might measure academic merit and introduce league

177

tables there. The hospital system was further centralized and given a host of new targets. The police, faced with a review of their pay and demands by the Home Secretary, Kenneth Clarke, for forces to be amalgamated, were given their own performance league tables. The Tories had spent 74 per cent more, in real terms, on law and order since 1979 yet crime was at an all-time high, as a doleful list of high-profile murders reminded the public. Clarke's contempt for many of the police as 'vested interests' was not calculated to win them round to reform. Across England and Wales elected councillors were turfed off police boards and replaced by businessmen. Clarke's hostility to local control had been confirmed by his time as Health Secretary when, according to one department insider, he showed himself as 'a leading exponent of the Stalinist side of the Tory party. He castrated the regional health authority chairmen.'[7]

In 1993 Clarke defended his new police league tables in language that was eerily echoed by New Labour later: 'The new accountability that we seek from our public services will not be achieved simply because men of good will and reasonableness wish that it to be so. The new accountability is the new radicalism.' Accountability: once the word had implied a contest of ideas and achievements, played out in front of the voters. Now it meant something very different. Across the country, from the auditing of local government to the running of courts or the working hours of nurses, an army of civil servants, accountants, auditors and number-crunchers marched in. Once, long ago in the 1940s, Labour had been mocked for saying that the man in

178

Whitehall knew best. Now the auditors and accountants hired by Whitehall ruled instead. Weakly, from time to time, ministers would claim that the cult of central control and measurement had been imposed by Brussels. Some had been, but this was mostly a homegrown 'superstate'.

Major called his headline policy the Citizen's Charter, though he himself did not like the name very much because of its 'unconscious echoes of Revolutionary France'. Every part of government dealing with public service was ordered to come up with proposals for improvement at grass-roots level, to be pursued from the centre by inspections, questionnaires, league tables and ultimately the system of awards, Charter Marks, for organizations that did well. Throughout, Major spoke of 'empowering' teachers and doctors, 'helping the customer' and 'devolving'. He thought his great system of regulation from the centre would not last long: it was 'a regulatory goad to raise standards … over time, I anticipated formal regulation steadily withering away, as the effects of growing competition are felt.' But how would this happen? In practice, the regulators grew more powerful, not less so. If people are paid to respond to regulators' targets and jump through hoops, they become excellent at target-practice and hoop-jumping. This does not make them wise administrators. Despite the rhetoric, public servants were not being given real freedom to manage. Elected office-holders were being sacked. Major's hopes for central regulation withering away echo Lenin, who hoped for a 'withering away' of the Soviet State, with similar success.

Above. The Iron Lady
on manoeuvres.
Margaret Thatcher
at the peak of her power,
with tank and flag, 1986.

Right. The Tories had
another blonde who felt
the call of destiny:
Michael Heseltine,
Conservative conference
darling.

FRONT OF BRASS AND FEET OF CLAY

When Thatcher took on the moderate 'wets' in her own cabinet, she could rely on the support of much of the press. But it was the Falklands that changed everything: a soldier aboard the 1982 task force waits for the shooting to start.

Rebel faces: picketing miners
caught and handcuffed to a
lamp-post by police, 1986,
and the notoriously violent
poll-tax riot of 1990 in
Trafalgar Square.

Above. Two lost leaders:
Labour's Neil Kinnock attacking
left-wing Militants at the party
conference in 1985 and his
successor John Smith, who would
probably have become prime
minister in 1997, but died
of a heart attack.

Left. In June 1988, 185 men died
when a North Sea oil platform,
Piper Alpha, blew up – yet the
extraordinary story of the oil boom
is little mentioned in politicians'
memoirs.

Bitter-sweet: Tory chairman Chris Patten helped John Major win a triumphant electoral victory in 1992, but lost his own seat at Bath, and was sent as the last governor to Hong Kong.

The death of Diana in 1997 produced an almost Mediterranean outpouring of grief across the country. A small field of flowers lies outside Kensington Palace.

What's waiting in the wings?
Alastair Campbell guards his
master's back (*opposite, top*).
New Labour was famously
image-obsessed, but (*above*)
by 2005 neither Tony Blair nor
Gordon Brown could be bothered
to disguise their mutual enmity.

Tony Blair's legacy?
Anti-war protestors became
a familiar sight on the streets
of Britain (*opposite*), while British
troops did their utmost in the
devastated and violence-plagued
world of post-war Iraq. By 2007,
(*right*) they were still not welcomed
by many Iraqis.

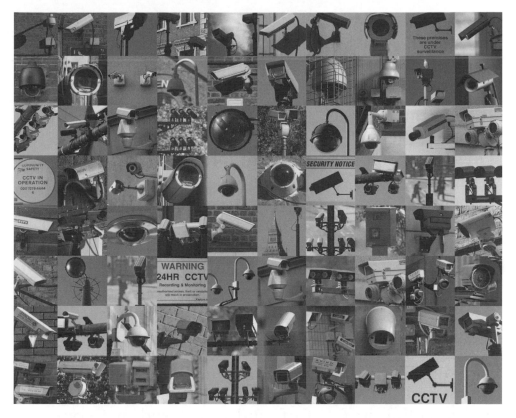

More than four-million closed-circuit television cameras now watch the British: a surveillance society that echoes the wartime world of identity cards and observation with which this history began.

The biggest social change continues to be migration, latterly from eastern Europe: Polish road signs to help drivers in Cheshire, February 2007.

Small Wars, Big Questions

In December 1993 John Major stood outside the black-painted, steel-armoured door of Number Ten Downing Street with the affable Taoiseach of the Irish Republic, Albeit Reynolds. He declared a new principle which offended many traditional Conservatives and Unionists. If both parts of Ireland voted to be reunited, Britain would not stand in the way. She had, said Major, 'no selfish strategic or economic interest in Northern Ireland'. Thus a long strand of Tory thinking, which was that the party was dedicated to the United Kingdom, consciously and proudly biased in its favour, was torn up. There was more. If the Provisional IRA, which had so lately bombed the very building Major was standing in front of, and murdered two young boys in Cheshire, renounced violence, it could be welcomed into the sunlight as a legitimate political party.

In the run-up to this Downing Street Declaration, the government was also conducting top-secret 'back channel' negotiations with the terrorist organization. The Provisional IRA leadership proved slippery and frustrating but in August 1994 they declared 'a complete cessation of military operations' which, though it was a long way short of renouncing violence, was widely welcomed. It was followed a month later by a Loyalist ceasefire. A complicated dance of three-strand talks, framework documents and arguments about the decommissioning of weapons followed. The road to peace would be tortuous, involving many walkouts and public arguments. On the streets, extortion, knee-capping and occasional murders continued. But whereas the number of people killed in 1993 had been eighty-four, the toll fell to sixty-one the following year and nine in 1995. The contradictory demands of Irish republicanism and Unionism meant that Major failed to get a final agreement, even on paper. That was left for Tony Blair, unfinished business. But Major's achievement was substantial: he was a good peacemaker.

And he made a dramatic bid for peace at home. In July 1995, tormented by yet more rumours of right-wing conspiracies against him, Major riposted with a theatrical coup all of his own, one his music-hall father would have applauded. He resigned as leader of the Conservative Party and invited all comers to take him on. He told journalists gathered in the sunshine in the Number Ten garden it was 'put up or shut up' time. If he lost, he would resign as Prime Minister. If he won, he expected the party to rally around him. This was a risk, for there were other plausible leaders. One was Michael Heseltine, who had become Deputy Prime Minister and who loyally supported Major. Another was Michael Portillo, then a pin-up boy of the Thatcherite right, whose supporters prepared a campaign headquarters for him but who decided against standing. In the event the challenger was John Redwood, the Welsh Secretary, known to many as 'the Vulcan' because of his glassy extraterrestrial demeanour but a highly intelligent Thatcherite. At a catastrophic press launch of his campaign he was surrounded by a celebratory, luridly dressed collection of supportive MPs swiftly dubbed 'the barmy army'. Major won his fight, though not gloriously. In the end 109 Tory MPs failed to back him. Nevertheless, in a clever political operation, victory was swiftly declared and he lived to be defeated finally by the real electorate two years later. By then defeat had been made inevitable by the self-destructive European war of the previous years.

Major was also a cautious warmaker. Blair would inherit not only the Northern Irish peace process but also the bubbling ethnic wars breaking out in former Yugoslavia, following the recognition of Slovenia, Croatia and Bosnia as independent states in the early nineties. The worst violence followed the Serbian assault on Bosnia and the three-year siege of its capital, Sarajevo. The term 'ethnic cleansing' was heard for the first time as woeful columns of refugees fled in different directions. A nightmare which Europeans thought had vanished in 1945 was returning, only a couple of days' drive away from London. Major asked his military advisers how many troops it would take to keep the sides apart and was told the answer was 400,000, three times the total size of the British Army. He sent 1,800 men to protect the humanitarian convoys that were rumbling south. Many British people proved ready to collect parcels of food, warm clothes, medicine and blankets, which were loaded onto trucks and driven south by volunteers. A London conference tried to get a peace deal and failed.

This new war went on, ever nastier. Many in the government were dubious about Britain being further involved. But the evening news bulletins showed pictures of starving refugees, the uncovered mass graves of civilians shot by death squads, and children with appalling injuries. There was a frenzied campaign for Western intervention. But what kind? In the United States President Clinton was determined not to risk American soldiers on the ground, but a swelling of outrage about the behaviour of the Serbs persuaded him to consider less costly alternatives, such as air strikes and lifting the arms embargo on the Bosnians. This would have put others who were on the ground, including the British, directly in the line of fire when the Serbs retaliated. There were rows between London and Washington. Hideous attacks in Sarajevo, notably a mysterious mortar strike at the market, finally provoked the Nato air strikes. In response the Serbs took UN troops hostage, including British soldiers who were then used as human shields. The Serb capture of the town of Srebrenica was followed by disgusting slaughter, and renewed demands for full-scale military intervention.

It never came. After three years of war, sanctions on Serbia and the success of Croats in fighting back, a peace agreement was finally made in Dayton, Ohio. Major was the first British Prime Minister of the post-Cold War world, grappling with what the proper role of the West should be. The Balkan wars, a result of the fall of communism, showed perfectly the dangers and limits of intervention. When a civil conflict is relayed in all its horror to tens of millions of voters every night by television, the pressure to do something, to separate the sides and succour the suffering, is intense. But mostly this requires not air attacks but a full-scale ground force, which will be drawn into the war, and must be followed by years of aid and rebuilding. Will the same voters be happy to keep paying, and keep accepting the casualties that follow? Major and his colleagues were accused of moral cowardice and cynicism in allowing the revival of fascist behaviour in one corner of Europe. This was nobody's finest hour. Yet Western leaders were wary about whether their voters would have accepted a full-scale war and the thankless neo-colonial responsibilities that would follow. They may have been right.

A Very English Coup

Tony Blair was an Establishment figure, more so than Thatcher, Major or Smith. He had been a mild teenage rebel, worn his hair long, broken school rules and imitated Mick Jagger in a rock band. His father had been brought up by a Communist on Clydeside and had suffered an early and severe stroke which brought his children uncertainty and a bump down in the world. Far more importantly, though, Blair was the son of a Tory lawyer and went to a preparatory school in Durham, then the grand fee-paying boarding school Fettes in Edinburgh, then Oxford University, and then the Bar, before becoming an MP. There was more Gothic architecture in his early history than in most volumes of Pevsner's architectural guide. Though he rebelled, the lessons of politeness, deference and a quiet knowledge about where power lay, were in place from the start. Gifted with a natural charm, infectious good humour and a great skill in acting, he was a young man whose seriousness and principle were also evident. His father's stroke had happened when he was still young: he lost his adored Irish-born mother when he was a student and turned increasingly to religion, in its activist, not contemplative form.

Much ink has been spilled about why he joined the Labour Party rather than the Conservatives. It is not a ridiculous question. Falling for a young Liverpudlian socialist called Cherie Booth sharpened his politics but he had joined Labour before he met her. There is a widespread belief that it was mere calculation. In the early eighties, the Tories were awash with bright lawyers looking for seats and political careers while Labour seemed on its last legs. If you wanted to get into the Commons and then rise, Labour offered an easier if riskier route. While this is possible, joining Labour at its lowest ebb would show uncanny prescience for a pure careerist. The likeliest explanation is simply that he believed in political action and that, though flawed, Labour's belief in social justice was nearest to the Christian social views he had formed. Once in the party, working his way through local branches in London, he displayed the full kit of soft-left beliefs of the time, being hostile to the European Community and privatization, pro-CND and high taxes, the rights of illegal immigrants and greater freedom for the press. He would ditch all of these views later but this does not mean they were insincerely held at the time; for the Labour Party of Foot's time they were considered moderate, and Blair was always opposed to the hard-left Bennite and Militant groups.

After fighting a hopeless by-election, Blair won a safe Labour seat in the north-east of England with his combination of chutzpah and charm and, in the

Commons from 1983, quickly fell in with another new MP. Gordon Brown was much that Blair was not. He was a tribal Labour Party man from a strongly political family, who had barely glimpsed the crenellated English Establishment which produced Blair. Brown had been Scotland's best-known student politician and a player in Scottish Labour politics from the age of twenty-three, followed by a stint in television. Yet the two men had some things in common. They were both Christians and they were both deeply impatient with the condition of the Labour Party. For seven or eight years they seemed inseparable, working mostly from a tiny, windowless office they shared. Brown tutored Blair in the darker ways of politics, treating him like a sweetly naive kid brother. (He would learn.) Blair was also a vital sounding-board for Brown, however, teaching him what the mysterious English middle classes might be thinking. No working relationship in politics was closer. Brown summed it up in 1991: 'I think Blair could well be leader of the party after me.' Together, they made friends with Westminster journalists, together they matured as Commons performers, together they shared their frustration about older Labour politicians, together they worked their way up the ranks of the shadow cabinet.

Then Blair began to pull ahead. After the 1992 defeat he made a bleak public judgement about why Labour had lost so badly. The reason was not complicated, but simple: 'Labour has not been trusted to fulfil the aspirations of the majority of people in a modern world.' As shadow home secretary he began to try to put that right, promising (in words borrowed from Brown) to be 'tough on crime and tough on the causes of crime'. His response to the horror of the 1993 murder of the toddler James Bulger by two young boys, which provoked a frenzy of national debate, was particularly resonant. In general Blair tried to return his party to the common-sense language of morality. He drank deep from the mix of socially conservative and economically liberal messages used by the great communicator Bill Clinton and his team of 'New Democrats'.

So too did Brown. But he had a harder brief, since as shadow chancellor his job was to demolish cherished spending plans and say no to Labour MPs. Brown's support for the ERM meant he was ineffective when Major and Lamont suffered their great defeat. The Brown and Blair relationship was less close than it had been earlier but it was still strong. Together they visited the United States to learn a new political style from the Democrats. Awkwardly for Brown, it relied heavily on leadership charisma. At home Blair pushed Smith aggressively over reforming the party rulebook, falling out with him badly. Watching media commentators and some Labour MPs began to tip him as the next leader, Brown's team began to ask whether Blair was now manoeuvring and briefing against his old mentor. It was a grim time for Brown and he did not bother to reach out, or show a sunny side. Slowly but perceptibly, Brown-Blair was turning into Blair-Brown.

The days after John Smith died have produced more analysis and speculation than almost any other short period in modern British politics. But the basic story is clear. Blair decided almost

187

immediately that he would run as leader. Brown, perhaps more grief-stricken than Blair or perhaps more cautious, hesitated. But he had assumed he would inherit and when he heard Blair's plans, he was aghast. In at least ten face-to-face meetings in Edinburgh and London, the two men argued. On Blair's side were opinion polls showing him much more popular, the support of greater numbers of Labour MPs and greater backing in the press. This was not all a plot by Peter Mandelson, as Brown people later claimed; it was a widespread assessment come to independently by many people who disagreed about other things. Crucial to the case for Blair was that he was a well-spoken Englishman who would reassure those parts of the country which were the main electoral battleground. On Brown's side were his deeper knowledge of Labour, stronger support among the unions and his more thought-through policy agenda for change. Had the two fought each other, given Labour's complicated electoral college it is impossible to say just what would have happened. Blairites say their man would have crushed and 'humiliated' Brown; Brown's people reply that his formidable campaigning skills would have taken the metropolitan Blairites by surprise. On only one subject were they both agreed. For the two modernizers to fight would be disastrous. Personal attacks would be impossible to avoid. If Brown had any hope of winning, he would have to attack Blair from the left.

So Brown came to a deal, culminating in a notorious dinner at the chic, now defunct Islington restaurant Granita. (Some sense of the cultural gap between the two men can be drawn from the fact that Brown had to go and have a proper meal afterwards.) Again, the outcome is much disputed, except that Blair acknowledged Brown's authority over a wide range of policy which he would direct from the Treasury, including the 'social justice' agenda. Did he also promise to limit his prime ministership to seven years and then make way? It would be an extraordinarily arrogant thing for one Opposition politician to say to another; the Conservatives would be in power for years yet. But probably some form of words about a transition in power was exchanged, if only to salve Brown's hurt. Looking back many years later it can be seen that the true significance of the Granita deal and the meetings that preceded it, was that it gifted Britain's mightiest government department, the Treasury, even more power than it had in the Conservative years. Blair would be, as Prime Minister, more concerned with foreign affairs than he could ever have guessed, and Brown's Treasury would become a grand Department for British Affairs, beyond its mandarins' wildest dreams. Gordon Brown would be the Treasury's final victory over George Brown.

The Killer Cows of Old England

John Selwyn Gummer, a devout Christian and environmentalist, was one of the nicest men in British politics. On a sunny May morning in 1990, he paraded his daughter Cordelia before the cameras in Suffolk and tried to persuade her to eat a beefburger. The four-year-old Cordelia was nobody's fool and absolutely refused. Gummer quickly swallowed his embarrassment, and then the cooling burger too, pronouncing it 'absolutely delicious'. He was of course trying to make a political point. There was rising disquiet about a mysterious and unpleasant disease of the brain found in cattle, which caused them to stagger, fall over and expire. It was called BSE, for bovine spongiform encephalopathy. The disease was being found all across Britain at the rate of 300 cases a week. The Ministry of Agriculture, Fisheries and Food, with Mr Gummer at its head, was more the department of farmers than the department of shoppers and it discouraged alarm about the new disease. Could it be spread to humans? At that stage the answer was no. Still, because it seemed to be spread by the use of mashed-up cow offal in feed, a kind of grisly if unwitting cow cannibalism, new rules were put in place. Farmers were told to destroy BSE-infected cattle. Gummer's stunt was intended to show how safe British beef, even in beefburgers, now was. Prior to Cordelia's rejected burger, cow brains, spleen, tonsils and gut had already been banned for human consumption.

But the problem would not go away. Among those refusing to eat British beef were the Germans, some schools, and a majority of doctors. Various other animals, including a cat, a cheetah and a monkey, died of BSE. By the mid-nineties, the government was spending tens of millions on compensation for farmers who were burning or burying their dead cattle. The line that humans could not contract the brain disease was beginning to crumble. Victoria Rimmer, a teenager from North Wales, was dying of Creutzfeld-Jakob

Disease (CJD) which was closely related to BSE and said to have been caused by eating infected beef. More human cases were reported, from, amongst others, farmers, butchers and people who had had blood transfusions. It began to be clear that many slaughterhouses were not following the new rules and that some BSE-infected cattle still ended up for human consumption. The EU started to take a close interest. In March 1996 ministers admitted that a new form of CJD had been found in ten people, of whom eight had died, and that this was probably due to BSE being in food.

There was, rightly, an eruption of anger and the credibility of the department was questioned. British beef was banned by the EU. New rules about the deboning of beef before it was eaten were introduced and a massive programme of slaughtering all cows over thirty months began. Beef on the bone was off the menu and parts of the British countryside were studded with oily pyres of swollen dead corpses, an unappetizing spectacle. The slaughter was extended to 147,000 animals but Europe remained steely, and extended the ban to exported British beef outside the EU as well. 'Mad cow disease' became as emblematic of the end of the Tory years as union militancy or punk rock had been of the late seventies. The government's anger was mainly directed at continental Europe, seen as gleefully exaggerating the lethal infection in the Roast Beef of Old England in order to sell their own meat. Yet the anger might have been as profitably directed elsewhere – to the farming-dominated government department that had acted slowly, the farmers who had refused to report the full extent of the disease, the sloppy slaughterhouses and, in general, a form of industrial farming that fed dead cows' brains to cows, apparently heedless of whether this was nice, safe or healthy. The science was still sketchy and the media was hysterical, but government and industry were to blame as well.

The Sword of Truth

For British voters, the Major years were remembered as much for the sad, petty and lurid personal scandals that attended so many of his ministers, after he made an unwise speech remembered as a call for old-style morality. In fact 'back to basics' referred to almost everything except personal sexual morality – he spoke of public service, industry, sound money, free trade, traditional teaching, respect for the family and law, and a campaign to defeat crime. 'Back to basics', however, gave the press a fail-safe headline charge of hypocrisy whenever ministers were caught out, and caught out they were. A series of adulteries exposed, children born out of wedlock, a sex death after a kinky stunt went wrong, rumours about Major's own affairs (truer than was realized, though the press had the wrong person) and then an inquiry into whether Parliament had been misled over the sale of arms to Iraq, were knitted together into a single pattern of misbehaviour, which got an old name, 'sleaze'.

In 1996 a three-year inquiry into whether the government had allowed a trial to go ahead against directors of an arms company, Matrix Churchill, knowing that they were in fact acting inside privately accepted guidelines, resulted in two ministers being publicly criticized. It showed that the government had allowed a more relaxed regime of military-related exports to Saddam Hussein even after the horrific gassing of 5,000 Kurds at Falluja, and revealed a culture of secrecy and double standards. Other 'sleaze' related stories were more personal. One of the more flamboyant Thatcherite MPs, the bow-tied and flippant Neil Hamilton, was accused of taking cash in brown paper envelopes from the owner of Harrods, Mohamed al-Fayed, to ask questions for him in Parliament. In a libel case which followed he vociferously denied this, but lost the action and was financially ruined. Jonathan Aitken, a Treasury minister, was accused of taking improper hospitality from an Arab business contact. He resigned to fight the *Guardian* over the claims, with 'the simple sword of truth and the trusty shield of fair play', was found guilty of perjury and served eighteen months in prison.

There is no logical link between a minister who forms improper links with a sexual partner, and a minister who forms improper links with a businessman. Never mind. All of this was expertly packaged together by the New Labour Opposition, working closely with the media. In the late nineties, sleaze was as ubiquitous and smug a word as 'spin' would be later. It set the tone of the times. One of the more dramatic episodes in the 1997 election was the overwhelming defeat of Hamilton in his Tatton constituency by the former BBC war reporter, who had been badly injured at Sarajevo, Martin Bell. Clad in his familiar white suit, helped by a decision to stand aside by the Labour and Liberal Democrat candidates, and advised by the Labour spin doctor Alastair Campbell, Bell succeeded in overturning Hamilton's enormous majority, emerging with an 11,000 majority of his own. He became Britain's first independent MP for nearly fifty years. It is worth recalling that there was a time not so long ago when it seemed that white suits, if not swords of truth, would cleanse British politics.

By the end of Major's government, it seemed that some lessons had been learned about politics in Britain, broadly defined. The European Union was perilous, a potential party-splitter. Their single currency was as toxic as our beef. There was a mood of contempt for politicians. The press had lost any sense of deference. Busy reforms directed at the health service, police and schools had produced surprisingly little improvement. The post Cold War world was turning out to be nastier and less predictable than the days of the 'peace dividend' had promised. And finally, when your luck turned, it turned dramatically. There was, in all this, material for a thoughtful and wary Opposition to reflect on. How might the country be better governed? What was the right British approach to peace-keeping and intervention now that the United States was the last superpower left standing? How could the promises of an end to cynicism be fulfilled? But by 1997, New Labour had no time to reflect on all that. It was moving in for the kill.

Team Tony

The 1997 general election demonstrated just what a stunningly effective election-winning machine Tony Blair now led. New Labour won 419 seats, the largest number ever for the party and comparable only with the number of seats for the 1935 National government. Its majority in the Commons was also a modern record, 179 seats, and thirty-three more than Attlee's landslide majority of 1945. The swing of 10 per cent from the Conservatives was yet another post-war record, roughly double that which the Thatcher victory of 1979 had produced in the other direction. A record number of women were elected to Parliament, 119 of them, of whom 101 were Labour, 'Blair's babes'. The party also won heavily across the south and in London, in parts of Britain from which it had recently been hardly represented. Yet among this slew of heart-stopping statistics, which had Blair shaking his head with disbelief and exclaiming 'it can't be real', there were some small warning signs. The turnout was very low, at 71 per cent the lowest since 1935. Labour had won a famous victory but nothing like as many actual votes as the reviled John Major had won five years before. Still, as the sun came up on a jubilant, celebrating party there was much wet-eyed rhapsodizing about a new dawn for Britain. Alastair Campbell had assembled crowds of party workers and supporters to stand along Downing Street waving Union Jacks as the Blairs strode up to claim their inheritance. Briefly, it looked as if the country itself had turned out to cheer.

The victory was due to a small group of self-styled modernizers who seized the Labour Party, and then took it far further to the right than anyone expected. The language used tells its own story. New Labour was to be a party of the 'left and centre left', then one of the 'centre left', then the 'centre and centre left' and in Blair's later years simply of 'the centre'. Blair was the leading man in this drama but he was not the only player. He needed the support and encouragement of admirers and friends who would coax and goad him, rebuke him and encourage him, and do his will, whether he knew what they were up to or not. Who were they? There was Mandelson, the brilliant but temperamental former media boss, by now an MP. Once fixated by Gordon Brown, he was adored by Blair and returned the sentiment. Yet he was so mistrusted by other members of the team that his central role in Blair's leadership election was disguised from them under the name 'Bobby' (for Bobby Kennedy, working to Blair's JFK: modesty was never a hallmark of the inner circle).

There was Alastair Campbell, Blair's press officer and attack-dog. A former journalist, natural propagandist, ex-alcoholic and all-round alpha male, Campbell would chew the ears of everyone who criticized Blair and helped devise the campaign of mockery against Major. He behaved in private towards the Labour leader (and on one occasion was filmed doing so) with the cheery aggression of a personal trainer working over a nervous young housewife. There was Philip Gould, a working-class boy whose admiration for US political techniques knew no bounds; he would bring his focus group expertise, his polling and ruthless analysis to the party. There was Deny Irvine, the rotund, intimidating, brilliant and surprisingly sensitive Highlands lawyer who had first found a place in his chambers for Blair and Cherie Booth. He advised on constitutional change and would become Lord Chancellor. And there was Anji Hunter, the contralto charmer who had known Blair as a youth and who remained his best hotline to *Daily Mail*-reading middle England.

These people, with Brown and his team working (almost) alongside them, formed the inner core. The young David Miliband, whose father was a famous Marxist political philosopher, provided research help. They would be joined by Jonathan Powell, a diplomat who had been observing the Clintons in the United States, and whose older brother Charles had been one of Thatcher's most important aides. By the end of the Blair years, with so many others fallen by the wayside, he was undoubtedly the second most important man in Downing Street. Among the MPs who were initially close were Marjorie (better known as Mo) Mowlam and Jack Straw. The money for Blair's leadership campaign was raised from a clutch of mainly media millionaires, including Greg Dyke, later Director General of the BBC, and Michael Levy, a record promoter who would later be ennobled and later still face a police investigation and arrest on corruption charges. The first striking thing about Team Blair is how few elected Labour politicians it included. The second is how many of its original members would later fall out with him. He had a capacity to charm and pull in people whom he needed, and then to drop them briskly once they were surplus or embarrassing.

Blair had won 57 per cent of the vote in the leadership election, easily beating two more left-wing candidates, one of whom, John Prescott, was elected as his deputy. In his campaign Blair had stuck mostly to generalities about modernization and the instincts of the British people, but had sounded approving of the regime of centralized testing and quangos the Conservatives had pursued in public services. To that extent people had due warning. By the time the party congregated again for its annual conference, the Labour Party had become 'New Labour'. In his first conference speech Blair made a veiled reference to the need for an up-to-date statement of Labour values. What he actually meant was that he planned to scrap clause four of its constitution, which declared that public ownership of the means of production, distribution and exchange was necessary to 'secure for the workers by hand or by brain the full fruit of their industry'. Clause four, part four, was a household god for Labour, its 1918 commitment to destroy capitalism, which sat in a corner covered in cobwebs. Hugh Gaitskell had wanted to abolish it, but had drawn back and the ambition had slumbered for decades. Blair killed it. His new statement of aims began with the assertion that 'the Labour Party is a democratic socialist party' which, by then, was going it a bit. In his next conference speech Blair used the word 'new' fifty-nine times, referred to socialism just once and omitted to mention the working class at all.

Though politics is a serious business, there is an undeniably comic side to the Blair coup. With his impish grin he suddenly behaved as if everything was possible, and no political allegiance was impossible to shift. He became the playful magician of political life. He took to warmly praising Margaret Thatcher. He opened private talks with the Liberal Democrats about some grand new alliance of the centre. In Fleet Street he took to charming every rheumy proprietorial troll and crusty prophet of the right he could lay his smile on. Later he would continue the practice in government, appointing Tory statesmen to big jobs, gleefully ushering in defectors and keeping close for a while to the Lib-Dem leader Paddy Ashdown, and its elder statesman Roy Jenkins (though he would later disappoint both by his conservatism). He went to visit Rupert Murdoch's News International team in Australia and impressed them too. What manner of man was this Tony Blair? Where did he stand? Where were his limits? There were not many. In the election campaign the pro-European Blair cheerfully put his name to an article in Murdoch's *Sun*, ghost-written by Campbell, promising 'to slay the dragon' of federalism. Later relations would be so close that Murdoch would complain of the amount of time he wasted in London drinking tea with Blair and coffee with Brown. He searched out Lord Rothermere, proprietor of the *Daily Mail*, traditionally Labour's bitterest critic in the British press, and dined him privately, promising him that he abhorred high taxes, uppity unions and sleaze. It was as if, freed by winning the leadership, Blair was rattling the handle of every door in town to see if it opened. As he was on a roll and Labour was desperate to win at all costs, the traditionalists looked on in silent, helpless disbelief. Was nothing sacred? Apparently not.

Yet when it came to serious policy formation, the story was less amusing. Blair talked of his priority being 'education, education, education', of his ambition to make Britain a 'young country' and of his own belief in 'power for a purpose'. He identified the broad areas he wanted to concentrate on, but when it came to clearer proposals said little. Blair has been mocked so richly since for the airy blandness of his promises that it is worth recalling an example of the 'optimism-lite' rhetoric which was taken at least half-seriously in 1997. A few early sentences from Labour's manifesto give a flavour of this:

> I believe in Britain. It is a great country with a great history. The British people are a great people. But I believe Britain can and must be better: better schools, better hospitals, better ways of tackling crime, of building a modern welfare state, of equipping ourselves for a new world economy. I want a Britain that is one nation, with shared values and purpose, where merit comes before privilege, run for the many not the few, strong and sure of itself at home and abroad. I want a Britain that does not shuffle into the new millennium afraid of the future, but strides into it with confidence.

Britons would stride with a purpose, and in their hands they would hold New Labour's first pledge card, a credit-card-sized rectangle of coloured cardboard. Produced in time for the election, its five pledges were rather clearer than the early rhetoric. In government Labour would cut class sizes to thirty or below for five- to seven-year-olds, by scrapping the assisted places scheme that helped people from poor families go to private schools. It would speed up punishment for persistent young offenders, halving the time from arrest to sentencing. It would cut health service waiting times 'by treating an extra 100,000 patients as a first step' paid for by cutting red tape (the last resort of political accountancy). A quarter of a million young people would be put to work through a windfall tax on the privatized utility companies. There would be no rise in income tax rates and inflation and interest rates would be kept 'as low as possible'. The last seemed entirely meaningless since no government has tried to raise inflation, but now seems like a coded reference to Gordon Brown's decision to hand control over interest rates to a committee of the Bank of England. Looking back, the pledge card revealed a lot about the strengths and weaknesses of New Labour. It was modest in promise, and costed. Its promises, however, were so simple they often turned out to be damaging in practice; the waiting times pledge was one example. And there was a yearning for numerical simplicity – all those suspiciously round numbers – which suggested the purpose of the pledges was propagandists, not governmental, easy ideas to spoon into voters who could not be bothered to concentrate.

Most damaging of all for a campaign which so relentlessly accused the Conservatives of deceit and destroying people's trust in politics, Labour made promises which it would promptly break when it won power. It promised not to privatize the air traffic control system, but did so. It promised not to levy tuition fees for students and a year later did exactly that – and would repeat the trick with student top-up fees during the 2001 election. It promised an end to sleaze and to deception. It implied that the overall tax burden would not increase, yet it would. The most important pledges were the negative ones, coming from Brown and his Treasury team; that there would be no increase in rates of income tax, while for two years a New Labour government would stick to the Conservatives' spending totals. Those promises were stuck to, though there were big and unmentioned stings to come.

But why were so many other pledges broken? Team Tony, the group who put together the New Labour 'project', were intelligent people who wanted to find a way of ruling which helped the worse off, particularly by giving them better chances in education and to find jobs, while not alienating the mass of middle-class voters. They exuded a strange, unstable mix of anxiety and arrogance. They were extraordinarily worried by newspapers. They were bruised by what had happened to Kinnock, whom they had all worked with, and ruthlessly focused on winning over anyone who could be won. Yet there was arrogance too. They were utterly ignorant of what governing would be like. The early success of Blair's leadership victory and his short time as Opposition leader produced a sense that everything was possible for people of determination. If they promised something, no doubt it would happen. It they said something, of course it was true. They weren't Tories, after all. The pity of all this was that they were about to take power at a golden moment when it would have been possible to fulfil the pledges they had made and when it was not necessary to give different messages to different people in order to win power. Blair had the wind at his back. The Conservatives would pose no serious threat to him for many years to come. Far from inheriting a weak or crisis-ridden economy, he was actually taking over at the best possible time when the country was recovering strongly, but had not yet quite noticed. Blair won by being focused and ruthless, and never forgot it. But he also had incredible, historic luck, and never seemed to realize quite what an opportunity it gave him.

Celebrity Life, Celebrity Death

Tony Blair arrived in power in 1997 in a country spangled and sugar-coated by a revived fashion for celebrity. It offered a few politicians new opportunities but at a high cost. The glamour industry had always been with us, under different names, but had become super-charged during the sixties when rock stars, Hollywood actors and television performers were feted by the tabloid press and a new generation of women's and urban magazines. Such interviews and profiles spread more widely during the seventies and eighties but it was not until 1988 that the shape of the modern celebrity culture became fully apparent. That year saw the first of the true modern celebrity glossies in Britain when *Hello!* magazine was launched on 17 May. It was the English-language version of the Spanish magazine *Hola!* which had already made its owner Eduardo Sanchez Junco a multi-millionaire. Its success is often credited to the exotic Marquesa de Varela, who allegedly owns 200 dogs and has four luxury homes in Uruguay, as well as New York and London. The *Hello!* formula would copied by *OK!* from 1993 and many other magazines, to the point where yards of coloured mimicry occupied newsagents' shelves in every town and village in the country. It sheds a sidelight on Britain's changing public culture.

The essence of its sweetheart deal was that celebrities would be paid handsomely to be interviewed and photographed, in return for coverage that was generally fawning and never hostile. *Hello!* allowed the flawed-famous to shun the mean-minded sniping of the regular press, while it scooped up access to the most famous names, time after time. The sunny, good-time, upbeat, airbrushed world of *Hello!* was much mocked. In the real world the relentless optimism of its coverage of grinning couples and their lovely homes was inevitably followed by divorces, drunken rows, accidents and ordinary scandals. But it was hugely successful. People seemed happy to read good news about the famous and beautiful even if they knew in their hearts there was more to it than that. In the same year as *Hello!* arrived, 1988, the BBC put the Australian soap opera *Neighbours* into a prime teatime slot. At its height this show, which had been a failure on its home patch, was attracting 15 million British viewers. It too portrayed a youthful, sunny alternative to grey Britain[8] and its early stars, notably Kylie Minogue and Jason Donovan, went on to become celebrities themselves. In the same year as *Hello!* and

204

Neighbours, ITV launched the most successful of the daytime television shows, *This Morning,* hosted from Liverpool by Richard Madeley and Judy Finnigan, a live magazine programme of frothy features and celebrity interviews. Daytime television had existed since 1983 when BBC One's breakfast show with Frank Bough and Selina Scott arrived alongside the independent *TVam.* These, though, were high-minded and mainstream compared to the more popular *This Morning* show, television's celebrity breakthrough moment.

What did this celebrity fantasy world, which continued to open up in all directions in the media through the nineties, have to do with anything else? For one thing it re-emphasized to alert politicians, broadcasting executives and advertisers the considerable if recently unfashionable power of optimism. Mainstream news in the nineties might be giving the British an unending stream of bleakness, burning cattle carcasses, awful murders and disasters on railway lines; millions turned all the more urgently to celebrity. They did not think that celebrities had universally happy lives, or always behaved well, or did not age.

But in celebrity-land, everyone meant well, everyone could forgive themselves and be forgiven, and there was always a new dawn breaking over the swimming pool. The celebrity who emoted, who was prepared to expose inner pain, enjoyed a land of power. And in eighties and nineties Britain, no celebrity gleamed more brightly than the beautiful, troubled Princess Diana. For fifteen years she was an ever-present presence. As an aristocratic girl, no intellectual, whose childhood had been blighted by a bad divorce, her fairytale

205

marriage in 1981 found her pledging her life to an older man who shared few of her interests and did not seem to be in love with her.

The slow disintegration of this marriage transfixed Britain, as Diana moved from china-doll, whispery-voiced debutante, to painfully thin young mother, to increasingly charismatic and confident public figure, working crowds and seducing cameras like a new Marilyn Monroe. As eighties fashions grew more exuberant and glossy, so did she. Her eating disorder, bulimia, was one suffered by growing numbers of girls. When she admitted later to acts of self-harm, she sounded like teenagers and young women in many less privileged homes. When plagues and cruelties of the age were in the news, she appeared as visual commentator, hugging AIDS victims to show that it was safe, or campaigning against land-mines. Rumours spread of her affairs. Britain was now a divorce-prone country, in which 'what's best for the kids' and 'I deserve to be happy' were batted across kitchen tables. So Diana was not simply a pretty woman married to a king-in-waiting, but became a kind of Barbie of the emotions, who could be dressed up in the private pain of millions. People felt, possibly wrongly, that she would understand them. Her glance was as potent as the monarch's touch had once been for scrofula. A feverish, obsessive quality attached to her admirers, something not seen before by the Royal Family, who found all this uncomfortable and alarming. They were living symbols. She was a living icon.

After the birth of her second son Harry in 1987 Diana's marriage was visibly failing. In 1992 the journalist Andrew Morton, to general huffing, claimed to tell *Diana – the True Story* in a book which described suicide attempts, blazing rows, her bulimia and her growing certainty that Prince Charles had resumed an affair with his old love, Camilla Parker Bowles, something he later confirmed in a television interview with Jonathan Dimbleby. In the December after Morton's publication John Major announced that Charles and Diana were to separate. A wily manipulator of the media, Diana became simultaneously a huntress in the media jungle, pursuing stories that flattered her, and the hunted, both haunted and haunting. Then came her revelatory 1995 interview on *Panorama*. Breaking every taboo left in royal circles, she freely discussed the breakup of her marriage ('there were three of us'), attacked the Windsors for their cruelty and promised to be 'a queen in people's hearts'. Finally divorced in 1996, she continued her charity work around the world and began a relationship with Dodi al-Fayed, son of the owner of Harrods. To many she was a selfish and unhinged woman endangering the monarchy. To millions her painful life-story and her fashionable readiness to share that pain, made her more valuable than formal monarchy. She was followed with close attention all round the world, her face and name a sure seller of papers and magazines. By the summer of 1997 Britain had two super-celebrities. One was Tony Blair and the other was Princess Diana.

It is therefore grimly fitting that Tony Blair's most resonant words as Prime Minister and the moment when he reached the very height of his popularity came on the morning when Diana was killed with Dodi in a Paris underpass after their car

207

crashed. Blair had been woken from a deep sleep at his Trimdon constituency home, first to be warned about the accident, and then to be told that Diana was dead. He was deeply shocked, and worried about what his proper role should be. After pacing round in his pyjamas and having expletive-ridden conversations with Campbell, Blair spoke to the Queen, who said that neither she nor any other senior would make a statement. He decided he had to say something. Later that morning, standing in front of his local church, looking shattered, and transmitted live around the world, he spoke for Britain. 'I feel, like everyone else in this country today, utterly devastated. Our thoughts and prayers are with Princess Diana's family – in particular her two sons, her two boys – our hearts go out to them. We are today a nation in a state of shock …' As he continued, his hands clenched, his voice broke and he showed he understood why she achieved her special status: 'Her own life was often sadly touched by tragedy. She touched the lives of so many others in Britain and throughout the world with joy and with comfort. How many times shall we remember her in how many different ways, with the sick, the dying, with children, with the needy? With just a look or a gesture that spoke so much more than words, she would reveal to all of us the depth of her compassion and her humanity.'

Looking back at the words many years on, they seem strangely close to what might be said of a religious figure, someone about to be declared a saint by the Catholic Church a holy figure whose glance or touch could heal. At the time, though, they were much welcomed and assented to. Blair went on: 'People everywhere, not just here in

Britain, kept faith with Princess Diana. They liked her, they loved her, they regarded her as one of the people. She was – the People's Princess and that is how she will stay, how she will remain in our hearts and our memories for ever.' These are the sentiments of one natural charismatic paying tribute to another. Blair regarded himself as the people's Prime Minister, leading the people's party, beyond left and right, beyond faction or ideology, a political miracle-worker with a direct line to the people's instincts. And in the country after his impromptu eulogy to Diana, astonishingly, his approval rating rose to over 90 per cent, a figure we do not normally witness in democracies.

Blair and Campbell then paid their greatest service to an institution which represented Old Britain, or the forces of conservatism, the monarchy itself. The Queen, still angry and upset about Diana's behaviour, wanted a quiet private funeral and wanted, also, to remain away from the scenes of public mourning in London. She stayed at Balmoral, looking after her devastated grandsons. This may well have been the grandmotherly thing to do, and the best thing for them but it could have been disastrous for her public image. There was a strange mood in the country, a frantic edge to the mourning which Blair had predicted from the first. The lack of publicly mourning Windsors, the lack of a flag at half-mast over Buckingham Palace, any suggestion of a quiet funeral, all seemed to confirm all Diana's most bitter thoughts about a cold and unfeeling Royal Family. With Prince Charles's full agreement Blair and his aides cajoled the Palace first into accepting that this would have to be a huge public funeral so the country's grief could be expressed, and second that the Queen should return to London. She did, just in time to quieten a growing mood of anger about her behaviour.

This was a generational problem as well as a class one. The Queen had been brought up in a land of buttoned lips, stoicism and private grieving. She now reigned over a country which expected and almost required exhibitionism. To let it all loll out had become a guarantee of authenticity. For some years in Britain the deaths of children, or the scenes of fatal accidents, had been marked by little shrines of cellophane-wrapped flowers, cards and soft toys. In the run-up to Diana's funeral parts of central London seemed Mediterranean in their public grieving. There were vast mounds of flowers, people sleeping out, holding placards, weeping in the streets. Strangers hugged strangers. If Blair's words in Trimdon suggested Diana was a living saint, a sub-religious hysteria responded to the thought. People queuing to sign a book of condolence at St James's Palace reported that her image was appearing, supernaturally, in the background of an oil painting.

The funeral itself was like no other before, and will never be mimicked. The capital was at a standstill. Among the lucky ones invited to Westminster Abbey, gay men in matching sado-masochistic leather outfits queued up with members of the Household Cavalry, in long leather boots and jangling spurs. Campaigners stood with earls, entertainers shared programmes with elderly politicians as the worlds of rock music and aristocracy, charity work and politics, jostled together. Elton John performed a hastily rewritten version of 'Candle in the Wind', his lament for

Marilyn Monroe, and Princess Diana's brother Earl Spencer made an angrily half-coded attack from the pulpit on the Windsors' treatment of his sister. This was applauded when it was relayed outside, and then disloyal clapping was heard in the Abbey itself. Diana's body was driven to her last resting place and showered with flowers all the way.

In another echo of Marilyn Monroe, Diana's death would begin a worldwide rumour that she had been murdered, either because she was pregnant by Dodi or because she was about to marry a Muslim. Wild theories about British secret service agents would ripple through cyberspace, reappearing regularly in newspapers. Those same papers, implicated in the hounding of Diana by paparazzi photographers whose work they bought eagerly, were more obvious to blame. Less was said about that. Nearly a decade later an inquiry headed by a former Metropolitan Police commissioner concluded that she had died because her driver was drunk and trying to throw off pursuing photographers; this was greeted by the conspiracy theorists as another Establishment cover-up. The Queen recovered her standing after making a grim live broadcast about her wayward former daughter-in-law. She would later rise again in public esteem to be seen as one of the most successful as well as longest-serving sovereigns for centuries. A popular film about these events sealed the verdict. Blair never again quite captured the mood of the country as he did that late summer. It may be that his advice and help to the Queen in 1997 was vital to her, as well as being, in the view of some officials, thoroughly impertinent.

What did Tony Blair take from the force of the

Diana cult, and of charismatic celebrity generally? His instinct for popular culture when he arrived in power was uncanny. He too would soon launch himself onto daytime television programmes, spinning an engaging and chirpy story about his life and interests, not always accurate in every detail. The New Age spiritualism which came out into the open when Diana died, with its shrines and its charms, its wide-eyed-ness, was echoed by the influence of people such as Carole Caplin in Blair's Downing Street circle. But it went further. What other politicians failed to grasp, and he did grasp, was the power of optimism expressed by the glossy world of celebrity, and people's readiness to forgive their favourites not just once, but again and again. In celebrity-land, if you had charisma and you apologized, or better still, bared a little of your soul, you could get away with most things short of murder. Interesting. But the world of politics would prove to be a little tougher.

Days of Hope

Optimism was the only real force behind the Northern Ireland peace process. Too often, this is now remembered by one of Blair's greatest soundbites as the talks reached a climax: 'This is no time for soundbites ... I feel the hand of history on my shoulder.' While irresistibly comic, it would be a horribly unfair thing to hold on to from one of Blair's biggest achievements. As we have seen, John Major had been tenacious in trying to bring Republicans and Unionists to the table but there had been a stalemate contributed to by both IRA bloody-mindedness and his own parliamentary weakness. Encouraged by Bill Clinton, Blair had decided in Opposition that an Irish peace settlement would be one of his top priorities in government. He went to the province as his first visit after winning power and focused Number Ten on the negotiations as soon as the IRA, sensing a new opportunity, announced a further ceasefire. In Mo Mowlam, the pugnacious, earthy and spectacularly brave new Northern Ireland Secretary, he had someone prepared to eff and blind at Unionists and coo or hug Sinn Feiners in pursuit of a deal. Mowlam was, after Blair himself, the nearest the new government had to a charismatic celebrity.

Quite soon the Ulster Unionist politicians found her a bit much, and suspected she was basically 'Green'. She concentrated her charm and bullying on the Republicans, while a Number Ten team run by Blair's chief aides concentrated their work on the Unionists. Blair would emphasize his own family's Unionist roots to try to win trust. As under Major, there were three separate negotiations taking place simultaneously. There was direct talking between the Northern Irish political parties, aimed at producing a power-sharing assembly in which they could all sit. This was chaired by former US Senator George Mitchell, and was the toughest part. There were the talks between the Northern Irish parties and the British and Irish governments about the border and the constitutional position of Northern Ireland in the future. And finally there were direct talks between London and Dublin on the wider constitutional and security settlement.

The story of the negotiations in detail is gripping but cannot be given here. Suffice it to say that this was a long, intensely difficult process which appeared to have broken down at numerous points, and was kept going mainly thanks to Blair himself. His advisers grumbled that he spent a ludicrously disproportionate amount of time on Northern Ireland, expending charm, energy, long days and late nights for months at a time. He also took big personal risks, as when early on he invited Gerry Adams and Martin McGuinness of Sinn Fein, the latter also a top Provisional IRA commander, to Downing Street. Some in the Northern Ireland Office, as well as in Unionist politics, believe Blair personally gave too much away to the Republicans, particularly over the release of terrorist prisoners. His former Northern Ireland Secretary and friend Peter Mandelson later said as much. But he spent most of his time trying to keep the Unionists with him, having moved Labour policy away from a position of support for Irish unification and in Washington, Blair was seen as too Unionist. At one point, when talks had broken down again, Mowlam made the astonishing personal decision to go into the notorious Maze prison herself and talk to Republican and Loyalist terrorist prisoners. Hiding behind their politicians, the imprisoned hard men still called the shots, at a time when this was not a metaphorical expression.

Given a deadline for Easter 1998, after last-gasp setbacks, a deal was finally struck. Northern Ireland would stay part of the UK for as long as the majority there wished it. The Republic of Ireland would give up the territorial claim to Northern Ireland, amending its constitution. The parties would combine in a power-sharing executive, based on a new elected assembly. There would be a new North–South body, knitting the two parts of Ireland together in various practical, undramatic ways. The paramilitary organizations would surrender or destroy their weapons, monitored by an independent body. Prisoners would be released. The policing of Northern Ireland, long a sore point, would be made fairer. This deal involved much pain, particularly for the Unionists. It was only the start of true peace and would be threatened frequently afterwards. The horrific bombing of the centre of Omagh a few months after the signing of the Good Friday Agreement was the worst setback. A renegade IRA splinter group murdered twenty-nine people and injured two hundred. Yet this time the extremists seemed unable to stop the rest from talking.

Once the agreement had been ratified by referendums on both sides of the border, the decommissioning of arms proved an endless and wearisome game of bluff. Though the two leaders of the moderate parties in Northern Ireland, David Trimble of the Ulster Unionists and John Hume of the SDLP, won the Nobel Prize for Peace, the agreement was to elbow both their parties aside. With electorates nervous, they lost out at the ballot box to the harder-line Democratic Unionists of Dr Ian Paisley and to Sinn Fein, under Adams and McGuinness. This made it harder to set up an effective power-sharing executive and assembly in Belfast. Yet, astonishingly, the so-called 'Dr No' of Unionism, Paisley, and his republican enemy, Adams, would eventually sit down together. The thuggery and crime attendant on years of terrorist activity has not yet disappeared. Yet because of the agreement hundreds of people who would have died had the 'troubles' continued, are alive and living peaceful lives. Investment has returned. Belfast is a transformed, cleaner, busier, more confident city. Large businesses increasingly work on an all-Ireland basis, despite the existence of two currencies and a border. Tony Blair can take a sizeable slice of the credit. As one of his biographers wrote: 'He was exploring his own ability to take a deep-seated problem and deal with it. It was a life-changing experience for him.'[9]

The Tartan Pizza

If the Good Friday Agreement changed the UK, Scottish and Welsh devolution plans changed Britain. Through the Tory years, the case for a Scottish parliament had been bubbling north of the border. Margaret Thatcher was seen as a conspicuously English figure imposing harsh economic penalties on Scotland, which considered itself inherently more egalitarian and democratic. This did not stop Scots buying their council houses (when she came to power the proportion of people living in state housing was higher than in many Eastern European countries under Communism), nor did they send back their tax cuts or fail to use the new legislation to choose which schools their children went to. But Scotland did have a public culture further to the left than that of southern England and the real action came from the respectable middle classes. A group of pro-devolution activists, including SNP, Labour and Liberal people, churchmen, former civil servants and trade unionists formed the Campaign for a Scottish Assembly. In due course this produced a 'Constitutional Convention' meant to bring in a wider cross-section of Scottish life behind their Claim of Right. It argued that if the Scots were to stand on their own two feet as Mrs Thatcher insisted, they needed control over their own affairs.

Momentum increased when the Scottish Tories lost half their remaining seats in the 1987 election, and when the poll tax was introduced there first to stave off a rebellion among homeowners about higher-rates bills. Over the next three years a staggering 2.5 million summary warrants for non-payment of the poll tax were issued in Scotland, a country of some five million people. The Constitutional Convention got going in March 1989, after Donald Dewar, Labour's leader in Scotland, decided to work with other parties. The Convention brought together the vast majority of Scottish MPs, all but two of Scotland's regional, district and island councils, the trade unions, churches, charities and many more – almost everyone indeed except the Conservatives, who were sticking with the original Union, and the SNP, who wanted full independence. Great marches were held. The newspapers became highly excited. A detailed blueprint was produced for the first Scottish parliament since 1707, very like the one later established.

Scottish Tories, finding themselves increasingly isolated, fought back vainly. They argued that 'Thatcherism' bore a close family resemblance to many of the ideas of the Scottish Enlightenment.

217

Was not Scotland's time of greatness based on thrift, hard work and enterprise? One of the cradles of Thatcherism more recently had been in Scotland, at St Andrews University. They pointed out that if a Tory government, based on English votes, was regarded as illegitimate by the Scots, then in future a Labour government based on Scottish constituencies might be regarded as illegitimate by the English. In the 1992 election, John Major made a passionate plea for the survival of the Union. Had the four countries never come together, their joint history would have never been as great: 'are we, in our generation, to throw all that away?'. He won back a single Scottish seat. Various minor sops were offered to the Scots in his years, including the return of the Stone of Destiny, with much ceremony. In 1997, the party, which had once had a majority of seats in Scotland, had not a single one left.

So by the time Tony Blair became leader, Labour's commitment to devolution was long-standing. Unlike most of Labour's commitments this was not a manifesto promise by a single party. It had been agreed away from Westminster, outside the New Labour hub, with a host of other bodies. John Smith, whose funeral in Scotland was a great gathering of the country's establishment, united in grief, had been a particularly passionate supporter. Dewar, now in charge of the project, was Smith's great friend. Blair could not simply tear this up. He was not much interested in devolution or impressed by it, particularly not for Wales, where support had been far more muted. The only thing he could do was to insist that the Scottish Parliament and Welsh assembly would only happen after referendums in the two countries, which in Scotland's case would include a second question as to whether the parliament should be allowed the power to vary the rate of income tax by 3p in the pound. This proved to be a great service to devolution, because it entrenched the legitimacy of the parliament. In September 1997, shortly after the death of Diana, which interrupted campaigning, Scotland voted by three to one for the new Parliament, and by 63.5 per cent to 36.5 per cent to give it tax-raising powers. The vote for the Welsh assembly was far closer, indeed wafer-thin. The Edinburgh parliament would have clearly defined authority over a wide spread of public life – education, health, welfare, local government, transport, housing – while Westminster kept taxation, defence, foreign affairs and some lesser issues. Wales's assembly had fewer powers, and no tax-raising rights. Only six Labour MPs said they would leave London and make a career in politics at home.

In 1999, after nearly 300 years, Scotland got her parliament with 129 MSPs, and Wales her assembly, with sixty members. Both were elected by proportional representation, making coalition governments almost inevitable. In Scotland, Labour provided the first 'first minister' ('prime minister' being considered too provocative a title). He was Donald Dewar, a lanky, pessimistic and much-loved intellectual who looked a little like a dyspeptic heron. He took charge of a small pond of Labour and Liberal Democrat ministers. To start with, Scotland was governed from the Church of Scotland's general assembly buildings, the forbidding gothic affair in Edinburgh. Later it would move to a new building by a Catalan architect, Enrico Miralles, who died of a heart attack at an early stage. A brewery opposite the Palace of Holyroodhouse was demolished and the complex new structure, with a roof meant to look like overturned fishing boats, was finally ready for use in 2004. It is architecturally impressive with a lightness and openness millions of miles removed from Westminster, but it was originally budgeted to cost £55 million and ended up costing £470 million, producing a vitriolic public argument in Scotland about wasted money. Dewar never lived to see it opened, collapsing and dying from a brain haemorrhage in 2000. Wales got her new assembly building, by Richard Rogers, in Cardiff Bay, in 2006 with much less controversy.

Few predictions about the Scottish Parliament proved right. It was said that it would cause an early crisis at Westminster because of the unfairness of Scottish MPs being able to vote on England-only business, particularly when the cabinet was so dominated by Scots. This did not happen, though it may yet. It was said that home rule would put paid to the Scottish National Party. Under Alex Salmond, their pugnacious leader, they were by 2007 so popular they were ousting Labour from its old Scottish hegemony. It was assumed that the Scottish Parliament would be popular in Scotland. A long and tawdry series of minor scandals, plus the cost of the building, meant that it became a butt of ridicule instead. This too may change, as Scots experience new laws it has passed. Among the policies the Edinburgh parliament has implemented are more generous provision for older people; no up-front top-up fees for students from Scotland, though English students at Scottish universities must pay; new property laws to allow Highland communities to compulsorily purchase the land they occupy; and a ban on smoking in public places. In all these Scotland has reinforced her reputation for being to the left of England, though extra taxes have not yet been levied on the Scots.

The most striking change, however, has been how quickly Scottish public life has diverged from that of the rest of Britain since the parliament was established. Scotland always had a separate legal system, schools, newspapers and football leagues. Now she had separate politics too, with her own controversies and personalities, a news agenda increasingly different from that of England. This part of post-war Britain's story is still developing. Like England's, Scotland's economy has moved steadily towards services and away from manufacturing. After many years of decline, Scotland's population has begun to rise gently since 2003, with net immigration from the rest of the UK. When large numbers of asylum seekers began arriving in Britain those who were sent to Scotland found that the Scots were considerably less welcoming than their piously democratic self-image suggested they would be. And anti-English feeling was not much quietened by home rule.

Wales too has her own politics, but feels not radically different, a change of emphasis, not direction. Scotland feels more like a different country, and London now seems a lot more than 400 miles from Edinburgh. By the winter of 2006–7 some polls showed more than half of Scots prepared to vote for independence. This may be a blip, a reaction to an unpopular government in London. There had been earlier warnings of a coming break-up of Britain, a great topic of debate from the late sixties, when the oil was discovered, right through to the final years of John Major's administration in the mid-nineties. It may be that a slow, soft separation is now taking place instead. There has been no constitutional chopper coming down to separate Scotland and England. It is more like two pieces of pizza being gently pulled apart, still together but now connected only by strings of molten cheese.

The Dawning of a New Era?

Margaret Thatcher had been a celebrity strictly on her own terms, never big on forgiveness or peace-making but always understanding the importance of optimism. Blair was learning from her. He quickly invited her back to see him in Downing Street and during his first years in office showed that he had picked up some of her bad traits too. She was unreasonably suspicious of the civil service. So was he. She was unimpressed by her first cabinet. He felt the same about his. Like her, when it might have voted him down on a pet idea, he simply went round it. Like her, he toyed with and then discarded the ideologies of intellectuals as he saw fit. With Thatcher it was the radicals of the new right, urging her to sell off hospitals or motorways. With Blair, it was the more gentle spirits urging him to adopt 'stakeholding' or 'communitarianism,' novel ways of reordering or taming capitalism. For their authors these were new political philosophies, for New Labour, briefly useful fads. Blair was no more of an intellectual than she was. He shared middle-class instincts, just like her. She took to praising him, if in qualified terms. They were really quite similar. Yet when Thatcher became Prime Minister she had years of Whitehall experience. Blair had none. She may not have enjoyed the boozy male dubbiness of Parliament but she respected the institution. Blair gave every sign of disliking the place intensely.

But the biggest difference between the two was Blair's obsession with journalism. Thatcher did her best to cope with the media, a little flattery here, a blunderbuss-blast from Bernard Ingham there. Blair during his first years in power was a fully engaged media politician. She sailed on the stuff, he swam in it. She knew who her press enemies were, and who were her friends, and more or less kept both throughout. Blair tried to make everyone his friend, and would lose almost all of them. Campbell was more powerful in the Blair court than Ingham had been in the Thatcher one. Again it was a generational thing: she had come into politics when newspapers were comparatively deferential and it was beneath a rising minister to court journalists. Blair learned the dangers of schmoozing media people, but slowly. More a problem of his early years, his relationship with the press and his misused press briefings hurt him and his reputation badly.

One example of how, came in the debate over British membership of the euro, the single currency finally taking shape at the beginning of 1999. Though never a fanatic on the subject, Blair's pro-European instincts and his desire to be the lead figure inside the EU predisposed him to announce that Britain would join – not in the first wave, perhaps, but soon afterwards. He briefed that this would happen. British business seemed generally in favour. But, as the former Liberal Democrat leader Paddy Ashdown revealed in his diaries, Blair had a problem. According to Ashdown, Roy Jenkins told Blair in the autumn of 1997: 'I will be very blunt about this. You have to choose between leading in Europe or having Murdoch on your side. You can have one but not both.' Ouch. Pro-euro journalists went to see him and came away thinking he was on their side. Anti-euro journalists had the same experience. He had a pro-euro adviser, Roger Liddle. But he also had an anti-euro adviser, Derek Scott. The briefing and guesswork in the press was completely baffling. Lord Simon, the former BP boss now in government working on euro matters, held up a wodge of papers at one evening speech, announcing that they represented the speech about the euro that had been written for him, before putting it down and confessing that he would not bother to read it; it had been completed an hour before so the policy had probably changed. It was a joke, but meant to sting.

Gordon Brown, who had been generally in favour of the euro, munched his way through Treasury reports. For him, stability came first. He concluded that it was not likely Britain could safely enter in the first Parliament. He warned Blair. The two argued. Eventually they agreed a fudge. Britain would probably stay out during the 1997 Parliament but the door should be left slightly ajar. Pro-European business people and those Tories who had lent Blair and Brown conditional support, as well as Blair's continental partners, should be kept on board. So should the anti-euro press. The terms of the delicate compromise were meant to be revealed in an interview given by Brown to *The Times*. Being more hostile to entry than Blair, and talking to an anti-euro paper, his team briefed more strongly than Blair would have liked. By the time the story was written, the pound had been saved from extinction for the lifetime of the Parliament. When Blair discovered this he was aghast and began to phone desperately around until he reached Brown's press officer, the affable Charlie Whelan (a man Blair detested and had tried vainly to have sacked earlier in the year). Whelan was in the Red Lion public house in Whitehall and cheerfully confirmed to the Prime Minister on his mobile phone that his government's policy was indeed that Britain would not enter during the lifetime of the Parliament. As Whelan put it later, 'he was completely gobsmacked'. Blair told him to 'row back'. Whelan replied it was too late.

The chaos surrounding such an important matter was ended and patched up by Brown as he and his adviser Ed Balls quickly produced five economic tests which would be applied before Britain entered the euro. They required more detailed work by the Treasury; the underlying point was that the British and continental economies must be properly aligned first. Brown then told the Commons that though it was likely for economic reasons Britain would wait until after the next election, there was no constitutional or political reason not to join. Preparations for British entry would begin. It all gave the impression, not least to Blair, that once the tests were met there would be a postelection referendum, followed by the demise of sterling. In 1999, with tantantaras and a full-scale public launch at a London cinema, Blair was joined by the Liberal Democrat leader Charles Kennedy and the two former Tory cabinet ministers Ken Clarke and Michael Heseltine to launch 'Britain in Europe'. This was to be a counterblast to the anti-euro campaign, 'Business for Sterling'. Blair promised that together they would demolish the arguments against the euro, and there was alarmist coverage about the loss of 8 million jobs if Britain pulled out of the EU.

But this expensive, brightly coloured and crowded bandwagon was going nowhere at all. The real significance of the Red Lion kerfuffle was that the power to decide over membership of the euro passed decisively and for ever from Blair in Downing Street to Brown, whose Treasury fortress became the guardian of the economic tests. Brown would keep Britain out, something which won him great personal credit among Conservative press barons. There would be no referendum in the Blair years, however much the Prime Minister fretted. During his second administration, according to the former cabinet minister Clare Short, Blair offered Brown an astonishing deal: he would leave Number Ten soon if Brown would 'deliver' the euro. Brown brusquely rejected the offer, telling Short that he didn't make policy that way and in any case, could not trust Blair to keep his side of a bargain.

But other historic changes went ahead. Both devolution and the Irish peace process reshaped the country and produced clear results. So did other constitutional initiatives, such as the expulsion of most hereditary peers from the Lords, ending its huge inbuilt Conservative majority, and the incorporation of the European human rights convention into British law, allowing cases to come to court here. Neither produced the outcomes ministers expected. The Lords became more assertive and more of a problem for Blair, not less of one. British judges' interpretation of the human rights of asylum seekers and suspected terrorists caused much anguish to successive home secretaries; and the 'human rights culture' was widely criticized by newspapers. But at least, in each case, serious shifts in the balance of power were made, changes intended to make Britain fairer and more open.

Other early initiatives would crumble to dust and ashes. One of the most interesting examples is the Dome, centrepiece of millennium celebrations inherited from the Conservatives. Blair was initially unsure about whether to forge ahead with the £1bn gamble. He was argued into the Dome project by Peter Mandelson who wanted to be its impresario, and by John Prescott, who liked the new money it would bring to a blighted part of east London. Prescott suggested New Labour wouldn't be much of a government if it could not make a success of this. Blair agreed, though had the Dome ever come to a cabinet vote he would have lost. Architecturally the Dome was striking and elegant, a landmark for London which can be seen by almost every air passenger arriving in the capital. Public money was spent on cleaning up a poisoned semicircle of derelict land and bringing new Tube and road links. The millennium was certainly worth celebrating. But the problem ministers and their advisers could not solve was what their pleasure Dome should contain. Should it be for a great national party? Should it be educational?

Beautiful? Thought-provoking? A fun park? Nobody could decide. The instinct of the British towards satire was irresistible as the project continued surrounded by cranes and political hullabaloo. The Dome would be magnificent, unique, a tribute to daring and can-do. Blair himself said it would provide the first paragraph of his next election manifesto.

A well-funded, self-confident management was put in place but the bright child's question – yes, but what's it for? – would not go away. When the Dome finally opened, at New Year, the Queen, Prime Minister and hundreds of donors, business people and celebrities were treated to a mishmash of a show which embarrassed many of them. Bad organization meant most of the guests had a long, freezing and damp wait to get in for the celebrations. Xanadu this was not. The fiasco meant the Dome was roasted in most newspapers and when it opened to the public, the range of mildly interesting exhibits was greeted as a huge disappointment. Far fewer people came and bought tickets than was hoped. It turned out to be a theme park without a theme, morphing in the public imagination into the earliest and most damaging symbol of what was wrong with New Labour: an impressively constructed big tent containing not very much at all. It was produced by some of the people closest to the Prime Minister and therefore boomeranged particularly badly on him and the group already known as 'Tony's cronies'. Optimism and daring, it seemed, were not enough.

Squeeze, Relax:
New Labour Economics

The events described so far were all, in different ways, secondary to the transformation of Britain that Blair had promised. Northern Ireland was a crisis needing solving. Scotland and Wales were inherited commitments which did not engage much of the Prime Minister's time, nor any of his passion. The Dome was also inherited, a sally of optimism and opportunism which went terribly wrong. The death of Diana was one of Macmillan's 'events', brilliantly handled. But none of this was what New Labour was really about. Its intended purpose was a more secure economy, radically better public services and a new deal for the people at the bottom. And much of this was in the lap not of Tony Blair, but of Gordon Brown. The saturnine Chancellor would become a controversial figure later in the government too but his early months in the Treasury were rumbustious, as he overruled mandarins and imposed a new way of governing. Like Blair, Brown had no experience of government and, like Blair, he had run his life in Opposition with a tight team of his own, dominated by his economic adviser (later an MP and Treasury minister) Ed Balls. Relations between Team Brown and the Treasury officials began badly and stayed frosty for a long time, rather as other civil service bosses resented the arrival of the rule of special advisers at Number Ten.

Brown's handing of interest rate control to the Bank of England was a theatrical coup, planned secretly in Opposition and unleashed to widespread astonishment immediately New Labour won. Other countries, including Germany and the United States, had long run monetary policy independently of politicians, but this was an unexpected step for a left-of-centre British Chancellor. It turned out to be particularly helpful to Labour ministers since it removed at a stroke the old suspicion that they would favour high employment over low inflation. It reassured the money markets that Brown would not (because he could not) debauch the currency. In a curious way this gave him more freedom to tax and spend. As one of Brown's biographers put it, he 'could only give expression to his socialist instincts after playing the role of uber-guardian of the capitalist system'.[10] The Bank move has gone down as one of the clearest achievements of the New Labour era – tellingly, like the devolution referendums, actions taken immediately after winning power. Brown also stripped the Bank of England of its old job of overseeing the rest of the banking sector. If it was worried about the health of commercial banks but also in sole charge of interest rates, the two functions might conflict. His speed in doing so infuriated the Bank's governor Eddie George who came close to resigning and so spoiling Brown's early period as Chancellor.

Labour won an early reputation for being economically trustworthy. Brown was the granite-and-iron Chancellor. Then a bachelor, his only mistress was the pinched-cheeked, pursed-mouthed Prudence. Income tax rates did not move. The middle classes could relax and feel free to vote Labour a second time, as they duly did in their droves in 2001. Even when Brown found money growing on trees he did not spend it. In 2000, at the most iridescent swollen glossiness of the dotcom bubble, when Britain was erupting with childlike candy-coloured names for companies promising magical profits, when anyone would pay anything for anything allegedly digital, Brown sold off licences for the next generation of mobile phones for £22.5 bn, vastly more than they were soon worth. The fruit went not into new public spending but into repaying the public debt, £37 bn of it. By 2002 government interest payments as a proportion of its income, were the lowest since 1914. Brown's stock soared.

Another consequence of the early squeeze was more immediately controversial. What became known as 'stealth taxes', like the stealth bomber itself, made a lot of noise and did not always hit the targeted area. Stealth taxes included the freezing of income tax thresholds, so an extra 1.5 million people found themselves paying the top rate; the freezing of personal allowances; rises in stamp duty on houses and a hike in national insurance (both of which provided huge new tax streams in the Labour years); the palming off of costs onto council tax, which rose sharply; and most famously the removal of tax credits for share dividends in 1997. This was sold at the time as a sensible technical reform, removing distortions and encouraging companies to reinvest in their core businesses. In fact it had a devastating effect on the portfolios of pension funds.

By 2006, according to a paper for the Institute of Actuaries, this measure was responsible for cutting the value of retirement pensions by £100 bn, a staggering sum, more than twice as much as the combined pension deficits of Britain's top 350 companies. Pensioners and older workers facing great holes in their pension funds were outraged. What is more, Treasury papers released in 2007 showed that Brown was given ample warning of the effect. The destruction of a once proud pension industry is a more complicated story than the simple 'blame Brown' charge. The actuarial industry, rule changes in pensions during the Major years, a court ruling about guaranteed pay-outs and Britain's fast-ageing population are also part of the tale. But the pension fund hit produced more anger, directed personally against Brown, than any other single act in his time as Chancellor.

Longer term, perhaps the most striking aspect of Brown's running of the economy was the stark, dramatic shape of public spending. For his first two years he stuck fiercely to the promise he had made about continuing Conservative spending levels. These were so tight that even the former Chancellor Ken Clarke said he would not have actually kept to them had he been re-elected. But Brown brought down the State's share of public spending from nearly 41 per cent of gross domestic product to 37.4 per cent by 1999–2000, the lowest percentage since 1960 and far below anything achieved under Thatcher. He was doing the opposite of what earlier Labour chancellors had done. They had arrived in office, immediately started spending, and then had to stop and raise taxes later on. He began as Scrooge and quietly fattened up for Santa. Then there was an abrupt and dramatic shift and public spending soared, particularly on health, back up to 43 per cent. So there were the lean years followed by the fat years, famine then feast, squeeze then relax.

Prudence was a stern mistress. The first consequence of her reign was that the 1997–2001 Labour government achieved far less in public services than it had promised. During the 2001 election Blair was confronted outside a Birmingham hospital when a postmistress called Sharon Storer exploded with rage at him over the poor care being given to her partner who had cancer. Vainly he tried to stem the flow and usher her away from microphones and cameras. New Labour's choreography was usually slick but for once Blair was pinned down and harangued by someone who was no longer prepared to hear his excuses. John Prescott had promised a vast boost in public transport, telling the Commons in 1997, 'I will have failed if in five years' time there are not many more people using public transport and far fewer journeys by car. It's a tall order but I urge you to hold me to it.' Because of Prudence, and Blair's worries about being seen as anti-car, Prescott had nothing like the investment to follow through and failed completely. Prudence meant that Brown ploughed ahead with cuts in benefit for lone-parent families, angering Labour MPs and resulting in a Scottish Labour conference vote which called them 'economically inept, morally repugnant and spiritually bereft'.

Reform costs money, and without money it barely happened in the first term, except in isolated areas where Blair or Brown put their heads down and concentrated. The most dramatic programme was in raising literacy and numeracy among younger children, where Number Ten worked closely with the Education Secretary, David Blunkett, and scored real successes. But unequivocally successful public service reforms were rare. And the real drawback of the squeeze-then-relax Brown guide to fiscal fitness was that he did not entirely conform to it himself. Some new money had to be raised and it was.

One curious thing a time-traveller from the seventies might notice in the Britain of the early twenty-first century would be unfamiliar uniforms and symbols in public offices, by roadsides, in hospitals and outside schools. The men and women on security duty in the Treasury in not-quite-official caps and jackets, the badges on construction workers' jackets and helmets, the little logos of jumping manikins, bright flowers, bean-like blobs, and the new names, Carillion, Vinci or Serco, were all visual hints about the greatest change in how government was working. The name for it, public finance initiative, or PFI, was dull. Yet the change was big enough to arouse worry even outside the small tribes of political obsessives. The underlying idea was simple. It had started life under Norman Lamont, five years before Labour came to power, when he experimented with privatizing public projects and allowing private companies to run them, keeping the revenue. A group led by the Bank of America built and ran a new bridge connecting the Isle of Skye to the mainland. There were outraged protests from some islanders about paying tolls to a private consortium and eventually the Scottish Executive bought the bridge back. At the opposite corner of the country, another bridge was built joining Kent and Essex across the Thames at Dartford, the first bridge across the river in a new place for more than half a century; it was run by a company called Le Crossing and successfully took tolls from motorists.

To start with Labour hated this idea. PFIs were a mix of two things, the privatization of capital projects, with government paying a fee over many years; and the contracting-out of services – waste-collection, school meals, cleaning – to private companies, which had been imposed on unwilling socialist councils from the eighties. Once in power, Labour ministers began to realize that those three little letters were political magic. For the other thing about PFI is that it allows today's ministers to announce and oversee exciting new projects, and take the credit for them, while the full bill is left for taxpayers twenty or fifty years in the future. Today's spending on schools or hospitals is a problem that will eventually land on the desk of an education minister who is presently still at primary school, or a Chancellor who has not yet arrived at the maternity unit. This was government on tick. It was invented in Britain. And for better or worse, it is now spreading round the world. PFIs were particularly attractive when so many other kinds of spending were so tightly controlled by Prudence. At the same time large swathes of money for new schools, hospitals, prisons and the like were declared to be investment, not spending, and put to one side of the national accounts. Was this clever, or merely clever-clever? The justification was that private companies would build things and run them so much more efficiently than the State, that profits paid to them by taxpayers would be more than compensated for.

There is no doubt that sometimes this has been so, but assertions tail off into guesswork because they depend on misty unknowables – how well a modern civil service might have run such projects itself, whether the contract was drawn up tightly enough to fully protect the taxpayer, and so on. Committees of MPs certainly thought they had found incompetence and inefficiency in PFI deals. Ministers, pressed against a wall, tended to reply that since without PFIs Britain would not have got the shiny new school buildings or health centres that were so desperately needed by the late nineties, it was by definition a good thing. It was certainly a big thing. By the end of 2006 a total of £53 bn of such contracts had been signed, with another £28 bn in the pipeline, for fire stations, army barracks, helicopter training schools, psychiatric units, prisons, roads, bridges, government offices, computer programmes, immigration systems, as well as hundreds of schools and hospitals. The biggest was for the modernization of the London Underground, hugely expensive in legal fees and hugely complex in contracts. Tellingly, the peak year for PFIs was 2000, just as the early Treasury stringency on conventional spending had bitten most.

The cost of the forward contracts for running these places, sometimes half a century ahead, is hard to estimate but there is certainly over £100 bn of rent due to be paid by tomorrow's taxpayers. In the private sector lawyers, company managers and accountants began to specialize in PFIs. A whole new business sector arose. In the public sector civil servants struggled to grapple with the new skills they would need to negotiate with unfamiliar private sector partners. There is an obvious problem about defining the real risk of these projects. If a firm is commissioned to build a prized new hospital at a certain budget and falls behind, to the point where failure looms unless the taxpayer intervenes again, is it likely the hospital will simply be abandoned? Risk is a routine business idea but means something else in politics. How do you blend the culture of ministerial promises and that of construction and IT firms? Yet another white-collar industry arose to try. And by the mid-2000s the number of PFI contracts being sold on from one company to another, a booming secondary market in subcontracted government, was well over four-fifths of the total. How to keep a grip on sold-on PFIs? Another mini-profession popped up to try that, too. All of it, of course, paid for by the taxpayer.

Yet, PFIs did not make quite the noise one might have expected. Most politicians from most parties reflected that one day, they too might find them useful.

The Moment of Truth

So when did Brown's great shift in policy happen? When did straightforward, on-balance-sheet, old-fashioned public spending, financed by old-fashioned taxes, return to the political agenda? And why did the great romance between Gordon and Prudence end? It occurred, appropriately, just as Brown's real-life romance with Sarah Macaulay, a very bright public relations businesswoman, was becoming public. They would marry in August 2000, six months after Prudence had been told to make other arrangements. And despite Sharon Storer's disappointment the following year, it was indeed the National Health Service which triggered the change of pace. In its first election manifesto New Labour promised to 'safeguard the basic principles of the NHS, which we founded'. It protested that under the Tories there had been 50,000 fewer nurses but a rise of no fewer than 20,000 managers – red tape which Labour would pull away and burn. Though critical of the Tory internal market, Blair promised to keep a split between those who commissioned health and those who provided it. The overall message was less fiddling and a bit more money.

Under Frank Dobson, Labour's new Health Secretary, a staunch traditionalist and the man with the filthiest sense of humour in British politics, this is what happened. There was little reform but there was, year by year, just enough extra money to buy off the winter crises. But then a quite different crisis hit the headlines. As often happens, it began with individual human stories which rapidly came together and expanded toward a general truth. First there was a particularly awful case of an old lady whose cancer was made inoperable after repeated delays. Then came a furious denunciation of his elderly mother's treatment by Professor Robert Winston, the Labour peer and fertility expert much admired by Blair. Winston said that Britain's health service was much the worst in Europe, was getting worse still, and that the government had been deceitful about the true picture. This set off something close to panic in Whitehall not only because Winston was about the most authentic witness anyone could imagine but also because he was, in general terms, right. And Labour's polling showed the country knew it. So after a difficult haggle with Brown, Blair declared on Sir David Frost's Sunday morning television show in January 2000 that the NHS badly needed more money and he would bring Britain's health spending up to the European average within five years.

That was a huge promise, a third as much again in real terms (close to what actually happened). Gordon Brown was unhappy. He thought that Blair had pre-empted his decision, had not spoken to Frost enough about the need for health service reform to accompany the money, and according to Downing Street rumour, had 'stolen my bloody budget'. Brown made up for this on the day itself when he promised that from then until 2004 health spending would rise at above 6 per cent beyond inflation every year, 'by far the largest sustained increase in NHS funding in any period in its fifty-year history' and 'half as much again for health care for every family in this country'. The tilt away from tight spending controls and towards expansion had started. There was more to come. With an election looming in 2001, Brown also announced a review into the NHS and its future by a former banker called Derek Wanless.

As soon as the election was over, broad hints about necessary tax rises began to be dropped. When Wanless finally reported, he confirmed much that the winter crisis of nearly two years earlier had shown. The NHS was not, whatever Britons fondly believed, as good as health systems in other similar countries, and it needed a lot more money. Wanless also rejected a radical change in funding, such as a move to insurance-based or semi-private health care. Brown immediately used this as objective proof that taxes had to rise to save the NHS, something Wanless felt a little uneasy about. Was he being used, in the words of one writer, as Brown's human shield? At any rate, in his next Budget of March 2002, Brown broke with a political convention which had reigned since the eighties, that direct taxes may never be put up again. He raised a special 1 per cent national insurance levy, equivalent to a penny on income tax, to fund the huge reinvestment in Britain's health.

Public spending shot up, above all on health. In some ways, it paid off. By 2006, there were around 300,000 extra NHS staff compared to 1997. That included more than 10,000 extra senior hospital doctors (about a quarter more) and 85,000 more nurses. But there were also nearly 40,000 managers, twice as many as Brown and Blair had ridiculed the Conservatives for hiring in the days when they were campaigning against red tape. An ambitious computer project for the whole NHS became an expensive catastrophe. Meanwhile, the health service budget rose from £37bn to more than £92 bn a year. That vast investment produced results. Waiting lists, a source of great public anger in the mid-nineties, fell by 200,000. By 2005, Blair was able to talk of the best waiting list figures since 1988. Hardly anyone was left waiting for an inpatient treatment for more than six months. Death rates from cancer for people under the age of seventy-five fell by 15.7 per cent between 1996 and 2006 and death rates from heart disease fell by just under 36 per cent. The public finance initiative meanwhile meant that new hospitals were being built around the country.

If only that was the full story. 'Czars', quangos, agencies, commissions, access teams and planners hunched over the NHS as Whitehall, having promised to devolve power, now imposed a new round of mind-dazing control. By the autumn of 2004 hospitals were subject to an astonishing 100-plus inspection regimes. A great war broke out between Brown in the Treasury and the Blairite Health Secretary, Alan Milburn, about the basic principles of running hospitals. Milburn, backed by Blair, wanted more independence and competition. Brown asked how you could have competition when for most people there was just one big local hospital. If it lost the competition, it could hardly shut down. Polling suggested that in this Brown was making a popular point. Most people wanted better hospitals, not more choice. Blair's team responded that they would only get better hospitals if there was choice. A truce was eventually declared with the establishment of a small number only of independent, or foundation, hospitals. Britain was back to the old argument. Do you try to run everything from the centre, using targets as your flails and unelected quangos as your legionaries? Or do you mimic the private sector, allowing hospitals to rise and fall, expand and close?

By the 2005 general election, Michael Howard's Conservatives were attacking Labour for wasting money and allowing people's lives to be put at risk in dirty, badly run hospitals. Just like Labour once had, they were promising to cut bureaucracy and slash the number of organizations inside the Health Service. By the summer of 2006, despite that huge increase in money, the health service was facing a cash crisis. The amount of money involved was not large as a percentage of the total budget but trusts in some of the most vulnerable parts of the country were on the edge, from Hartlepool to Cornwall to London. Across Britain, 7,000 jobs had gone and the Royal College of Nursing was predicting 13,000 more would go soon. Many expensively qualified new doctors and specialists could not find work. After the great spending U-turn of 2000–2 and historic amounts of new money, it seemed that wage costs, pricey new drugs, poor management and the vast bureaucratic expense of endless 'reforms' had resulted in a health service which was irritating people as much as ever. Less fashionable health causes, such as mental health, felt left out and outside the NHS there was a vast growth in the reach of private insurance and private health. Bupa, the leading private operator, was covering around 2.3 million people in 1999. Six years later the figure was more than 8 million. This partly reflects greater affluence but it is not a resounding vote of confidence on the success of Labour's investment in the NHS.

A parallel story could be told about schools. Here too traditional socialists wanted a single system for every child, comprehensive across the country, and run directly from Whitehall (except, of course, in now-devolved Scotland and Wales). Those dangerously semi-independent institutions, the Tories' grant-maintained schools, though there were few enough of them, were abolished. In education the government did everything that enthusiasm, hard work and determination could, to improve things from Whitehall. First under David Blunkett, and then his successors, a stream of plans on every aspect of school life poured out of the department. By 2001, in a single year, 3,840 pages of instructions were being sent to schools. One headteacher settled down and counted 525 separate targets for his school. This, literal, wheelbarrow-load of paperwork no more transformed the schools than the revised NHS bureaucracy was transforming hospitals. Blair tried a new tack and returned to the idea of semi-independent schools. There were already 'specialist schools' in the state sector with say over their admissions but this was to be at a different level. Businesses, faith groups and rich local businessmen would endow part of the cost and be allowed some involvement in their 'ethos'. As with hospitals, there was great Labour resistance. Did this not mean a possible return to some kind of selection? Another great battle began and, under pressure from Labour MPs, it was written into law that such schools could not select by academic ability. Links with local education authorities were also to be kept.

Yet it seemed possible in the early years of the new century that Britain was moving back towards an educational model half remembered from long ago. Schools were being sponsored by evangelical Christians, computer companies or firms of accountants. Was this so different from the ancient schools set up by local worthies, livery companies and religious orders? Some even favoured a teaching of life's origins which edged Darwin aside in favour of the Bible. There was a great growth too in Muslim schools, closed to faithless outsiders. The government tried to make faith schools open up a little to people from other communities but were forced to pull back. For some this was a betrayal of the idea of one nation implicit in comprehensives, a retreat to ghetto schooling. Others asked, if locally elected councillors oversaw such independent schools, and if they were restrained from being too aggressive in ramming doctrines down young throats, was that such a bad thing? Polls suggested parents were less worried about structures than lax discipline and too-easy exams. Such schools are certainly a decisive break from the direction of education in the sixties and seventies, and far nearer the dreams of Thatcher and her Conservative successors. As in health, private schools boomed.

As the public spending had begun to flow during the second Blair administration, vast amounts of money had gone in pay rises, new bureaucracies and on bills for outside consultants. Ministries had been unused to spending again, and did not always do it well. There were other unfortunate consequences. Brown and his team resorted to double and triple counting early spending increases to give the impression they were doing more for hospitals, schools and transport than they actually could. They were, rightly, roasted for it.

A fascinating insight into the problems faced by the Blair government in public service reform came in 2005 when a former spin doctor published a book. Peter Hyman, a young, serious-minded man, had worked for Tony Blair since he became leader, rising to head the Number Ten strategic communications unit. He wrote speeches, spun for him, argued with him and saw the power game at its highest, most exhilarating level. In 2003, after sweating hard at Blair's conference speech, he decided it was time to make the favoured buzzword 'renewal' personal. He resigned and became a teacher at a tough inner London comprehensive school, Islington Green. His book about the reality-jolt this produced remains one of the best texts on modern British politics available. Late on, he is arguing with a pupil about why when the Prime Minister says something, it does not just happen: 'I look him in the eye and say, "When Tony promises to deliver on education what needs to happen is that you pass your exams. How can he guarantee that? You may not even turn up for them."' Hyman reflects that his old way of doing politics, dealing frantically with 24-hour media, is useless for delivering a better school. Instead of conflict and novelty, consistency is needed; not battles but partnership. 'Now, looking through the other end of the telescope I see how unequal is the relationship between politicians and the people ... Those at the centre relish ideas and, in the main, are bored by practicalities. Those who suggest better ways of making policy work are too often dismissed as whingers ... Why can't politicians acknowledge that those on the front line might know more?'[11]

It is a good question. In trying to achieve better policing, more effective planning, healthier school food, prettier town centres and a hundred other hopes, the centre of government ordered and cajoled, hassled and harangued, always high-minded, always speaking for 'the people'. The railways, after yet another disaster, were shaken up again. In very controversial circumstances Railtrack, the once-profitable monopoly company operating the lines, was driven to bankruptcy and a new system of detailed Whitehall control was imposed. At one point Tony Blair boasted of

245

having 500 targets for the public sector, and later his deputy had found five times that number for local government and transport alone.[12] Parish councils, small businesses and charities found they were loaded with directives – not as many as schools or hospitals, but always more, interfering with much of what they wanted to do. The interference was always well meant but it clogged up the arteries of free decision-taking and frustrated responsible public life. Blair famously complained, early in his time as Prime Minister, that he had 'scars on my back' from trying to get reform in the public sector. Perhaps with a little less auto-flagellation and a little more conversation, both he and the country would have been happier.

Rebel British

Meanwhile the British people, the end-point of this frantic activity, proved as unpredictably stroppy as they always had been. In general, it was moral and cultural protest that took the place of the economic controversies of earlier decades. Through most of the Blair years the fox-hunting struggle engorged month after month of parliamentary time and unbelievable amounts of political energy. Polling suggested the country cared almost as little about it as the Prime Minister – plenty of people had views, but few held them strongly. Behind this, though, was the determination of animal rights activists to get something out of an avowedly radical government, while the Countryside Alliance (which expanded its campaigning to include fishing, organic food and much else) represented a feeling that part of the historic nation was being ignored, that there were people of all classes who did not fit into the New Labour world-view.

Fox hunting was a country pursuit since medieval times; the poem *Sir Gawain and the Green Knight* contains a description from around the year 1370 which is recognizable in its essentials today. By the 1670s, its rituals, red coats, language and literature were a part of British culture known around the world. Only a part, however: hunting always had its detractors. In the eighteenth century, the fox-hunting Tory squire, red-faced and stupid, was a staple of urban Whig propaganda. (The hunting nickname for the fox, Charlie, refers to the great Whig radical Charles James Fox.) Towards the end of the nineteenth century, the thunderous passage of whooping huntsmen became an emblem among radicals of oppressive aristocracy riding roughshod over the people. In Oscar Wilde's phrase they were 'the unspeakable in full pursuit of the uneatable'. Little followed from this until the arrival in the middle of the twentieth century of a militant animal rights movement, determined to frustrate hunting by using scent sprays, horns and human barriers. The first example of saboteurs at work seems to have been in August 1958 when members of the League Against Cruel Sports (which had been founded much earlier, in 1927) used chemicals to try to disrupt the Devon and Somerset Staghounds. Direct action like this began to be used against fox hunters too, with the North Warwickshire and the Old Berkeley at Amersham confronted in 1962–3. In December 1963 the Hunt Saboteurs Association was formed by a young journalist in Brixham, Devon, and the practice quickly spread.

Confrontations between hunt supporters and 'Sabs', often violent with the police in full pursuit, became a regular feature of country life from then on. Sabs would compare themselves to the hunters, needing quick wits, courage and good tactics to confuse the hounds and allow the fox or stag to escape. They were accused of thuggery. They accused the hunt supporters of being brutal to them, and many bones and noses were broken in the bracken. There was a bit of class conflict and of city-against-country in it all. Over time it became clear that while the Sabs might save some foxes, they were unable to stop the hunts, so animal rights activists turned increasingly to Parliament to get it banned. Labour voters and MPs tended to be against hunting, and the party took a £100,000 donation from the animal rights lobby before the 1997 election. When New Labour won with a massive majority it was clear that a parliamentary move to ban hunting with hounds was inevitable. With so many MPs committed, it would probably become law. This directly affected the 200,000 people who were hunting regularly and with those who watched and supported them, perhaps half a million in all. A new organization, the Countryside Alliance, was formed to campaign against a ban and held its first big rally, with 120,000 people present, at Hyde Park, six weeks after the election.

From then on pro-hunting protests were continual and varied. There were marches at Labour Party conferences, in Scotland where a separate and earlier ban was being passed, outside Parliament and in many other towns throughout

Britain. People had always been on the march about something, but whereas before it had been students in duffel-coats, coalminers or left-wingers in leather jackets, this time it was ruddy-faced women in tweed skirts, farm-workers and former public schoolboys – Boden and loden, Barbour and brogue. In the Blair years, the sound of hunting horns, the excited yelping of hounds and even the clatter of hooves became part of the backdrop of parliamentary life. After a noisy march in Bournemouth, Blair himself joined in the argument, telling his conference in 1999 that he would sweep away the 'forces of conservatism' and branding the Conservatives 'the party of fox hunting, Pinochet and hereditary peers – the uneatable, the unspeakable and the unelectable'.

This was a rare and quickly regretted Blair incursion into the language of leftism. He never much cared about hunting one way or another, and wished the issue would vanish. It did not. John Prescott, more of a class warrior than his leader, enlivened the 2001 election when a burly Countryside protester threw an egg at him during a visit to Rhyl, Wales, and was rewarded with a hefty punch. After the election Labour MPs pressed ahead while on the other side, vigils were mounted, topless women delivered petitions to Whitehall and a thousand horses rode through Leicester as part of a 'summer of discontent' in 2002. That September, the Alliance claimed more than 400,000 supporters in its biggest 'Liberty and Livelihood' protest outside the Commons, a protest which saw violent confrontations between the police and angry young men in tweed caps and waxed olive jackets.

On 18 November 2004 a law banning hunting

with hounds finally passed its parliamentary hurdles. After legal challenges it became law the following February though the many loopholes, allowing riders with hounds to flush out foxes, which could then be shot, meant hunts carried on across England and Wales. The day after the ban took effect, thousands were out again and ninety-one foxes were killed. There, as in Scotland, the hunts continue and Sabs still follow with cameras, trying to find evidence of law-breaking. There have been very few prosecutions. Bloody predictions of masters of foxhounds shooting their dogs and then hanging themselves, a nightmare hanging over Labour spin-doctors for several years, were never realized. The fox hunting story can serve as a symbol for much else in the New Labour years: a long and noisy confrontation at Westminster, which in the end had surprisingly little effect on the ground.

The first intimation that protest could go further under New Labour than noisy pro-hunting demonstrations came in 2000, when a nationwide revolt by truckers against high petrol prices brought the country to a standstill. The automatic increase in fuel duty had in fact been briefly halted, but rising world oil prices and the high petrol taxes already in place meant unheard-of prices at the petrol pumps. A group of irate truckers, men who owned their own lorries, held a protest meeting in Wales and decided to mount a brief blockade of a giant oil refinery in Cheshire. They attracted widespread news coverage and an enthusiastic reaction from ordinary drivers. To begin with, Blair and his ministers concluded that it was not a serious challenge and continued with their plans. A command centre was established at Cobra, the bland meeting-room below Downing Street from where national crises are directed.

The Prime Minister himself went ahead with a tour of the English Midlands, due to end with a celebration of John Prescott's thirty years in Parliament in a Hull Chinese restaurant. On the way, officials and journalists noted V-formations of slow-moving lorries blocking motorways in other parts of the country and followed reports of petrol stations in the north of England running dry, or being besieged by queues of panicky motorists. More refineries were blockaded. Still Blair and his team insisted that nothing was really wrong and the tour would go on. He would not be diverted. By that evening, with Prescott in a Hull town hall surrounded by countryside protesters, he was getting a different message. Told that he could not be guaranteed a getaway from the splendid Chinese restaurant, he apologized to his deputy and headed for Sheffield, still insisting the show would go on. On the following morning, after overnight briefings, he gave in, turned tail and sped back to London to take charge.

Blair was generally good in a crisis and began trying to knock heads together. But this time the oil company bosses would not help him by ordering drivers of petrol tankers, who were both self-employed and sympathetic to the fuel protesters, to break through the pickets. Blair raged, threatened and begged. Now all across Britain, petrol stations ran dry. Wherever petrol remained, vast queues formed. It was all perfectly good-humoured but the crisis was spinning out of Blair's hands. Food shortages were reported. Bread was going, milk was going and the nation's egg-laying chickens were in danger. What was left of Britain's manufacturing industry was close to being forced to suspend working. Yet all tests of public opinion showed the majority of the country was with the protesters not the government. Brown repeatedly refused to pre-announce his March Budget by promising cuts in fuel taxes, in response to blackmail by two thousand to three thousand hauliers. There was private talk of bringing in the army, forcing the blockades. Panicky-sounding government papers were leaked and Blair came close to begging the protesters to stop: 'This is not on, you know. This is just not right ...'; Eventually, after health service managers had warned that people would soon die, and with even the anti-Blair press telling the protesters that enough was enough, the blockades were lifted and life returned to normal. Brown made a crabwise but generous-enough move on petrol duty in his Budget and something close to honour was restored. Yet Britain had come very close to the kind of collapse not seen since the winter of 1978–9.

The country quickly bounced back – there was no threatening undertow in the 2001 election. The combination of early Prudence and the public spending promised had played well with the electorate. John Major was succeeded as party leader by the most talented Tory of his generation, the young, bright, bald and witty Yorkshireman, William Hague. A natural Thatcherite since his schooldays and a political obsessive, he had done his best to make his leadership seem trendier and more in touch with modern Britain, donning a baseball cap and visiting the Notting Hill carnival.

He was mocked for it, and learned. Hague was a man of some political experience, having been with Norman Lamont at the Treasury and later Welsh Secretary, and his greatest achievement was that he stopped a bewildered and defeated party tearing itself apart. At his best in the Commons, he had been a sparkling Opposition leader, discomfiting Blair and leading the charge on Labour 'stealth taxes', the Dome and the new issue of bogus asylum-seekers. But heavily concentrating his election campaign on saving the pound, promising voters 'we will give you back your country' and attacking the still-popular Blair as a slimy liar, he allowed New Labour to portray his party as xenophobic and nasty. By any standard, the Tory attack failed. Labour was returned with a majority of 166, having lost just six seats net, and the Conservatives, after all their energy and hard work, managed a single net gain. It was an important election because it cemented the New Labour achievement of 1997 and showed the country had moved towards Blair's agenda. Yet this general election will be remembered for one other ominous statistic too. The turnout was – just – below 60 per cent. Since Britain had first become a democracy, the public had never been less interested in voting.

Pre-Iraq Wars and Foreign Policy

The Iraq War will remain for ever the most important and controversial part of Tony Blair's legacy. But long before it, during the dog-days of the Clinton administration, two events had taken

253

place which primed his response and explain some of what followed. The first was the bombing of Iraq by the RAF and US air force as punishment for Saddam Hussein's dodging of UN inspections. The second was the bombing of Serbia during the Kosovo crisis, and the threat of a ground force invasion. These crises made Blair believe he had to be involved personally and directly in overseas wars. They caused dark nights of self-doubt, and toughened him to criticism. They emphasized the limitations of air power and the importance to him of media management. Without them, Blair's reaction to the changing of world politics on September 11 2001 would have been different.

Evidence of Saddam Hussein's interest in weapons of mass destruction was shown to Blair soon after he took office. He raised it in speeches and privately with other leaders. Most countries in Nato and at the United Nations security council were angry about the dictator's expulsion of UN inspectors when they tried to probe his huge palace compounds for biological and chemical weapons. But the initial instinct was for more diplomacy. Iraq was suffering from sanctions already; Saddam eventually allowed the inspectors back. He was playing cat and mouse, however, and in October 1998 Britain and the United States finally lost patience and decided to smash Iraq's military establishment with missiles and bombing raids. In a foretaste of things to come, Blair even presented MPs with a dossier about Saddam's weapons of mass destruction. Again, at the last minute, the Iraqi leader backed down and the raids were postponed. The United States soon concluded this was another trick and, in December, British and

American planes attacked, hitting 250 targets over four days. Operation Desert Fox, as they called it, probably only delayed Saddam's weapons programmes by a year or so though it was sold as a huge success. As later, Britain and the United States were operating without a fresh UN resolution. Among their publics there was a widespread suspicion that Clinton had ordered the raids to distract from his embarrassing 'Monica-gate' travails. Congress was debating impeachment proceedings during the attacks and did indeed formally impeach Clinton on the final day of the raids. Over this episode, however, Blair faced little trouble in Parliament or outside it.

The second bombing campaign happened as a result of the breakup of Yugoslavia in the later stages of the long Balkan tragedy that had haunted John Major's time in office. Kosovo, a province of Serbia, was dominated by Albanian-speaking Muslims but was considered almost a holy site by history-minded Serbs, who had fought a famous medieval battle there against the Ottomans. The Serbian ex-communist leader Slobodan Milosevic had made himself the hero of the minority Kosovar Serbs. The Dayton peace agreement had calmed things down in 1995 but the newly formed Kosovo Liberation Army triggered a vicious new conflict, marked by increasingly savage Serb reprisals from 1998–9. Despite the use of international monitors and a brief ceasefire violence returned with the slaughter of forty-five civilians in the town of Racak, provoking comparisons with Nazi crimes. Ethnic cleansing and the forced migration of tens of thousands of people across wintry mountain tracks produced uproar around the world. In Chicago

Blair declared a new 'doctrine of the international community' which allowed 'a just war, based ... on values'. When talks with the Yugoslavs broke down, Nato duly launched a massive bombing campaign. British and American jets attacked targets first in Kosovo and then the rest of Serbia, hitting factories, television stations, bridges, power stations, railway lines, hospitals and many government buildings.

It was, however, a complete failure. Many innocent civilians were killed and daily life was disrupted across much of Serbia and Kosovo. Sixty people were killed by an American cluster bomb in a market. An allegedly stealthy US bomber blew down half the Chinese embassy in Belgrade, causing a huge international row. Meanwhile, low cloud and the use of decoys by Milosevic's generals limited the military damage and he used the attacks to increase his ethnic cleansing massively. The death squads went back to work. Hundreds of thousands of people were on the move – eventually roughly a million ethnic Albanians fled Kosovo and an estimated 10,000–12,000 were killed. Blair began to think he might not survive as Prime Minister if nothing was done. (So Downing Street staff said at the time: if they were right, the reader will notice that Mr Blair believed he might be ousted much more often than any level-headed observer might have predicted.) The real problem was that only the genuine threat of an invasion by ground troops might convince Milosevic to pull back; air power by itself was not enough. Blair tried desperately to persuade Clinton to agree. He visited a refugee camp and angrily said: 'This is obscene. It's criminal ... How can anyone think we shouldn't intervene?'

It would be the Americans whose troops would bear the brunt of a new war, since the European Union was far away from any coherent military structure and lacked the basic tools for carrying armies to other theatres. There was alarm in Washington about the British Prime Minister's moral posturing and it was only after many weeks of shuttle diplomacy that things began to move. Blair ordered that 50,000 British soldiers, most of the available army, should be made available to invade Kosovo. This would mean a huge call-up of reserves and if it was a bluff, was one on a massive scale, since other European countries had no intention of taking part. For whatever reason, the Americans began to toughen their language and finally, at the last minute, the Serb parliament buckled. The Americans and Russians worked together to apply pressure and Milosevic withdrew his forces from Kosovo and accepted its virtual independence, under an international mandate. Blair declared a kind of victory. Good had triumphed over evil, civilization over barbarism. Eight months later, Milosevic was toppled from power and ended up in The Hague charged with war crimes.

First Desert Fox and then Kosovo are vital in appreciating Blair's behaviour when it came to the full-scale Iraq War. They taught him that bombing rarely works. They suggested that, threatened with ground invasion by superior forces, dictators will back down. They played to his sense of himself as a moral war leader, combating dictators as wicked in their way as Hitler; something that was underpinned by the successful, life-saving intervention in Sierra Leone in 2000. After working well with Clinton over Desert Fox, he worried that he had tried to bounce him too obviously over Kosovo. He learned that American presidents need tactful handling. He learned not to rely on Britain's European allies very much, though he pressed the case later for the establishment of a European 'rapid reaction force' to shoulder more of the burden in future wars. He learned to ignore criticism from the left and right, which became deafening during the Kosovo bombing. He learned to cope with giving orders which resulted in much loss of life. He learned an abiding hostility to the media, and in particular the BBC whose reporting of the Kosovo bombing campaign infuriated him. The Irish peace process had convinced him of his potency as a deal-maker. Desert Fox, Kosovo and Sierra Leone convinced him of his ability to lead in war, to take big gambles, and to get them right.

Dubya

Most of those around the Prime Minister, certainly including his wife, had hoped that the Democrats' Al Gore would win the 2000 presidential election. Blair himself had been careful to open up early lines of communication to George W. Bush, sending diplomats to his ranch and passing a friendly message to the Texan governor via his father, ahead of the election campaign. His first phone conversation with the new President had been friendly enough but Blair was uneasy. With reason; he had enjoyed extraordinarily close relations with Clinton, an intellectual romance with the charismatic reshaper of Democratic politics which had survived their disagreements and the embarrassment of the Lewinsky affair. Bush had been elected to wipe away all that. Blair's first visit to see Bush at Camp David in February 2001 has been remembered for an uneasy photo-opportunity stroll when Blair was wearing embarrassingly tight jeans, and for Bush's awkward joke that the two of them did agree about issues – they both used the same brand of toothpaste, Colgate.

Away from the cameras, however, something more significant had happened. The two had established a relaxed private relationship which would grow into one of mutual trust, close enough to be controversial right around the world. Blair agreed to back Bush's proposed new US missile defence system, opposed by most European leaders and most Labour Party people. He would allow the upgrading of sites in Britain necessary to make it work. Bush, in turn, grudgingly agreed to support the latest British-French defence initiative to create a rapid reaction force in case of future Kosovos. More important than this bargain though, was the chemistry. Blair's aides were almost star-struck by the quality of Bush's team, particularly Condoleezza Rice, Donald Rumsfeld and Colin Powell. Blair found the new President clear, businesslike, brisk and easy to do business with – rather easier in fact than the loquacious, undisciplined Clinton. Even Cherie Blair, who had arrived on the plane still asking crossly why they had to be nice to 'these people', did her best to get on with Laura.

Those who have not met him underrate Bush's

instinctive skill with people and his ability to dominate a room. Kosovo had already taught Blair the importance of sticking with the US President if he wanted to fight 'moral' conflicts. Clinton himself had told Blair to make Bush 'your best friend'. Blair decided he liked Bush (but then, did he have any choice?) and rebuked anyone from then on who described the US President as stupid or badly informed. Relations between a US President and a British Prime Minister can never be between equals, but the groundwork had been done. At the time it all seemed rather humdrum. The consequences would be awesome.

From New York to Kabul

When the al Qaeda attack on New York and Washington took place, Blair was on the point of addressing the TUC in Brighton about his public sector reforms. It seemed an important speech. Campbell had been briefing journalists that he would confront the dinosaur instincts of the unions; it would be a 'belter', and highly dramatic. Just then the 24-hour news channels, which had become a feature in every ministerial office and wherever journalists gathered, began showing repeated film of a burning building. As speculation spread about some dreadful accident involving a light plane, the second tower was hit. Blair reacted to the news like everyone else, with disbelief. He was quickly advised that this was a terrorist attack on an unprecedented scale. Whatever his failures of analysis, Blair is very fast on his feet and, as

Diana's death had shown, quick to find words for moments of drama and grief. Inside the TUC there had been scenes of farce as journalists and others began taking phone calls and leaving the room. Its president rebuked them and called for order, only to find ripples of horror and speculation all round. When Blair arrived he said he was cancelling his speech, briefly described what had happened, expressed his great sympathy and support for America, and sped back to London by train with his advisers.

There, he found little preparation to defend the capital from a similar attack, which might be imminent. The airspace over London was closed, RAF jets were sent up on patrol, and the thinking began in the secure basement below Downing Street. Throughout the crisis Blair would work more closely with his military and intelligence advisers than he would with his ministers. He found he could not reach Bush by phone for more than twenty-four hours and there was a flurry of anxiety in London that the President had panicked or 'gone AWOL'. But as soon as contact was made with Bush at lunchtime on 12 September Blair was able to present not only his sympathy but also his hastily gathered briefing and thoughts about Osama bin Laden. The two resumed their mutually admiring partnership, emotionally charged by what had happened. This was a time when American flags fluttered across London, the band outside Buckingham Palace played 'The Star Spangled Banner', a carpet of flowers appeared outside the US embassy and the Last Night of the Proms became an act of solidarity with New York.

Not since 1945 had America been as popular in Britain.

By phone, Bush had promised that he was not going to act precipitously – 'pounding sand' – but told Blair he would make no distinction between the terrorists and those who harboured them. This implied first an ultimatum to the Taliban in Afghanistan and then a war. Blair agreed and made clear to the Commons soon afterwards that he believed the rules had changed, and that 'rogue states' harbouring terrorists, who might use chemical, nuclear or biological weapons, now had to choose whose side they were on. This emphatically did not mean that Iraq was to be attacked, certainly not by Number Ten's reckoning. We now know that at Camp David, four days after the September 11 attacks, Bush was advised by Donald Rumsfeld, his Defense Secretary, that he had an opportunity to attack Iraq but decided, for then, to concentrate on Afghanistan.

Nine days after the attack, in the midst of a frenzy of diplomacy, talking to the Germans, French, Chinese and Iranians, Blair went to pay tribute to the victims of what was already being called '9/11', struggling through torrential rain to the still-smoking ruins of ground zero and making an emotional cathedral oration for the British dead. In Washington afterwards, Bush told him that Iraq was for another day. Then in his speech to Congress laying out America's new 'war on terror' Bush warned that he would start with al Qaeda but not end there – another reference to Iraq. He also publicly praised Blair for showing such solidarity, turning to him theatrically, and saying: 'Thank you for coming, friend.' Congress rose to give Blair an ovation. Blair was using all his political capital, and the accumulated knowledge of the Foreign Office to help the United States, beyond the commitment of any other country and was receiving the emotional thanks of a President who now divided the rest of the world into friends and enemies. It was a high point of British prestige in America, certainly on a par with the Reagan-Thatcher age. Whether the mutual affection was truly influential is a moot point. For now, it encouraged the Americans to involve other countries in the attack on Afghanistan.

The strikes on the Taliban were launched less than a month after September 11, beginning with British submarines' cruise missiles and heavy bombing by US aircraft. Immensely destructive weaponry was dropped on al Qaeda training camps and Taliban defenders, including the notorious 'daisy-cutter' bombs. On the ground the war was conducted by the Northern Alliance and Afghan warlords, paid and supplied by the Americans and aided by Special Forces. This was a war of the twenty-first century against the nineteenth and it was over quickly, Kabul being deserted by the Taliban just five weeks after it had begun. The several thousand remaining al Qaeda Arab fighters and their Taliban hosts retreated to a cave complex near the Pakistan border, at Tora Bora, where even the Americans were unable to dislodge and capture all of them. Bin Laden, after calling for a war by the Muslim world against the West, disappeared. Throughout this, Blair had continued his diplomacy, helping win Pakistan round to the American cause and protesting to a wide range of Arab and Muslim leaders that the conflict was

263

emphatically not aimed at Islam. In Oman, Egypt, Syria and Palestine, he and his aides assured everyone who would listen that there would be no further war against Iraq unless evidence was uncovered of a link between al Qaeda and Saddam Hussein. Meanwhile, Blair's attempts to bring the other main European leaders nearer to close support for President Bush, and to kick-start a new phase of the peace process between Israel and her neighbours, were largely unsuccessful.

During these weeks of frantic activity, Blair was trying to build support for the new 'war on terror' but also to begin to give substance to his remarkable speech at Labour's conference in October, when he suggested the ills of the globe could be addressed in the aftermath of September 11. It remains the single most important speech he made and the best reference point for his failures and successes as a foreign affairs Prime Minister. Though advisers contributed key phrases, the thrust of the speech was his own, the product of the Christian moralism he had developed as an Oxford student, a growing belief in his personal ability as a global leader, and a hot concentration of excited thinking, utterly unlike his vaguer grasp of domestic policy. The Twin Towers attack had simply been a turning point in world history, he told his party. After movingly describing the aftermath in New York, he tied war-making and aid-giving together as Bush certainly would not have done. Defeat the terrorists, was his message, and then deal with the refugees; take on poverty and the terrorism would drain away. From the slums of Gaza to Africa itself which he was already describing as 'a scar on the conscience of the world', a new world could be made:

'From out of the shadow of this evil should emerge lasting good: destruction of the machinery of terrorism wherever it is found; hope amongst all nations of a new beginning where we seek to resolve differences in a calm and ordered way; greater understanding between nations and between faiths; and above all justice and prosperity for the poor and dispossessed.'

Some laughed in disbelief; others felt their eyes mist and their hearts beat faster. Blair was in some areas specific. He promised to make the Middle East peace process a personal priority from now on. But mostly he was visionary. The starving, the wretched, the dispossessed, the ignorant, could be saved. 'This is a moment to seize. The kaleidoscope has been shaken. The pieces are in flux. Soon they will settle again. Before they do, let us reorder the world around us.' It was an undeniably powerful act of rhetoric. But was Blair already reaching too far, allowing the intoxicating moral certainty of the hour to persuade him that he could play a messianic role round the world, part Gladstone, part Gandhi? Iraq was the bloody rock which would shatter these hopes, though Blair pursued his aims doggedly in Israel and Africa too.

The Joy of Trivia

Throughout the Blair years, Alastair Campbell would berate journalists for their tiny-minded obsession with trivia rather than substance. By trivia he meant a series of scandals involving ministers and money or, less often, ministers and

265

sex. Resignations from government punctuated the Blair years. Perhaps the most single damaging thing Tony Blair ever said was this: 'We are on the side of ordinary people against privilege. We must be purer than pure.' There were few instances of personal corruption but in trying to raise money for politics without going cap in hand to the trade unions, the Blair circle became deeply enmeshed with business and privilege, a world where favours were exchanged without anything explicit necessarily being said. The Blairs themselves enjoyed luxurious surroundings and the company of wealthy people. And after the huge endorsement of the 1997 election, lacking any restraint from a threatening opposition party, a certain swagger was soon apparent among the inner circle. From the word go, New Labour's high command, nose in the air, eyes aglitter with opportunity, was riding for a fall.

The Bernie Ecclestone affair of 1997, when the diminutive owner of Formula 1 racing around the world won an exemption from a tobacco advertising ban for his sport after giving a £1m donation to Labour, was the first rebuke to 'purer than pure'. In Opposition, Blair had been driven round the Silverstone racing circuit as the crowd waved Union Jacks at him; the two men were acquaintances.[13] The suggested link between a let-out clause in government policy for motor racing and Ecclestone's personal influence on him was hotly denied by Blair in public. Behind the scenes, he and his advisers knew how it looked. There was panic. Though nobody could finally prove wrongdoing, lies were told as Number Ten tried to cover up the detail of the story. On Campbell's advice Blair allowed himself to be interviewed by the BBC's premier attack-dog interviewer John Humphrys, to whom he made a lame half-apology and appealed to viewers: 'I hope that people know me well enough and realise the type of person I am to realise I would never do anything to harm the country or anything improper ... I think that most people who have dealt with me think that I am a pretty straight sort of guy.' Blair got away with it at the time, just about. But a dangerous impression had been left that the fresh-faced new administration which had so vigorously attacked Tory sleaze was not quite as clean-handed as it had seemed.

If Blair could still play his public reputation for niceness, the same could not in all fairness be said of Peter Mandelson. He had revelled in his reputation as 'the sinister minister', the all-seeing, omnipresent Machiavelli of New Britain. He could be stagey, camp, bullying, charming and for a man supposed to swirl around in the dark, was rather touchingly attracted by the spotlight. It was said that his arrival in a restaurant could turn soup to ice as he passed enemies, while he could raise an ally's blood temperature with just the flicker of a smile. He was less efficient than overwrought enemies thought him. As a dark manipulator he had his Inspector Clouseau moments. Yet in the early days of New Labour, Mandelson and the people around him felt they were masters of the universe. One of his aides, Derek Draper, boasted darkly to someone working undercover for a newspaper about 'the Circle'. There were, he said (no doubt tapping the side of his nose) only 'seventeen people who count'. Perhaps the Mandelson circle was sending itself up just a little; but it was setting itself up too. Mandelson himself had a strongly developed taste for good living and had borrowed £373,000 to buy a house before the election from Geoffrey Robinson, a cheery MP and supporter of Gordon Brown's. Robinson had a fortune secreted offshore in a Channel Island tax haven, money from a long business career and also from the bequest of a Belgian widow, happily called Madam Bourgeois. In government he became Paymaster General and in due course Mandelson became Secretary of State for Trade & Industry, the job which meant he was in overall charge of investigations into – among others – one Geoffrey Robinson, the man to whom he was indebted for his West End home.

There was an obvious conflict of interest. Mandelson tried to deflect enquiries about where he had got the money, suggesting it came from his mother. But the Brown camp both loathed him and knew the truth. So it was bound to come out. When it did so Blair was furious, not least because his close friend Peter had said nothing to warn him; nor had any of his staff. After a tearful scene with two Downing Street press officers, and Blair off-stage looking cross, Mandelson agreed that he would have to resign. The Prime Minister, though determined to see him go, then had him and his partner to stay at Chequers and gave him advice about rebuilding his life and the art of making friends. Characteristically, Mandelson's sad but noble letter of resignation and Blair's memorably moving reply were both written by Alastair Campbell. Then Robinson went too. So in due course did Charlie Whelan, Brown's press officer and the man blamed by Mandelson for revealing the story of his loan.

Had that been all it would have been bad enough. The mantra was established that nothing wrong had been done, but because of the appearance of wrongdoing, resignation was called for. But there followed a roll-call of scandals, all different in their detail, together devastating in their effect. Blair was accused of lying when he denied knowledge of any connection between a Labour donation made by Lakshmi Mittal, an Indian businessman, and his help for Mittal in trying to buy a Romanian steel company. Mandelson returned to government just ten months after his resignation and threw himself into the new job of Northern Ireland Secretary. Then came questions about whether two Indian businessmen who had helped fund the Dome had tried to obtain British citizenship via Mandelson. He was later cleared of wrongdoing but had to resign again. After Blair again showed himself entirely steely about this, Mandelson, who eventually turned up again as Britain's Commissioner in Brussels, felt badly betrayed. (Connections between ministers and business people who 'know the form' and protect one another by never explicitly asking or offering, depend on a shared culture. It is interesting that so many of the rows that broke surface concerned Asian business people. They did not know the form. They could speak English, but not Unspoken English.)

For the same cabinet minister to have to resign twice within a year was unheard-of. But in the Blair years, twice happened twice. David Blunkett, the blind, tough-talking former leader of Sheffield council who had been Blair's enforcer in education, had to resign as Home Secretary in 2004 after a row over whether he had asked his private office to fast-track a visa application for his lover Kimberley Quinn's nanny. He had not exactly rallied colleagues to his side by confiding in a journalist his derisive views on much of the rest of the cabinet, duly published in a biography to his embarrassment and their fury. Press interest in the 'nannygate' story was whipped to fever pitch by Quinn's role as well-known publisher of the Tory-supporting *Spectator* magazine and the revelation that she had had a child by him. Even Blunkett described it as the tale of the socialite and the socialist. There followed a bitter custody battle between Quinn, supported by her long-suffering husband, and the increasingly agitated Blunkett. It was a story from the wilder years of the eighteenth century and was used as the subject of a musical, which hurt Blunkett very much, as well as a television drama. He was brought back into government after the 2005 election as Work & Pensions Secretary but had to resign again after a row over shares in a DNA testing company he had purchased while out of the government. His taped diaries which were published in 2006 then revealed divisions at the heart of government before the Iraq War, his coruscating views on senior civil servants, and implied that Blair had considered sacking Brown if he failed to properly support him over it.

The Blunkett and Mandelson 'doubles' were the most celebrated resignations of the Blair years but were only part of the story. Ron Davies, the Welsh Secretary, went after 'a moment of madness' involving another man on Clapham Common.

270

Estelle Morris, Education Secretary, went after a 'moment of sanity' – thoroughly honorably, she decided she was not up to the job. There were the Iraq resignations, first of Robin Cook, then Clare Short, the loss of a badly bruised Lord Irvine of Lairg as Lord Chancellor after Blair overruled him on constitutional reform, and the departure of Alan Milburn, Health Secretary, to spend more time with his family. Stephen Byers, a former hard leftist from the north-east of England, had been one of Blair's most trusted and loyal ministers. He was badly damaged when his special adviser Jo Moore callously emailed colleagues telling them 9/11 was a good day 'to bury bad news', not the most sensitive response to the murder of thousands. Then as Transport Secretary Byers ignited a huge row when he forced Railtrack into liquidation and took control of it back, without paying the compensation to its shareholders that straightforward nationalization would have entitled them to. They felt robbed and cheated, though Labour MPs were delighted. Byers was attacked for lying to Parliament about this, and about what he said to a meeting of survivors of the horrific Paddington train disaster about the railway's future. He resigned in May 2002.

The dirty tide washed through Number Ten too. Blair and his wife Cherie had been the butt of many attacks for the gusto with which they enjoyed free holidays at the expense of rich friends – Geoffrey Robinson, an Italian prince, Cliff Richard, a Bee Gee, and (briefly) Silvio Berlusconi, the scandal-mired Prime Minister of Italy. Cherie had been criticized frequently for free-loading more generally; though a high-paid lawyer she was

271

unreasonably frightened of not having enough money, which presumably dated from her insecure childhood. The Blairs were less wealthy than the Thatchers (though not, in office, the Majors or the Wilsons or the Callaghans) and had failed to capitalize on the house-price boom when they sold their private north London home. Yet they and their children were looked after in two homes paid for by the State and he was well paid by the standards of ordinary Britain. Not rich only by the standards of millennial London high society, the family was comfortable. And as soon as Blair resigned he knew that through book deals, speaking fees and corporate work he could become rich beyond the dreams of avarice. None of this seemed to cut much ice.

Carole Caplin, a health and beauty trainer, had known Cherie Blair from the nineties but became more influential with her after Labour won power. Disliked by Number Ten officials who regarded her as manipulative, and her New Age views as barmy, Caplin nevertheless helped Mrs Blair develop a style and self-confidence she felt she had not had before. Particularly after her pregnancy with Leo, and then a later miscarriage, a close feminine bond was established. With Blair constantly distracted by the 'war on terror' and domestic politics, Cherie took it more upon herself to organize family plans, including financial plans. Through Caplin, she arranged to buy two flats in Bristol where her son Euan was at university, one for him and one as an investment. The deal was negotiated by Caplin's lover, a pantomime Australian rogue and fraudster called Peter Foster. When the story broke, Cherie Blair failed to tell Campbell the full truth. Nor did she tell Fiona Miller, Campbell's partner, who had been Cherie's spokeswoman and who loathed Caplin. Nor, it seems, did her husband know the complete story either. As a result, Number Ten misled the press when stories in the *Daily Mail* and *Mail on Sunday* were put to them and were later forced to apologize. Stormy scenes erupted inside Downing Street when the link from Blair to a conman, via Cherie and Caplin, was finally established. It was a very bleak moment for the couple and media anger was only partially assuaged when at Campbell's insistence Cherie made a live televised apology, blaming her busy life and maternal pressure for what had happened. Some applauded her for a courageous performance and a life of difficult juggling. Others were unconvinced.

Britain had not become a corrupt country. But a sense of let-down, betrayal or perhaps just weary disappointment was felt by millions who had hoped for better. Why had Blair and his associates failed to show themselves purer than pure? First, by deciding to live with a system of business donations to help fund politics, they opened themselves to influence-peddling. Blair always replied that he had set up rules for the disclosure of party donations and the tightest ever code for ministerial behaviour. This was true. Yet there always seemed to be another loophole and another set of questions. By the end of his time in office his fundraiser Lord Levy had been arrested in a loans-for-peerages investigation and he was facing police questioning himself.

Second, the growth of a super-rich class of business people in London in the two decades after the Big Bang gave some politicians a wholly

273

unrealistic measurement of how 'people like us' live. Many did not fall for it. Brown did not. Most ministers went home to their constituencies and found themselves walking again on solid ground. But the temptation to think, 'I run the country, or part of the country, don't I deserve better?' was always present. Britain seemed to have become a society which measured success merely by money, rather than by public esteem. Finally, the way politicians were really monitored had changed. It was not the smooth expressions of warning from civil servants they had to worry about, or even tough questions from fellow MPs. A self-appointed, lively, impertinent and at times savage opposition did the job instead, a class of people courted by ministers and then despised by them: the media. After brilliantly using journalism to help discredit the Conservatives, Blair and his colleagues were themselves about to feel the rough edge of a rough trade.

Into the Furnace

Blair's biographer Anthony Seldon rightly emphasizes how worried Blair was about Saddam Hussein and weapons of mass destruction long before Bush became President, or decided to launch his war. This was not simply something Blair worried about privately. He spoke of it again and again. He was particularly worried about a nuclear-enhanced 'dirty bomb' being used by Iraqi-supported terrorists. By now his earlier experiences of Saddam, and Milosevic, and to a lesser extent

Mullah Omar of the Taliban, as well as his personal contact with leaders he liked, such as Bush and Russia's Vladimir Putin, meant that for Blair foreign affairs was personal. By focusing so fully on Saddam as a man of evil, and the moral case for dealing with him, he did not focus enough on the complexities of Iraq, the country.

The hardening of views inside the White House which finally led to the decision to invade Iraq are not part of this story. In Bush's State of the Union speech for 2002 he had listed Iraq, Iran and North Korea as an 'axis of evil', sending shivers across diplomatic Europe. Attempts by US intelligence to prove a link between the secularist Saddam and the fundamentalist al Qaeda failed but this hardly halted the process of lining up Iraq as next for the Bush treatment. Blair's promises to Arab leaders about proof had no purchase in Washington. There were philosophical links between Blair's Gladstonian speech to the Labour Party and the neo-conservatives around Bush, many of whom believed that by toppling Saddam they would bring an age of democracy and prosperity to the Middle East, solving the Palestinian problem along the way. But the dominant group around Bush were not keen on grand visions. They believed first and second in toppling Saddam. They did not believe in waiting for, or depending upon, other countries, even Britain. After 9/11 this was America's war. They did not believe in UN inspectors or promises by Baghdad. Above all the hopes of some of the more intellectual US officials and of Britain's Foreign Office for a detailed plan for the reconstruction of post-war Iraq would be dashed by the hawks, Cheney and Rumsfeld at their head.

'Regime change' meant regime change. It did not mean promises to bring clean water and food to foreigners by democratic missionaries.

From the time when he visited Bush at his dusty Texan ranch at Crawford, near Waco, in April 2002, Blair knew he intended to invade Iraq. That did not end the matter, since Blair spent much of the rest of the year arguing that Bush should go via the United Nations. Without this, under British interpretations of international law, the invasion would be illegal. The UN would also give a last chance for Saddam to disarm peacefully. Keeping the international community together would make it easier to rebuild Iraq afterwards, in the spirit of Blair's conference speech. He also wanted Bush to commit to spending plenty of time on the Middle East peace process. On 7 September 2002 at Camp David Blair finally got Bush's promise to go via the UN, and Bush got Blair's promise that Britain would fight alongside America in Iraq if that route failed. Bush praised Blair for having 'cojones' – Spanish for balls. When Bush publicly confirmed his willingness to try for a UN resolution, ad-libbing in a speech to the General Assembly a few days later, Blair was delighted. But he was also locked in. He had spent his capital with Bush, and won a battle with the Washington hawks about the United Nations. But he had not persuaded anyone to take the post-war situation seriously. At the time it looked like a good deal.

It would turn out to be a rotten deal, not least because to Blair's chagrin and amazement, the United States and Britain were eventually unable to get the extra UN resolution they wanted. In the meantime the UN route helped keep the number of

Labour's Commons rebels to fifty-six. That was still a lot. In Whitehall the Foreign Office and many ministers were growing worried about where Blair was leading them. Outside it, the anti war movement was mobilizing. To try to win public opinion round Blair turned to a device he had used twice before, ahead of Desert Fox and after 9/11, the publication of a dossier of facts proving the case for war. This one, though, was different. The American case against Saddam was that he was a bad, dangerous guy who in the context of the new war on terror had to be taken out. The UN case was that he was failing to cooperate fully with weapons inspectors, leading to a suspicion that he was still hiding stocks of weapons of mass destruction (WMD), particularly chemical and biological weapons, though to be fair some had been destroyed. To get the resolution, it was vital to concentrate on the WMD, about which as we have seen Blair had long been worried. The dossier, therefore, had to show they existed. To win round British opinion, it would have to show they were threatening to Britain too. Thus Blair laid the central case for war not on the moral cause for removing a tyrant but on narrow and unproven assertions about the condition of the tyrant's arsenal.

Blair's team had already enjoyed some success with journalists in feeding them bloodcurdling lines about the damage Saddam might wreak. There is no doubt that senior intelligence and defence people believed he had WMD but was cleverly hiding them, and that he was trying to get nuclear weapons. The trouble was that Saddam's regime of terror was so effective that there were very few sources of information from inside Iraq. Those Britain's MI6 dealt with were untrustworthy – they were after all dissidents with a strong reason to bring forward the war. Sir Richard Dearlove, the MI6 director general, brought Blair information from an Iraqi source who said he knew where chemical agent was being made – though the source was 'untried and untested'. Satellite intelligence, though used by Colin Powell at the UN, was unsatisfactorily unclear. Thus the dossier had to produce information from a vague and difficult source which was nevertheless hard-edged enough, at least at first glance, to fulfil a highly political role. It was drawn from a variety of sources, channelled through the Joint Intelligence Committee, which reported to the Prime Minister. Different texts were batted to and fro through Downing Street, as officials questioned parts of it, and wondered whether it was sufficiently convincing. Suspicions were raised also following the publication of a second dossier in February 2003 about the background to Iraq's concealment programme, which was later dubbed 'the dodgy dossier' and proved to have been lifted without attribution from a PhD thesis found on the Internet.

Whatever the final truth about the shaping of the September 2002 dossier, something strange had happened. Suspicions had been hardened, assertions sharpened, doubts trimmed out and belief converted into proof. Nobody knew for sure what Saddam had (that was the point of the UN inspection process) but when it was published the dossier gave the impression that he had multiple weapons of mass destruction which could be ready for use in forty-five minutes and threatened, among other places, British bases in Cyprus. The forty-five-minute claim turned out to refer to some short-range battlefield chemical weapons which could not reach other countries, though maps printed in the dossier confused readers about it. And when Iraq was finally invaded, and exhaustive searches conducted everywhere, the 'weapons' never turned up. For years Blair insisted hotly that they would. He would be publicly mocked by President Putin, MPs and the world's media for this. He kept telling his critics they would be proved wrong. So far they have not been.

A tense struggle at the United Nations, with British diplomats in the lead, produced Resolution 1441, declaring that Saddam was in 'material breach' of his obligation to show he had no banned weaponry, and giving him a last opportunity to comply or face 'serious consequences'. The Iraqi leader fudged and dodged, letting inspectors back in but without offering a full declaration of his weapons. For the Americans, this was the trigger for war. For other countries, notably France, it merely meant that there should be another discussion at the Security Council about what to do. In February 2003, as British and US forces waited to attack Iraq from the south, there was a vast 'Stop the War' march through London. It was the biggest ever demonstration in the capital, a carnival of protest that put even the Suez protests in its shade. Blair, Jack Straw, the Foreign Secretary who had swallowed private doubts and resolved to loyally support his boss, with their diplomatic team were fighting desperately to get a second UN resolution agreed which would give full legal cover for the attack on Iraq. This was something Blair had told Bush repeatedly that he needed to be sure of holding his party together (and by implication, staying in power). But President Chirac of France, angry at the behaviour of Washington's hawks and worried about the impact of the war on the Islamic world generally, suggested that France would never accept a second resolution, and it collapsed. Despite everything the Prime Minister was left without the real UN cover he always thought he needed. For Blair and Straw it was a low moment.

For others, it was the last straw. Robin Cook, who as the previous Foreign Secretary had been deeply involved in Desert Fox and Kosovo, had warned the cabinet that without a second resolution he could not support this third war. He duly resigned. For the time being Clare Short, another cabinet dissenter who had publicly described Blair's behaviour as 'reckless', stayed on. In the Commons Cook, its former leader, then gave one of the most icily eloquent speeches heard in the chamber in modern times. He applauded Blair and Straw for trying so hard for the second resolution, which only showed how important it had been. Many countries, not just France, had wanted more inspections before any fighting: 'The reality is that Britain is being asked to embark on a war without agreement in any of the international bodies of which we are a leading partner – not Nato, not the European Union and, now, not the Security Council.' The US was a superpower and could afford to go it alone, but Britain could not. Iraq probably had no weapons of mass destruction 'in the ordinarily understood sense' but was in fact militarily very weak: 'Ironically, it is only because Iraq's military

280

forces are so weak that we can even contemplate its invasion. We cannot base our military strategy on the assumption that Saddam is weak and at the same time justify pre-emptive action on the claim that he is a threat.' The British people, said Cook, possessed collective wisdom: 'On Iraq, I believe that the prevailing mood of the British people is sound. They do not doubt that Saddam is a brutal dictator, but they are not persuaded that he is a clear and present danger to Britain.' Almost uniquely, against its hallowed traditions, the Commons loudly clapped Cook as he sat down.

Blair felt he had to press ahead. Saddam had proved himself yet again untrustworthy and a liar. He had legal cover from his attorney general for the war, though it was hardly resounding, and disputed by other government lawyers, one of whom resigned. He had given his word to President Bush, who offered Blair the chance to pull out and send British troops in after the invasion, as peacekeepers. Blair turned the offer down as dishonourable and bad for army morale. He had staked his reputation on the war and felt that if he could not carry his party, he was finished as a leader. Privately, arrangements for his resignation were set in hand. In the Commons a ferocious political and media struggle began to win round doubters, emphasizing Saddam's brutality and abuse of human rights, rather than his weaponry. A backbencher and sometime left-wing firebrand, Ann Clwyd, made a particularly influential speech about Saddam's treatment of the Kurds and his use of torture. Eventually, after days of drama and one of his best parliamentary speeches ever, Blair won a majority of Labour MPs, though 139 rebelled. The overall Commons victory was never in doubt because of Conservative support, but Blair had been close to failing his private yardstick of being backed by at least half his MPs. With that overcome, the final barrier to war was lifted.

The war began on 20 March 2003 with a thunderous air attack on Baghdad, described with brutal clarity in Washington as 'shock and awe'. An early attempt by Saddam's information minister to assassinate Saddam failed. For the first weeks, calm declarations of great victories being won out in the desert by the Iraqi armed forces were broadcast almost nightly. In fact, sandstorms delayed the US advance. In Baghdad a coalition bomb killed fifty-seven people in a market-place and in Britain anger about the war grew. Yet while not quite the walkover the Pentagon had hoped, the invasion was over very quickly. By 7 April British forces had taken Basra, having surrounded it long before, and two days later the Americans were in Baghdad, first seizing the international airport and then Saddam's famous palaces. Soon his statues were being jubilantly torn down. Before the invasion, there had been speculation about Baghdad fighting to the last, surrounded by trenches of burning oil, tank regiments and possibly artillery with chemical shells – an Arab *Götterddämmerung* on the banks of the Tigris. By those standards, the war had been a great, one-sided military success. The war beyond the war would be something else entirely.

Mediaocracy

In the eighties and early nineties, Labour had been savaged by much of the press. Neil Kinnock had a terrible time. When Blair became leader the people immediately around Kinnock at the time, Mandelson and Campbell, remembered it well. Campbell had worked for the *Daily Mirror* in the dirtiest, most cynical end of the newspaper market and came away thinking that most journalists were idle liars, as well as biased against Labour. He was tribal and assumed the rest of the world was too. Mandelson, with a background in television, was a master of image, and later of the killer briefing. So it is hardly surprising that New Labour became the most media-obsessed political party in British history. We have seen how Blair opened out to Labour's traditional enemies in the press after becoming leader, and how he exploited 'sleaze' to destroy John Major's reputation. On the way to winning power, New Labour turned itself into a kind of perpetual media news-desk, with a plan for what every political headline should say every day, an endless 'grid' of announcements, images, soundbites and rebuttals, constantly pressing down on journalists, their editors and owners, fighting for every adjective and exclamation mark.

It is now incontestable that the same way of thinking was brought into power and did terrible damage to the government's reputation and that of politics generally. Bizarrely, it was assumed that rival newspaper groups with different views about say, law and order, could be kept friendly by Blair

283

telling them what they wanted to hear – even though they would later confer. The attempted bullying of journalists, which grew much worse when some of the scandals described above began to break, was met with increasing resistance. Number Ten's news machine began to be widely disbelieved. The word 'spin' was attached to almost everything it said. Diaries published by one of the former Downing Street spin-doctors, Lance Price, show how justified this suspicion was. On the first Mandelson resignation, he notes: 'We said (quite falsely) that Peter had rung TB last night and said he wanted to resign.' Of a Sunday newspaper interview which Blair had given calling for a new 'moral purpose', Price says: 'It was totally vacuous and was made up just to give us a good story after two twelve-year-old girls were found to have got themselves pregnant. But it worked ...'[14]

There are many other examples. Some, collected by the journalist Peter Oborne, include the smearing of Chris Patten, the former Tory chairman and Hong Kong governor for leaking intelligence reports, a false trail to deflect attention from the breakup of Robin Cook's marriage; the assertion by Peter Mandelson that the Dome would feature an exciting new game called 'surf-ball' (which never existed); and Blair's own deceptions, such as over Mandelson's own plans to become an MP.[15] While there are exceptional circumstances in which political leaders have to deceive, such as when soldiers' lives would be at risk from disclosure, or when a currency was about to be devalued, journalists came to believe the currency of truth was now devalued. Anything asserted by Number Ten, and later Blair himself, was picked over in minute semantic detail. Worryingly often, the picking-over turned out to be justified. The 'non-denial denial' became an essential phrase in reporting New Labour. At election time statistics were twisted even beyond the normal elastic rules of political debate. There was a spiral downwards. Journalists grew more aggressive in their assertions and began consigning the (disbelieved) official denials to the final paragraph of their stories. Some ministers drew the conclusion that the press was so hostile it was legitimate to use any trick or form of words to mislead them. Others complained that every time they were frank, their words were twisted and used against them: why bother? Before long a government which had arrived in office supported by almost all the national papers, was being attacked daily by almost all of them. And the papers themselves were selling fewer copies. Ultimately, cynicism is boring.

The most infamous confrontation between New Labour and the media, however, was not with a newspaper but with a broadcaster. One of the domestic consequences of the Iraq was the worst falling out between the BBC and the government since the Suez crisis. At issue was whether or not officials in Number Ten had 'sexed up' that dossier about Iraq's alleged weapons of mass destruction. As previously described, the dossier blended two cultures, the cautious, secretive, nuanced culture of intelligence gathering for internal government purposes, and the spin-doctors' culture of opinion-forming, in this case to win more of the public over to back a coming war. But the cultures did not blend, they curdled. At seven minutes after six one morning at the end of May 2003, Radio

Four's *Today* programme broadcast an interview between its presenter John Humphrys and its defence correspondent, a dishevelled digger of a journalist called Andrew Gilligan. He alleged that Downing Street had 'sexed up' the dossier beyond what intelligence sources thought was reasonable, particularly in saying that weapons of mass destruction could be ready for use within forty-five minutes. Campbell quickly and unequivocally denied the truth of Gilligan's assertion and demanded an apology. Gilligan went further, in an article for a newspaper in which he named Campbell. As Iraq burned, Number Ten and the BBC began a war of their own.

In general battles between journalists and politicians do not spill real blood. There is bitterness. There may be resignations. But when the smoke clears, everyone gets up again and goes back to work. When Campbell widened his criticism of the BBC to attack it for having an anti-war agenda, he had no idea quite what he was setting off. Yet there was a certain recklessness in his mood. He confided to his diary that he wanted to 'fuck Gilligan' and wanted 'a clear win' against the corporation. On the BBC side, it would turn out that Gilligan had been loose with his words, claiming rather more than he knew for sure, so opening a flank to Campbell; nor was Gilligan frank with his colleagues. The BBC's Director General, Greg Dyke, who had been hounded in the press as a Blair crony, was ferociously robust in defending the corporation against Campbell and was strongly supported by his Chairman, Gavyn Davies, whose wife was Gordon Brown's senior aide. He too was determined to demonstrate his independence.

Neither side gave way until eventually it was revealed that a government scientist with a high reputation as an arms inspector, Dr David Kelly, was probably the source of Gilligan's information. Downing Street did not name him but allowed journalists to keep throwing names at them until they confirmed who he was; a bizarre game. Because he was not involved directly in the joint intelligence committee or its work, 'outing' Kelly as the secret mole would, in the government's eyes, discredit the BBC story. Suddenly thrown into the cauldron of a media row, Kelly himself was evasive when aggressively questioned by a committee of MPs. Visibly nervous, he denied that he could have been Gilligan's informant. Yet he was. A fastidious, serious-minded man who had supported the toppling of Saddam and had served his country honourably as a weapons inspector, Kelly seems to have cracked under the strain. On a quiet July morning in 2003 he walked five miles to the edge of a wood near his Oxfordshire home where he took painkillers, opened up a pen-knife, and killed himself. This media battle had drawn blood in the most awful way. Blair, arriving in Tokyo after triumphantly addressing both houses of Congress about the fall of Saddam, was asked: 'Prime Minister, do you have blood on your hands?' He looked as if he was about to be sick.

Back home, he ordered an inquiry under a judge, Lord Hutton, which engaged the minute attention of the world of politics through the autumn of 2003. Much was revealed about Blair's informal, sloppily recorded and cliquish style of governing, and the involvement of his political staff in discussion which led to the final dossier. But with the head of the JIC and other officials insisting they had not been leant on, or obliged to say anything they did not believe, and a very strong public performance by Blair, Lord Hutton concluded Gilligan's assertion that the government knew its forty-five-minute claim was wrong, was unfounded. The intelligence committee might have 'subconsciously' been persuaded to strengthen its language because they knew what the Prime Minister wished the effect of the dossier to be; but it was consistent with the intelligence at the time. Hutton decided that Kelly had probably killed himself because of a loss of self-esteem and the threat to his reputation, but that nobody else was to blame. (There was a strongly held private belief among some doctors and journalists that Kelly had been murdered but so far, not a shred of hard evidence has come to light.) Hutton attacked the BBC's editorial controls. His findings had been leaked a day early to Rupert Murdoch's *Sun* newspaper, which robustly set the political mood: victory for Blair, humiliation for the BBC. With Blair defiant and claiming complete vindication in the Commons both Dyke and Davies resigned almost immediately. Distraught employees walked out from their offices to cheer them as they left. The corporation had suffered its worst day ever. Yet the stakes were high on both sides. Had Hutton found against the Prime Minister, it would have been Blair being applauded by his tearful staff as he walked into retirement.

Feeling vindicated and as aggressive as ever about the quality of journalism, Campbell then left Downing Street. Blair had concluded that the age of spin had done them all far more harm than good. It was time, despite his personal debt to Campbell, for a new broom. A widely trusted and traditionalist press officer who had worked for Roy Hattersley, called David Hill, was appointed. Slowly, painfully, both the BBC and Number Ten moved on – although there was plenty of trouble still ahead. By his last couple of years in office, Blair had come to realize that the frantic headline-chasing and rebuttal of the early years had merely helped stoke a mood of cynicism in the press. The habits of truth-shaving, subtle deception and syntactical evasion, which had once seemed magnificently clever, had done more harm than any brief newspaper victories they might have achieved. After Iraq, one of the most common jibes made about him was simply 'Bliar' For a Prime Minister who in his early days had been able to say that most people thought him 'a pretty straight kind of guy', it was a terrible come-down.

Always with us?

Through the New Labour years, with low inflation and steady growth, most of the country grew richer. Growth since 1997, at 2.8% a year, was above the post-war average, Britain's gross domestic product per head was above that of France and Germany, and she had the second-lowest jobless figures in the EU. The number of people in work increased by 2.4 million. Incomes grew, in real terms, by about a fifth. Pensions were in trouble but house price inflation soared, so that home-owners found their properties more than doubling in value and came to think themselves prosperous indeed. One study showed that Britain had a higher proportion of dollar millionaires than any other country. Family budgets are by definition tricky things to generalize about but by 2006 analysts were assessing the disposable wealth of the British, defined by the consultants KDP as 'the money people can really put their hands on if necessary' at £40,000 per household. The wealth was not evenly spread geographically, averaging £68,000 in the south-east of England and a little over £30,000 in Wales and north-east England. But even in historically poorer parts of the UK house prices had risen fast, so much so that government plans to bulldoze worthless northern terraces had to be abandoned when they started to become worth quite a lot. Cheap mortgages, easy borrowing and high property prices meant that millions of people felt far better off, despite the overall rise in the tax burden. Cheap air travel, which had first arrived in the seventies with Freddie Laker, gave the British opportunities for easy travel both to their traditional sun-kissed resorts and to every part of the European continent. A British expatriate house-price boom rippled slowly across the French countryside and roared through southern Spain. People began to commute weekly to their jobs in London or Manchester from villas by the Mediterranean. Small regional airports grew, then boomed.

Clever, constantly evolving consumer electronics and then cheap clothing from the Far East kept the shops thronged. The internet, advancing from colleges and geeks to the show-off upper middle classes, then to children's bedrooms everywhere, introduced new forms of shopping. It first began to attract popular interest in the mid-nineties:

Britain's first internet cafe and internet magazine, reviewing a few hundred early websites, were both launched in 1994. The following year saw the beginning of internet shopping as a major pastime, with both eBay and Amazon arriving, though for tiny numbers of people at first. It was a time of immense optimism, despite warnings that the whole digital world would collapse because of the 'millennium bug' – the alleged inability of computers to deal with the last two digits in '2000', which was taken very seriously at the time.

In fact, the bubble was burst by its own excessive expansion, like any bubble, and after a pause and a lot of ruined dreams, the 'new economy' roared on again. By 2000, according to the Office of National Statistics, around 40 per cent of Britons had accessed the internet at some time. Cyber frenzy swept the country, and business; three years later, nearly half of British homes were connected. By 2004 the spread of broadband had brought a new mass market in downloading music and video online. By 2006, three-quarters of British children had internet access at home. Simultaneously, new money arrived. The rich of America, Europe and Russia began buying up parts of London, and then other attractive parts of the country, including Edinburgh, the Scottish Highlands, Yorkshire and Cornwall. For all the problems and disappointments, and the longer-term problems with their financing, new schools and public buildings sprang up – new museums, galleries, vast shopping complexes, corporate headquarters, now biomorphic, not straight, full of lightness, airy atriums, thin skins of glass and steel. This was show-off architecture for a show-off material culture and not always dignified, but these buildings were better-looking and more imaginative than their predecessors had been in the dreary age of concrete.

At a more humdrum level, 'executive housing', with pebbled driveways, brick facing and dormer windows, was growing across farmland and by rivers with no thought of flood-plain constraints. Parts of the country far from London, such as the English south-west and Yorkshire, enjoyed a ripple of wealth that pushed their house prices to unheard-of levels. From Leith to Gateshead, Belfast to Cardiff Bay, once-derelict shorefront areas were transformed. Supermarkets, exercising huge market power, brought cheap meat and factory-made meals into almost everyone's budgets. The new global air freight market, and refrigerated lorries moving freely across a Europe shorn of internal barriers, carried out-of-season fruit and vegetables, fish from the Pacific, exotic foods of all kinds, to superstores everywhere. Hardly anyone was out of reach of a Tesco, a Morrison's, Sainsbury's or Asda. By the mid-2000s, the four supermarket giants owned more than 1,500 superstores. This provoked a new political row about their commercial influence but it also spread consumption of goods that had once been luxuries. Under Thatcher, millions had begun drinking wine. Under Blair they began drinking drinkable wine. Their children had to borrow to study but were more likely to go to college or university and to travel the world on a 'gap year', a holiday from ordinariness which had once meant working, occasionally abroad, but which by now might mean air-hopping across South America or to the beaches of Thailand. Materially, for the majority of people, this was a golden age, which perhaps explains why the real anger about earlier pensions decisions and stealth taxes failed to translate into anti-Labour voting in successive general elections.

Not everyone, of course, was invited to the party. New Labour's general pitch was to the well-doing middle but Gordon Brown, from the first, made much of its anti-poverty agenda. Labour in particular emphasized child poverty because, since the launch of the Child Poverty Action Group, it had become a particularly emotive problem. Labour policies took a million children out of relative poverty between 1997 and 2004, though the numbers rose again later. Brown's emphasis was also on the working poor, and the virtue of work. So his major innovations were the national minimum wage, the 'New Deal' for the young unemployed, and the working families' tax credit, as well as tax credits aimed at children. There was also a minimum income guarantee, and later a pension credit, for worse-off pensioners.

The minimum wage was first set at £3.60 an hour and rising year by year. (It stood at £5.35 an hour in 2006.) Because the figures were low the minimum wage did not destroy the 2 million jobs, or produce the higher inflation, which Conservatives and others claimed it would. Employment grew and inflation stayed low. It even appeared to have cut red tape, since the old Wages Councils had to inspect businesses more frequently than the new Inland Revenue minimum wage inspections. By the middle 2000s, the minimum wage covered 2 million people, the majority of them women. And because it was uprated slightly faster than inflation, the wages of the poor rose faster. The situation may change, particularly if unemployment worsens, but it appeared to have been an almost unqualified success, enough for the Conservative Party, which had so strongly opposed it, to embrace it under Michael Howard before the 2005 election.

The New Deal was funded by a windfall tax on privatized utility companies. By 2000, Blair said it had helped a quarter of a million young people back to work and it was being claimed as a major factor in lower unemployment as late as 2005. It was clearly less of a factor than the huge increase in the size of the state: in the Blair years, state employment grew by 700,000, funded by record amounts taken in tax. And the cost of goading, coaxing and educating people into jobs was very high. The National Audit Office, looking back at its effect in the first Parliament, reckoned the number of under 25-year-olds helped into real jobs could be as low as 25,000, at a cost per person of £8,000. All those new jobs which had to be created to help people into jobs came at a price. A second initiative was targeted at the youngest of all, the babies and young children of the most deprived families. Sure Start was meant to bring mothers together in family centres across Britain – 3,500 were planned for 2010, ten years after the scheme was launched – and help them to be more effective parents. A scheme in the United States had shown great success and Sure Start was another initiative backed in its essence by the Conservatives, though Blair himself appeared to be having second thoughts, as the most deprived families declined to turn up. He believed in sticks as well as carrots.

Abroad, the government's anti-poverty agenda

concentrated on Africa. In 2004 Blair initiated the Commission for Africa which worked to persuade the world's richest countries to back a wide plan for economic, political and social reform, supported by debt relief. By then it was estimated more than 50,000 people were dying every day from famine or bad water in Africa and the continent's AIDS epidemic was wiping out much of a generation. In 2005 Brown, struggling to persuade the United States to back his plans for an international finance facility – a global piggy bank – agreed to raise Britain's aid contribution to 0.7 per cent of GDP. Washington declined to follow suit. Enormous strength was added to the campaign by Make Poverty History, one of the two biggest examples of street politics in the Blair age. Here was extra-parliamentary action which showed people's readiness to engage with politics-as-unusual, a residual idealism. There is a tradition in Britain of moral protest and practical action for famine abroad. Oxfam had started as the Oxford Committee for Famine Relief in 1942, campaigning to persuade the wartime government to lift its blockade on German-occupied Greece, where the Nazis were allowing people to starve as they diverted food to their army in North Africa. (Churchill took the view that the starvation was the fault of the occupying power and the blockade should stay – the argument was strikingly similar to those made about sanctions imposed on Saddam Hussein's Iraq in the Major and Blair years.) What made the later movement different was the fusion of celebrity, music and television to raise unheard-of sums.

It began with the Irish rock star Bob Geldof, and

Midge Ure of the band Ultravox, who were shocked by news coverage of the 1984 Ethiopian famine by the BBC's Michael Buerk. They formed a thirty-strong 'supergroup' to make a fundraising Christmas single, 'Do They Know It's Christmas?' It raised £65 m and Geldof managed to persuade Margaret Thatcher to waive VAT for the famine victims. This success was followed by Live Aid, a linked global concert held in London and Philadephia in 1985. It was watched by an estimated 1.5 billion people in 160 countries, making it by far the biggest world television event to that point. Geldof continued to campaign on Africa, joining the Commission for Africa. Having sworn he would never try to repeat Live Aid, Geldof did so in 2005 with a host of rock stars, including U2 and the (briefly) reformed Pink Floyd, breaking more records for global audience numbers. This time, though, the focus was on lobbying the richest countries, meeting as the G8 under British chairmanship at Gleneagles in Scotland.

On 2 July 2005, some 225,000 people marched in Edinburgh calling for debt cancellation to help Africa's poorest countries. A week later a £28.8 bn aid deal and a debt cancellation programme for eighteen countries, plus new guarantees to fund anti-HIV drugs, were indeed agreed at Gleneagles. Because parts of the rich world remained hostile to opening up trade to Africa, essential to helping the continent recover, some campaigners were disappointed. And the announcement was greeted with cynicism by the anti-globalization movement which was also a feature of these years. Geldof said, however, that 'never before have so many people

296

forced a change of policy onto a global agenda' and his fellow campaigner, Bono of U2, claimed the deal would save the lives of 600,000 Africans, mostly children. The legacy of Live8 and the Commission for Africa will continue to be debated for years but it was a unique alliance between civil organizations, churches, rock musicians, actors, writers – and politicians. Both Blair and Gordon Brown were consciously trying to use the hundreds of thousands of marchers and the glamour of the rock stars to nudge other world leaders towards agreement, and they were at least partially successful. It showed what their partnership could do.

Poverty is hard to define, easy to smell. In a country like Britain, it is mostly relative. Though there are a few thousand people living rough or who genuinely do not have enough to keep them decently alive, and many more pensioners frightened of how they will pay for heating, the greater number of poor are those left behind the general material improvement in life. This is measured by income compared to the average and by this yardstick in 1997 there were three to four million children living in households of relative poverty, triple the number in 1979. This does not mean they were physically worse off than the children of the late seventies, since the country generally became much richer. But human happiness relates to how we see ourselves relative to those around us, so it was certainly real. Under their new leader David Cameron, the Conservatives declared that they too believed in the concept of relative poverty, as described by a left-of-centre commentator, Polly Toynbee. And a world of work remained below the minimum wage, in private homes, where migrant servants were exploited, and in other crannies. Some 336,000 jobs remained on 'poverty pay' rates.[16]

Nevertheless the City firm UBS believes redistribution of wealth – a phrase New Labour did not like to use in case it frightened middle-class voters – had been stronger in Britain than other major industrialized countries. Despite the growth of the super-rich, overall equality slightly increased in the Blair years. One factor was the return to means-testing of benefits, particularly for pensioners and through the working families' tax credit (which in 2003 was divided into a child tax credit and a working tax credit). This was a personal U-turn by Brown who in Opposition had opposed means-testing. As Chancellor he concluded that if he was to direct scarce money at the people in real poverty he had little choice. More and more pensioners were means-tested, eventually some 66 per cent of them, provoking a nationwide revolt and persuading the government to back down and promise an eventual return to a link between state pension rates and average earnings. The other drawback of means-testing was that a huge bureaucracy then had to track people's earnings and try to establish just what they should get. Billions were overpaid. As people getting tax credits rather than old-style benefits, did better, and earned a little more, they found themselves facing demands to hand back money they had already spent. Many thousands of civil servants were hurriedly sent to try to deal with a tidal wave of complaint, and the system became extremely expensive to administer. It was also hugely vulnerable to fraud, with gangs taking over people's identities (13,000 civil servants alone) and exploiting 'a culture of overpayment'.

In the New Labour years, as under John Major, a sickly tide of euphemism rose ever higher, depositing its oily linguistic scurf on every available surface. Passengers became customers; indeed everybody became customers. Bin-men became refuse operatives, people with mental disabilities became differently-abled. And the poor became the socially excluded. There were controversial drives to oblige more disabled (and sometimes shirking) people back into work. The 'socially excluded' were confronted by a wide range of initiatives designed to make them, in essence, more middle class. In theory, Labour was non-judgemental or liberal about behaviour. In practice, responding to the darkest areas of deprivation, an almost Victorian moralism began to reassert itself. Advice on diet, weight-loss and alcohol consumption followed earlier government campaigns on AIDS and drugs. Parenting classes were much trumpeted. And for the minority who made life hellish for their neighbours on housing estates or in the streets, Labour introduced a word which became one of its particular gifts to the language of the age, as essential as dotcom or texting, the Asbo.

The Anti-Social Behaviour Order, first introduced in 1998, was an updated system of injunctions for what earlier generations called hooligans. These had to be applied for by the police or local council and granted by magistrates. To break the curfew or restriction, which could be highly specific, became a criminal offence. Asbos could be given for swearing at people, harassing passers-by, vandalism, making too much noise, graffiti, organizing raves, flyposting, taking drugs or sniffing glue, joyriding, either offering yourself as a prostitute or kerb-crawling in your car to find a prostitute, hitting people, drinking in designated public places ... almost anything in fact that was annoying or frightening. More bizarre-sounding ones included giving an Asbo to an entire part of Skegness to allow police arrests of troublemakers there; a 13-year-old girl being banned from using the word 'grass' and an 87-year-old man being ordered not to make 'sarcastic remarks' to neighbours and their visitors. In one case a woman who kept trying to commit suicide was given an Asbo to prevent her jumping into rivers or canals.

Though almost every story about an unlikely-sounding Asbo as reported in newspapers turned out to have a reason behind it, Asbo-spotting became a minor national sport and there were fears that for the tougher children, they became a badge of honour. In their early years they were much mocked by Liberal Democrat and Conservative MPs for being ineffective and rarely used by local authorities, as well as being criticized strongly by civil libertarians. Since breaking an Asbo could result in a prison sentence, it meant extending the threat of prison to crimes that before had not warranted it. Yet the public when polled strongly supported Asbos and as they were refined and strengthened they were gradually used more frequently, becoming almost routine. Like the minimum wage, Bank independence and some of the anti-poverty initiatives they seemed to be a part of New Labour Britain that would stick. At the time of writing, 7,500 or so had been given out in England and Wales (Scotland followed in 2004 with its version). Was this part of a wider authoritarian and surveillance agenda changing life in the country?

The War on Privacy

At an educated guess, the British are currently being observed and recorded by 4.2 million closed circuit television (CCTV) cameras. Professor Clive Norris of Sheffield University, who did the educated guessing, has pointed out, 'That's more than anywhere else in the world, with the possible exception of China. It's one for every 14 citizens.' When they first appeared in the early nineties, gazing beadily down from a few high-security buildings, these remotely staring cameras were pointed out as novelties. They are now in almost every sizeable store, looking down at key points in most big streets, in railway and underground stations, buses, housing estates and even from the fronts of private homes. Londoners are said to be picked up on CCTV cameras on average 300 times a day; their cars are filmed and tracked by the cameras set up for the capital's congestion charge. The Home Office has spent three-quarters of its crime prevention budget on CCTV cameras and the face-recognition and 'smart' technology that goes with them. The number of mobile phones is now equivalent to the number of people in Britain; with global satellite positioning chips, they can show

301

where their users are, and the same of course goes for GPS systems in cars (by 2007 Britons were losing the art of map-reading). There are also more than 6,000 speed cameras on British roads.

Britain's information commissioner Richard Thomas warned that the country had becoming a 'surveillance society'. He thought future developments could include microchip implants to identify and track people; facial recognition cameras fitted into lampposts; and even unmanned surveillance aircraft over Britain's towns. Thomas suggested this could lead to discrimination and harassment: 'As ever more information is collected, shared and used, it intrudes into our private space and leads to decisions which directly influence people's lives.' Certainly, if being watched makes us good and safe, the British are now the goodest, safest people in the history of the world.

Who watches all the CCTV coverage? Court cases often demonstrated that either there was no film kept, or that to spot a face took many police officers many weeks. Though this can increasingly be done electronically, other kinds of surveillance were being done in person. A new force of council tax inspectors were given powers to enter any home in England and take photographs of any room, including bedrooms and bathrooms, on pain of a £1,000 fine for refusal or obstruction. This was to assess improvements including patios, conservatories and double glazing for revaluation purposes as soon as the government gave the go-ahead for such a revaluation, which was planned to include extra charges for people living in agreeable areas, or who could park their cars outside their homes. It was reported in early 2006 that discussions had taken place with the civil servant in charge of the surveillance programme about selling on the information his men had gleaned to insurance and mortgage companies. Paul Sanderson, director of modernization for the tax inspectors, said he thought privacy was 'an old-fashioned concept' and called for all the details, including photographs, to be shown online.

If anything could be more intimate than the insides of everyone's homes, it is their DNA, with its clues about heredity, vulnerability to disease and much else. In 2003 the law was changed to allow the police to take and store the DNA of anyone arrested for any imprisonable offence, whether or not they were later convicted. Previously the police had had to destroy the samples of anyone found innocent, or whose case was dropped. Three years later, by which time 3.6 million samples were being held, Tony Blair said the database should be extended to everybody: 'The number on the database should be the maximum number you can get' and there was 'no problem' with the general public providing their DNA as part of the wider fight against crime.

By then the public also knew they would be expected to give biometric data – iris recognition and perhaps eventually DNA – for new compulsory identity cards, due to be introduced from 2008 when people applied for new passports. David Blunkett had promoted the idea of compulsory ID cards despite a hostile reaction from his predecessor Jack Straw, the Chancellor Gordon Brown, and initial caution from the Prime Minister. But he won his fight in government essentially because he convinced Blair the technology was becoming safe, and that ID cards would be popular with the majority of voters. These cards would carry a range of personal information, forming yet another new database, the National Identity Register. The issue provoked rebellions in Parliament before and after the 2005 election, but seemed to have been finally resolved by a thirty-one-vote majority in the Commons in February 2006. The new cards would cost citizens at least £93 each though ministers did not initially make it an offence to fail to carry one at all times. What were they for? To combat fraud and crime, to make life easier for government, and for individuals to make it harder to lose money through 'identity fraud'. Yet compulsory ID cards would probably not have passed through Parliament had it not been for the terrorist threat.

Seven Seven

On 7 July 2005, at rush-hour, four young Muslim men from West Yorkshire and Buckinghamshire, Hasib Hussein, Mohammed Sidique Khan, Germaine Lindsay and Shezhad Tanweer, murdered fifty-two people and injured 770 more by blowing themselves up on London Underground trains and one London bus. The report into the worst such attack in Britain later concluded that they were not part of an al Qaeda cell, though two had visited Pakistan camps, and that the rucksack bombs had been constructed for a few hundred pounds. Despite government insistence that the war in Iraq – discussed below – had not made Britain more of a terrorist target, the Home Office investigation asserted that part of the four terrorists' motivation was British foreign policy.

They had picked up the information they needed for the attack from the internet. It was a particularly ghastly one, because of the terrifying and bloody conditions below the streets of London in tube tunnels and it vividly reminded the country that it was as much a target as the United States or Spain. Indeed the intimate relationship between Britain and Pakistan, with constant and heavy traffic between them, provoked fears that the British would prove uniquely vulnerable. Blair heard of the attack at the most poignant time, just following London's great success in winning the bid to host the 2012 Olympic Games. He rushed back from Gleneagles in Scotland, where the G8 summit was discussing the ambitious new aid plan for Africa, and differences between the United States and the rest over global warming.

The London bombings are unlikely to have been stopped by more CCTV coverage, for there was plenty of that, nor by ID cards, for the killers were British citizens, nor by 'follow the money' anti-terror legislation, for little money was involved. Only even better intelligence might have helped. The Security Service as well as the Secret Intelligence Service (MI5 and MI6 as they are still more familiarly known) were already in receipt of huge increases in their budgets as they struggled to track down other murderous cells. Richard Reid, the 'shoe bomber' from Bromley who tried to destroy a flight from Paris to Miami in 2001, was another example of the threat from home-grown extremists, visiting 'radical' mosques from Brixton to Yorkshire, and there were many more examples of plots uncovered in these years, though by no means every suspect finally made it to court. In August 2005 police arrested suspects in Birmingham, High Wycombe and Walthamstow, east London, believing there was a plan to blow up as many as ten passenger aircraft over the Atlantic. The threat was all too real, widespread and hard to grip.

After many years of allowing dissident clerics and activists from the Middle East asylum in London, Britain had more than its share of inflammatory and dangerous extremists, who admired al Qaeda and preached violent jihad. Once September 11 had changed the climate, new laws were introduced to allow the detention without trial of foreigners suspected of being involved in supporting or fomenting terrorism. They could not be deported because human rights legislation forbade sending back anyone to countries where they might face torture. Seventeen were picked up and kept at Belmarsh high security prison. But in December 2004 the House of Lords ruled that these detentions were discriminatory and disproportionate and therefore illegal. Five weeks later the Home Secretary, Charles Clarke, hit back with 'control orders' to limit the movement of men he could not prosecute or deport. They would also be used against home-grown terror suspects. A month later, in February 2005, sixty Labour MPs revolted against these powers too, and the government only narrowly survived the vote. Ten Belmarsh men were put under these new restraints but the battle was far from over. In April 2006 a judge ruled that such control orders were 'an affront to justice' because they gave the Home Secretary, a politician, too much power and two months later said curfews of eighteen hours a day on six Iraqis were 'a deprivation of liberty' and also illegal. The new Home Secretary, John Reid, lost his appeal and reluctantly had to loosen the orders. In other cases, meanwhile, two men under control orders vanished.

New Labour Britain found itself in a struggle between its old laws and liberties and a new borderless, dangerous world. As we have seen the Britain of the forties was a prying and regulation-heavy country, emerging from the extraordinary conditions of a fight for national survival. From the fifties to the end of the eighties, the Cold War had grown a shadowy security state, with the vetting of BBC employees, MI5 surveillance of political radicals, a secret network of bunkers and tunnels, and the suspension of British jurisdiction over those small parts of the country taken by the United States forces. Yet none of this seriously challenged hallowed principles such as habeas corpus, free speech, a presumption of innocence, asylum, the right of British citizens to travel freely in their country without identifying papers, and the sanctity of homes in which the law-abiding lived. In the 'war on terror' much of this was suddenly in jeopardy.

New forms of eavesdropping, new compulsions, new political powers seemed to the government the least they needed to deal with a new, sinuous threat which ministers said could last for another thirty years. They were sure that most British people agreed, and that the judiciary, media, campaigners and elected politicians who protested were a hand-

307

wringingly liberal, too-fastidious minority. Tony Blair, John Reid and Jack Straw were particularly emphatic about this and on the numbers were probably right. As Gordon Brown eyed the premiership, his rhetoric was similarly tough. Against recent historical tradition it was left to the Conservatives, as well as the Liberal Democrats, to mount the barriers in defence of civil liberties.

The Waning

This book is written under the shadow of a new politics of global warming, when the British were being urged to be environmentally friendly. This author's contribution, which may save a Nordic wood or small grove of some beauty, is to resist giving a detailed account of the decade-long feud between Tony Blair and Gordon Brown. It would, apart from anything else, require at least another volume the same size as this one. But it cannot be ignored because it has affected the country itself. The feud went on from New Labour's first days in power until the last months when the Prime Minister's fingertips, white with effort, were slipping from office. Sometimes there were oases of tranquillity and good humour, for months at a time. Yet the stories of door-slamming tantrums, four-lettered exchanges, make-ups, go-betweens, public snubs and cherished policies for Britain's future being tugged back and forth like disintegrating soft toys, were repeated in Whitehall private offices, pubs and newspaper columns almost weekly. Occasionally it seemed as if Blair was on the point of sacking his Chancellor. Brown was variously reported by Number Ten to have psychological flaws, to be a control-freak, a wrecker, a traditionalist 'playing to the gallery' and disloyal whenever the Prime Minister was in real trouble. Blair, retorted the Brownites, was a vain second-rater obsessed with money and glamour, who had betrayed the Chancellor over their original deal.

In the first term, Brown was defending his huge remit as Chancellor and Blair was trying to come to terms with how brutally he was being kept out of large policy areas; how little he knew of forthcoming Budgets; and how weak was his ability to push Britain towards the euro. Brown felt the second election victory in 2001 was mostly his own work, based on the strong economy. In the second term that followed it, he began pushing for a date when Blair would leave office. Blair, turning to the 'war on terror' and Iraq, failed to concentrate enough on domestic policy. Even so, he became ever more determined to hang on until he got the reforms he wanted. A gap seemed to open between Blair's enthusiasm for market-mimicking ideas to reform health and schools, and Brown's, for delivering better lives to the working poor. As we have seen, Brown was also keen on bringing private capital into public services, but there was a difference in emphasis which both men played up. 'Best when we are at our boldest,' said Blair. 'Best when we are Labour,' retorted Brown. Over Iraq, foundation hospitals and student top-up fees, Blair thought Brown came close to leaving him at the mercy of lethal backbench revolts, disappearing off into the rhododendron bushes just when he was most needed. Brown did give his support, and rally 'his people' to help Blair out of various self-excavated holes, but the Scotsman with the ladder tended to arrive as darkness was falling.

After six years in office he felt Blair was squandering the party's reputation on gimmicks and a too enthusiastic backing for Bush. He thought Blair had lied to him about when he would step down. John Prescott intervened first during November 2003, so worried that their feud would bring down the government that he knocked their heads together – metaphorically, despite his reputation – over a dinner of shepherd's pie, telling them they would destroy the Labour Party. This produced a truce but during 2004 things worsened rapidly again. Labour was badly hurt in local elections. With Iraq still smouldering, Labour MPs began to panic about what would happen at the next election. A mix of personal and political frustration brought Blair to another low ebb. For years he and Brown had dealt with each other through a range of intermediaries meeting on neutral ground and carrying white flags. Punctuating these regular arm's-length contacts, at roughly the chilly level one might expect between a Prime Minister and Leader of the Opposition, Blair and Brown had hotter private meetings. But by now they were barely speaking and Blair was deeply depressed about his legacy, as well as private troubles.

In July 2004 four cabinet ministers were so worried he was about to resign that they jointly pleaded with him to stay on. In the autumn Prescott was involved in further talks about whether there could be a 'peaceful transition'. On one occasion he met Brown at an oyster bar by Loch Fyne in Scotland. All the tables were taken. So for an hour and a half the two men talked in a black government limousine in the carpark, surrounded by armed guards, as if they were two businessmen of Sicilian extraction planning the carve-up of criminal territories. Prescott later talked of the (tectonic) plates moving and admitted that ministers were positioning themselves for the end of the Blair years. Brown was preparing himself for his looming premiership, briefing himself on foreign affairs, reaching out to groups well outside the Treasury's normal remit. Transition teams were prepared. Surely, finally, even this soap-opera was ending?

It was not. Blair gathered together his formidable internal resources and quietly determined that he would not go after all. Immediately after Labour's conference at Brighton he returned to Downing Street to make a triple announcement. He confirmed he was buying a house (an expensive, ugly, hard-to-let house) in Connaught Square which he and Cherie would eventually use for their retirement. After a heart scare the previous year, he was going into hospital for treatment using a thin wire to correct irregular heartbeat problems. This condition, which Blair was at pains to downplay, was known only to a few close friends. Like the house purchase, it tended to focus attention on his political mortality. Hence the third announcement, a bolt from the blue. He intended to fight the forthcoming election and if elected serve a full term. But as he told the author: 'I do not want to serve a fourth term – I do not think the British people would want a Prime Minister to serve so long – but I think it's sensible to make plain my intention now.' It was an unprecedented thing to say, and caught Brown on the hop – he was on his way to a meeting in Washington. In the short term it effectively killed off speculation that Blair was about to resign. To that extent it was clever. It may also have helped Labour in the 2005 election since Blair was promising his critics he would not, like Margaret Thatcher, try to 'go on and on'.

It certainly felt like a slap in the face for Brown. Just a day earlier in Brighton the two of them had had a long, tense talk about the future in which Blair warned him that his supporters were destabilizing the government and urged him to work with him. In response to a newspaper report that he was intending to serve a full third term, Blair told Brown this was wrong. He said nothing about his heart problem. When he discovered that Blair was planning a complete third term Brown was reported to be livid. Demoted from his old role running the forthcoming election campaign, he rejected an offer to chair Labour's press conferences during it. 'There is nothing that you could ever say to me now that I could ever believe,' he was said to have told the Prime Minister.[17] But life is full of surprises. Blair discovered that pre-announcing his political mortality, however protracted, was a draining and sapping mistake, the worst purely tactical decision of his premiership. It provoked a stream of further questions – yes, but when exactly? How many years is a full term? How long does your successor get in office before a further election? If you are going, what validity do your long-term plans for the country really have? And most pertinently, do you still want Gordon

Brown to take over? These questions pursued him, loud, irritating, distracting heckles. His authority was first subtly, then dramatically, weakened.

Always, there were moments of hope. After Bush declared the war over on 1 May 2003, a search began for pro-Western Iraqis to whom some authority could be given. Eventually Saddam Hussein was found hiding in a hole and taken prisoner. Some eighty other countries pledged £18 bn for reconstruction, while US and British companies worked hard on repairing infrastructure. In the south where British forces were in control, they were quick to take off their helmets, patrolling in berets and trying to build good relations with local people. To start with, this worked well. Across Iraq huge amounts of money, dollars in shrink-wrapped blocks, were sent to be disbursed locally by hastily recruited Western viceroys. The following year saw the naming of Ayad Allawi, an affable Shiite, as interim Prime Minister of Iraq. That June, the United States formally handed over sovereignty to his government and a few days later, an Iraqi court began the trial of Saddam Hussein and eventually sentenced him to death. A national assembly was chosen and a date for elections was set. In January 2005, Iraqis had their first multi-party election for fifty years, choosing a transitional government. Later a Kurd, Jalal Talabani, was sworn in as Iraq's interim President. In October Iraqis voted for a new constitution, establishing an Islamic republic. At the end of the year millions took part in the full election which by January 2006 resulted in victory going to a Shia-dominated party, though without an overall majority. These were the drumbeats of

313

democracy and renewal, much what Blair and Bush had hoped would happen.

What had not been predicted by them was the appalling dark side of Iraq after the conflict, which completely overshadowed the reconstruction and the creation of democratic structures. A long, numbing tale of insurrection followed by religious feud, slaughters, car and suicide bombings, the killing of civilians in heavy-handed military responses, the beheading of Western hostages, the revelation of brutality by US guards at the notorious Abu Graib prison, a full-scale assault on the rebel town of Falluja, a thousand dead in a panicked stampede ... every day brought more murders, more fighting, less hope. By 2004, child mortality had doubled compared to 1990. There was a shortage of doctors and teachers. According to the World Bank, about a quarter of Iraqi children no longer attended school. Universities reported that they were being infiltrated by Muslim militias; professors fled and female students were persecuted for failing to wear the hijab. According to the United Nations, some 750,000 people had fled their homes since the war, adding to the 800,000 refugees of the Saddam era, while an estimated 1.6 million Iraqis had moved across the borders. By 2006, electricity supply was running at below the pre-war level and only half of Iraqi homes had safe supplies of water. Baghdad was on the edge of full-scale war, her hospitals filthy and dangerous, while militias roamed the streets. The possible breakup of the country was being openly talked about. In spring 2007, the international Red Cross described the suffering of Iraqi civilians as 'unbearable and unacceptable.' According to polls most British voters wanted the troops home, whatever further mayhem was caused.

It was the same story in the United States where most voters, who had been sold the idea that the Iraq War followed on naturally from 9/11, now believed it was a mistake. Bush stopped talking about 'staying the course'. A report for a Ministry of Defence think tank described Iraq as a recruiting sergeant for Islamic extremism around the world. This reflected the view of the Washington organization which brings together America's nineteen intelligence agencies, who firmly concluded that Iraq had increased the global risk of terrorism. In December 2006 the US Iraq Study Group presented Bush with a bleak assessment of the mayhem and a series of unpalatable options, designed to slowly bring America's soldiers home while negotiating with her traditional enemies in an attempt to bring some kind of stability to the country.

So by almost any standard that can be applied, three years after the Iraq war, it looked like a catastrophe. The country was experiencing civil war. The lives of Iraqis were now even more at risk, and mostly more unpleasant, than under Saddam's dreadful regime. Terrorism had been encouraged, not defeated. Countries regarded by London and Washington as regional menaces, Syria and Iran, were stronger and more confident, not less. With 120 British military dead in Iraq, most people saw the war as the worst single mistake by a British government in recent times. Some believe that had Blair refused to give British support for the war, it would not have happened. The mood inside the White House after September 11 makes this unlikely. Even so, having committed Britain, Blair could not stand aside from the consequences. The kaleidoscope was shaken all right. The pieces were in flux.

A Crowd of New People

One result of the long Iraqi agony was the arrival of many Iraqi asylum-seekers in Britain, Kurds, Shiites and Sunnis. This was little commented on because they were only a small part of a large migration into the country which changed it during the Blair years. It was a multi-lingual, many-religioned migration which included Poles, Zimbabweans, Somalis, Nigerians, Russians and Afghans, Australians, white South Africans and Americans, as well as sizeable French and German inflows. In 2005, according to the Office for National Statistics, immigrants were arriving to live in Britain at the rate of 1,500 a day; and since Tony Blair had arrived in power, more than 1.3 million people had come. By the mid-2000s English was no longer the first language of half the primary school children in London, and the capital boasted 350 different separate language groups.

The poorer new migrant groups were almost entirely unrepresented in politics but radically changed the sights, sounds and scents of urban Britain. The veiled women of the Muslim world, or its more traditionalist and Arab quarters, became common sights even on the streets of many market towns, from Scotland to Kent. Polish tradesmen and factory workers were followed by shops

316

stocking up with Polish food and selling Polish magazines, and even by Polish road signs. Chinese villagers were involved in a tragedy when nineteen were caught by the tide while cockle-picking at Morecambe Bay and drowned; but many more were working in grim conditions for rural 'gang-masters' or as the then Home Secretary, David Blunkett, put it, 'as slaves'. Russian voices began to be as common on the London Underground as Irish ones. Through most of its history Britain had been abnormally open to the world, mostly imposing herself elsewhere. Now she found herself a 'world island' in a new way.

Throughout the twentieth century, Britain's foreign policy had been concerned to control the impact of outside forces on these busy, crowded islands. In its first half she had tried this by attempting to keep her imperial possessions while subduing her greatest rival, Germany. In its second half she had worked with America against the Soviet Union to preserve a system of democracy and the free market, hoping to avoid nuclear annihilation, determined to avoid European federalism. She was not a successful manufacturing country but became a popular place to do financial business. Compared to similar countries, she was unusually warlike, spending more on defence and fighting more, too. Britain had always gone out into the world. Now, increasingly, the world came to her, poor and migrant, rich and corporate, the people of Eastern Europe and the manufactures of China. As in Victorian times, she was on the edge of newness, at the global bow-wave of change, but now it was change experienced near at hand.

317

Immigration had been a constant of British life. What was new was the scale and variety. Earlier modern migrations had, as we have seen, provoked a racialist backlash, riots, the rise of the National Front and a series of new laws. These later migrations were controversial in different ways. The early arrivals from the Caribbean or India were people who looked different but spoke the same language and in many cases had had a similar education to native British people. Many of the later migrants looked similar to the white British but shared no linguistic or imperial history. There were other differences. Young educated Polish or Czech people had come to Britain to earn money before going home again to acquire good homes, marry and have children in their rapidly growing countries. The economic growth of the early 2000s was fuelled by the influx of energetic and talented people, often denuding their own countries of skills, making their way in Britain as quickly as the East African Asians had before.

But there are always two sides to such changes. Criminal gangs of Albanians, Kosovars and Turks appeared as novel and threatening as Jamaican criminality had thirty years earlier. The social service bill for the new migrants was a serious burden to local authorities; towns such as Slough protested to national government about the extra cost in housing, education and other services. Above everything else, there was the sheer scale of the new migrations and the inability of the machinery of government to regulate what was happening. The Home Office's immigration and nationality department (IND) seemed unable to prevent illegal migrants entering Britain, to spot

318

those abusing the asylum system in order to settle here, or to apprehend and deport people. An illegal and sometimes lethal trade in 'people smuggling' made it particularly hard. Even after airlines were made responsible for the status of those they carried, large articulated lorries filled with human beings who had paid over their life savings to be taken to Britain, rumbled through the Channel Tunnel.

A Red Cross camp at Sangatte, near its French entrance, was blamed by Britain for exacerbating the problem. By the end of 2002, when Blunkett finally managed to get a deal with the French to close it, an estimated 67,000 had passed through Sangatte into Britain. Many African, Asian and Balkan migrants, believing the British immigration and benefits systems to be easier than those of other EU countries, simply moved across the continent and waited patiently for their journey into the UK. Thermal-imaging devices, increased border staff and unwelcoming asylum centres were all deployed. Unknown numbers of migrants died through thirst, asphyxiation or cold; some were murdered en route. Successive home secretaries – Jack Straw, David Blunkett, Charles Clarke and John Reid – tried to grapple with the trade, introducing legislation which was criticized by civil liberties campaigners and challenged in the courts. None was much applauded for their efforts and the last of them eventually confessed that he believed his department was 'not fit for purpose'. He hived off the struggling IND as a separate agency and promised to clear a backlog of around 280,000 failed asylum-seekers still in the country within five years. Uniformed border security staff were promised, and the historic Home Office was to be split up.

Meanwhile, many straightforwardly illegal immigrants had bypassed the asylum system entirely. In July 2005 the Home Office produced its own estimate of what the illegal population of the UK had been four years earlier, reckoning it between 310,000 and 570,000 souls, or between 0.5 and 1 per cent of the total population. A year later unofficial estimates pushed the possible total higher, to 800,000. The truth was, with boxes of cardboard files still being uncovered and no national recording system, nobody had a clue. Even the Bank of England complained, asking how it could set interest rates without knowing roughly how many people were working in the country. Official figures showed the number applying for asylum falling, perhaps as former Yugoslavia returned to relative peace. Controversially, thousands were being sent back to Iraq. But there were always new desperate groups, in the Middle East or war-torn and hungry Africa: projections about the impact of global warming suggested there always would be.

The arrival of workers from the ten countries which joined the EU in 2004 was a different issue, though it involved an influx of roughly the same size. When the European Union expanded Britain decided that, unlike France or Germany, she would not try to delay opening the country to migrant workers. Ministers suggested that the likely number arriving would be around 26,000 over the first two years. This was wildly wrong. In 2006 a Home Office minister, Tony McNulty, announced that since 2004 when the European Union expanded

427,000 people from Poland and seven other new EU nations had applied to work in Britain. If the self-employed were included, he added, the real figure would be nearer 600,000. There were at least 36,000 spouses and children who had arrived too and 27,000 child benefit applications had been received. These were very large numbers indeed. The Ugandan Asian migration which caused such a storm in 1971 had, for instance, amounted to some 28,000 people. It was hardly surprising that Britain now faced an acute housing shortage and that government officials began scouring the South of England looking for new places where councils would be ordered to let the developers start building.

By the government's own 2006 figures, annual net migration for the previous year was 185,000 and had averaged 166,000 over the previous seven years. This compares to the 50,000 net inflow which Enoch Powell had criticized in his notorious 1968 speech as 'mad, literally mad'. Projections based on many different assumptions suggested the UK population would grow by more than seven million by 2031. Of that, 80 per cent would be due to immigration. The organization Migration Watch UK, set up by a former diplomat to campaign for less immigration, said this was equivalent to requiring the building of two new towns the size of Cambridge each year, or five new Birminghams over the quarter century. But was there a mood of unnecessary hysteria? As has been noted, many of the Eastern European migrants, like those from Australia, France or the United States, could be expected to return home eventually. Immigration was partially offset by the outward flow of around 60,000 British people moving abroad each year, mainly to Australia, the United States, France and Spain. By the winter of 2006–7 one policy institute, the IPPR, reckoned there were 5.5 million British people living permanently overseas – nearly one in ten of us, or more than the population of Scotland – and another half million living there for some of the year. Aside from the obvious destinations, the Middle East and Asia were seeing rising colonies of expatriate British. Who were they? A worrying proportion seemed to be graduates; Britain is believed to lose one in six graduates to emigration. Many were retired or better-off people looking for a life of sunlit ease, just as many immigrants to Britain were young, ambitious and keen to work. Government ministers tended to emphasize the benign economic effects of immigration. Their critics looked around and asked where all the extra people would go, and what spare road space, hospital beds or schools they would find to use.

Blair's Final Years

From Labour's arrival in power in 1997 right through to the 2005 election, Blair and his ministers had never been seriously worried about the Conservatives. After the heavy defeat in 2001, Hague had instantly resigned. The Conservatives then rejected the man who had seemed the obvious alternative, Michael Portillo. The son of a Spanish republican refugee and as a boy the advertising face of Ribena fruit juice, he had suffered the crippling fate of being regularly touted as a future leader from the mid-eighties, Mrs Thatcher's chosen one. But Portillo had feuded with Hague. More importantly, he was on a personal journey to a more metropolitan view of the world, had admitted homosexual affairs in his youth, and would not condescend to pretend to his party that he was anything other than socially liberal. He launched his campaign in an achingly trendy London restaurant, so the party in its first full democratic leadership vote instead chose Iain Duncan Smith. In 'IDS', a former soldier, businessman and, in Parliament, a Euro-sceptic rebel, MP for Norman Tebbit's old seat of Chingford, traditionalist Conservatives thought they had found someone who truly represented their core beliefs. Indeed they had. But they underestimated Duncan Smith's deep interest in helping the disadvantaged and, sadly, had overestimated his political skill. A thoroughly decent man, he was outclassed so badly as a speaker and on television that the Tories took fright. A growing rebellion persuaded him to resign as leader in December 2003.

A demoralized party did something rare. It chose its next leader without the customary vicious fight, returning the former cabinet minister Michael Howard to the colours. Howard had been controversial as Home Secretary but was part of the Tories' 'Cambridge mafia' and brought rivals from the liberal wing of the party back inside his leadership tent. He began brilliantly as leader, binding wounds and restoring morale. He was the first Tory leader to really worry Brown and Blair, a dangerous opponent. Like Hague, he performed well in the Commons, calling on the Prime Minister to resign over Iraq and making much of a series of Home Office scandals and failures. In 2005 his election focused on better public services and immigration. Conservative posters asked the question: 'Are you thinking what we're thinking?' Though they gained substantial numbers of seats and votes – a majority in England – the country's overall answer was 'No, not really'. Michael Howard resigned and was replaced by the bright young Old Etonian David Cameron. Taking the Tories in a green and liberal direction, he won high poll ratings and looked set, by 2007, to be the Conservative leader best placed to oust a sitting Labour government since Margaret Thatcher had the job thirty years earlier.

The Liberal Democrats might have hoped that the hugely unpopular Iraq War and the Blair government's growing reputation for illiberal and fiddly statism, would allow the third party to break through. Under Paddy Ashdown, there had been a long and fruitless courtship with Labour, ultimately made impossible to consummate by Blair's large majorities. Then the experience of the Scottish parliamentary elections turned Blair against voting reform, a key Lib-Dem demand. His old mentor Roy Jenkins wryly gave him up as a constitutional reformer of any kind, and that relationship cooled. Ashdown's successor Charles Kennedy had been the youngest MP when first elected for the Western Isles as an SDP member. He was popular with the party and the media. He took the Lib-Dems away from any proximity to New Labour and campaigned, after some encouragement, against the Iraq War. Under him the third party became a place where disaffected leftish Britons gathered, a pacific haven from Blair's bellicose certainties and the Home Secretary David Blunkett's enthusiasm for locking up asylum-seekers. In the 2001 election the Liberal Democrats won fifty-two seats and in 2005, sixty-two, a record performance. But after the heady optimism of the early eighties, they seemed to be back playing a long game. Charles Kennedy had a serious alcohol problem which could make him fuzzy and unconvincing and which, though his aides lied about it for years, eventually led to his resignation as party leader. He was replaced by Sir Menzies Campbell, a Scottish lawyer and former Olympic runner who was older but safer.

The 2005 election campaign ended with Labour's majority cut from 167 in the previous contest to just sixty-seven. For most previous prime ministers a majority of that size would have been considered handsome. Heath, Wilson, Callaghan or Major would have killed for it, and it was twenty-four more than Margaret Thatcher had enjoyed in her first, strife-ridden and tumultuous administration. But by the standards of New Labour's record the loss was a serious rebuke. The voters were noticing. But what? Blair thought they were noticing the habit of disloyalty among his MPs. Many of them thought they were noticing Blair. Certainly with so many disaffected former ministers and left-wing dissidents on the Labour benches it meant he would have an even harder time getting his own way. Then there was the further problem of his time-limited remaining tenure and the slow withdrawal of his personal authority. Brown had not been given his accustomed role in election planning but was far more involved than Blair had first intended in the 2005 fight. With their best false hearty smiles in place, and much criticized for making wild claims about the cuts planned by their Tory opponents, they had won their third mandate standing beside one another, if not hand in hand. As soon as the election was over Blair turned his mind to staying on rather longer than the Chancellor had hoped.

The latter stages of Blair's time as Prime Minister were overshadowed by the bloody aftermath of the Iraq War, and by renewed fighting in Afghanistan. After more bad local elections in 2006 he sacked his Home Secretary, Charles Clarke, who publicly protested; he demoted his Foreign Secretary, Jack Straw, and he stripped John Prescott, who had been hit by a scandal, of his departmental responsibilities. The embarrassing police inquiry into whether businessmen had been recommended for peerages as a result of offering loans to the Labour Party drew closer to Downing Street; shortly before Christmas 2006 Tony Blair became the first serving Prime Minister to be interviewed by the police as part of a criminal investigation. He was questioned in Downing Street for two hours by Detective Chief Inspector Graeme McNulty and a colleague. This occurred on the same day as the official police report into the death of Diana was finally published, and a controversial announcement was made about rural post offices. Downing Street denied there was any attempt to bury bad news but from the outside it looked like one New Labour tradition that should have been ditched.

But would it bring forward an earlier departure? After a rocky summer in 2006 there had been an organized round of junior ministerial resignations, and demands for Blair to quit, assumed by Number

Ten and most of the media to have been organized by supporters of Gordon Brown. Despite calling an open letter on the subject 'disloyal, discourteous and wrong', on 7 September the prime minister promised that the coming party conference would be his last, breaking under duress his earlier promise to serve a full term. Labour's conference, held unusually in Manchester, saw one of Blair's most eloquent speeches ever, a defiant farewell to the party which no longer wanted him, and which responded to him with largely hypocritical adulation. It did not look as if the parting would be particularly sweet, on either side. His wife was heard referring to Brown's earlier conference speech with the single word 'liar'. Soon, Blairites were attempting to persuade the young cabinet minister David Miliband to challenge Brown in a leadership contest. He was being bashful, but it was evidence of how deeply in trouble Labour now was. The polls showed Brown trailing the new Conservative leader David Cameron. Whatever this was, it was not glad confident morning again.

Britain After Blair

This history has told the story of the defeat of politics by shopping. The political visions of Attlee, and Churchill in his romantic-nostalgic mood, were overthrown by the consumer boom of the fifties. People generally wanted colour, variety and new tastes, not austere socialist egalitarianism or thigh-slapping New Elizabethan patriotism, though a large minority was drawn to each of these. In the

Wilson and Heath years, politicians promised a newly scientific, planned future, all straight lines and patriotism, drawn up in Whitehall with everyone sitting down together 'backing Britain'. Their Britain collapsed and Margaret Thatcher's revolution shovelled away the rubble. Her boot-sale of state enterprise, defeat of the unions, and her abandonment of politicians' controls over money led to a new boom. The old state retreated and the consumer society advanced. Far from remoralizing the British with the Victorian values of frugality, saving, orderliness and continence as she had hoped, Thatcher gave many of us the licence and credit to behave like Regency rakes on a spree. The country went shopping again, as it had in the fifties and sixties and would again in the nineties and beyond.

The new great powers in the land were organizations that had barely been noticed before the war. In 1924 an East End barrow boy called Jack Cohen had used part of his surname and the initials of a tea supplier to market his own-brand tea under the title Tesco. Five years later he opened his first shop, then the country's first all-purpose food warehouse and in 1956, when Tony Blair was three, a self-service store. Tesco leaped ahead. In the eighties Cohen's daughter, Dame Shirley Porter, became leader of Westminster Council and, after a highly controversial 'homes for votes' scandal, left the country. By the time Blair left office, Tesco was the country's leading retailer with 1,780 stores, sales of more than £37bn and profits of over £2bn. It was gaining one pound in every three the British spent on groceries and there was talk of Britain becoming a 'Tescopoly'. Asda, set up by

Yorkshire farmers in 1965 and now owned by Wal-Mart, the American behemoth and the world's biggest company, came second to Tesco, but was still serving more than 13 million people a week. Sainsbury's, which had originated in a Victorian dairy shop and had launched the first self-service supermarket in 1950, had sales of £17bn, and more than 750 stores. Such companies dominated farmers and other suppliers exercised great power in planning disputes, and were becoming increasingly controversial. Meanwhile, to enjoy the consumer economy, the British were borrowing: the average adult had credit card, finance-deal and unsecured personal loans amounting to more than £4,500.

Apart from generous planning laws, the shopping boom required the 'great car economy' lauded by Margaret Thatcher, which was now restrained only by rising petrol prices and congestion. London had deployed its own congestion charge and a national debate had begun about road pricing. Car use was huge by historic standards. At the beginning of the sixties when supermarkets first took off, there were 9 million vehicles on the roads; by the mid-2000s, there were 30 million. It was not all shopping, of course. Commuting by car had become mundane and the number of journeys to school by car had doubled in ten years. By the standards of the forties or fifties, the British now led strikingly privatized lives. They mostly shunned public transport and were far less likely to shop shoulder to shoulder with neighbours, using shopkeepers they knew by name. With television, digital or analogue, and the computer boom, entertainment was much likelier to remain in the home. The British were afloat on a tide of cheap imported goods, easy credit and new labour, both skilled and unskilled. House prices had by now nearly tripled in the Blair years. But politicians, still taxing vigorously, still struggling to deliver popular and efficient public services, were not given any credit for that.

Politics shrivelled – as an activity, as a source of status, as a way of ordering life that was respected or trusted. Lady Thatcher found no truly effective way to run the public services. Nor did her successors, John Major and Tony Blair. The great middling layer of public life, the independent-minded managers of schools, hospitals and towns, who had real freedom to manage, and the self-confident local politicians who could make waves, had gone. By most measures overall crime had fallen from the late nineties, at the cost of overcrowded prisons. But violent crime was as much feared as ever, and as present on the streets of the main cities. All this had a direct effect on people's hopes and fears about the country. One commentator from a conservative-minded think tank explained the exodus of 1,000 people a day to other countries: 'People are emigrating because of a sense of hopelessness … nothing is ever done about the big problems like education, health, crime. There is a growing sense that politicians will never deal with the problems.'[18] That was only one voice, and others had different views, but it reminds us why the policy problems discussed at length earlier are so critical to the country's notion of its future.

Yet, at the end of this story, the need for true politics seems to have returned. Towards the end of his time in office Tony Blair unveiled a report by an economist, Sir Nicholas Stern, which he described as more important than any report to government during the New Labour years – more important, therefore, than the debate over Iraq, or pensions, peace in Ireland or the future of Britain's health service. Few questioned this bold assertion. For the report was about climate change. We have already seen how radically new waves of migration were changing Britain but they were as nothing compared to what a new climate might do. An overwhelming preponderance of scientists believed not simply that the climate was changing (there was no room left for doubt about that) but that the change was man-made and potentially catastrophic. The polar ice was melting, weather patterns were disrupted around the globe, species were disappearing and yet, as China and India advanced, the gases causing these changes continued to pour upwards. Blair had tried to persuade his partner in Iraq, George Bush, to alter in some way his hostility to carbon limits but to no avail: compared to the agreements he had won on Africa, Blair's effort on climate change had been a failure.

American self-interest overrode what to others seemed proper and fair. And there was no bigger cultural challenge to Britons' sense of proportion and fairness than the one thrown down by militant Islam. After 9/11 and the London bombings, there were plenty of angry, narrow-minded young Muslim men running amuck, either literally or in their heads. Their views, and the veiled women of Arab tradition, provoked English politicians to ask whether their communities wanted to fully integrate. Britain did not have as high a proportion of Muslims as France, but large parts of the English Midlands and the South had long-established and third-generation urban villages of hundreds of thousands of Muslim people. Muslims felt they were being watched in a new way and they were perhaps right to feel a little uneasy. In the old industrial towns of the Pennines, and in stretches of West London near Heathrow there were such strong concentrations of incomers that the word ghetto was being used by ministers and civil servants. White working-class people had long been moving, quietly, to other areas: Essex, Hertfordshire, the towns of coastal Sussex, even Spain.

They were a minority, if polling was any guide: only a quarter of Britons said they would prefer to live in white-only areas. Yet multi-culturalism, if it was defined as more than simple 'live and let live', was being questioned. How much should new Britons integrate, and how much was the retention of traditions a matter of their human rights? Speaking in December 2006 Blair cited forced marriages, the importation of sharia law and the ban on women entering certain mosques as being on the wrong side of the line. In the same speech he used new, harder language. After the London bombings, 'for the first time in a generation there is an unease, an anxiety, even at points a resentment that our very openness, our willingness to welcome difference, our pride in being home to many cultures, is being used against us.' He went on to try to define the duty to integrate: 'Our tolerance is part of what makes Britain, Britain. So conform to it; or don't come here. We don't want the hate-mongers ... If you come here lawfully, we welcome you. If you are permitted to stay here permanently, you become an equal member of our community and become one of us.' Though Blair chose security as his ground, for others it was about more than the struggle against terrorism. Britain's strong economic growth, despite a weak manufacturing base, was partly the product of a long tradition of hospitality. The question was now whether the country was becoming so crowded – England had the highest population density of any major country in the Western world – that this tolerance was eroding. It would require wisdom from politicians and efficiency from Whitehall to keep things on an even keel.

Just the same is true of that larger threat, climate change. This threatened reshaping was physical, not demographic, the waves of water, not of people. It promised to alter the familiar splatter of Britain as she is seen from space or on any map. Nothing is more fundamental to a country's sense of itself than its shape, particularly when the country is an island. Rising sea levels could make Britain look different on every side. They could eat into the smooth billow of East Anglia, centuries after the wetlands were reclaimed with Dutch drainage, and submerge the concrete-crusted, terraced marshland of London, and drown idyllic Scottish islands and force the abandonment of coastal towns which had grown in Georgian and Victorian times. Wildlife would die out and be replaced by new species – there were already unfamiliar fish offshore and new birds and insects in British gardens. All this was beyond the power of Britain alone to deflect, since she was responsible for just 2 per cent of global emissions. Even if the British could be persuaded to give up their larger cars, their foreign holidays and their gadgets, would it really make a difference?

Without a frank, unheated conversation between the rest of us and elected politicians, who are then sent out into the world to do the bigger deals that must be done, what hope for action on climate change? It seems certain to involve the loss of new liberties, such as cheap, easy travel. It will change the countryside as grim-looking wind farms appear. It will change how we light and heat our homes and how we are taxed. All these changes are intensely political, in a way the British of the forties would have recognized. Politics is coming back as a big force in our lives, like it or not. It will require more frankness, less spin, and a more grown-up interest in policy, not scandal. Without this frankness, without trust on each side, what hope for a sensible settlement between Muslim and Christian, incomer and old timer? Without a rebuilding of strong local structures, what hope for better-run schools, councils or hospitals? Without level-headed politics, how will the future shape of the UK, if it continues, be negotiated? In the course of this history, most political leaders have arrived eager and optimistic, found themselves in trouble of one kind or another, and left disappointed. Such is the nature of political life. (Indeed, perhaps it is the nature of life.) But the rest of us need those optimistic politicians, the next leaders, the ones whom we'll laugh at and abuse. And we need them more than ever now.

The threats facing the British are large ones. But in the years since 1945, having escaped nuclear devastation, tyranny and economic collapse, we British have no reason to despair, or emigrate. In global terms, to be born British remains a wonderful stroke of luck.

NOTES

Part 4: The British Revolution

1. See Hugo Young, *One of Us,* Macmillan, 1989.
2. Margaret Thatcher, *The Downing Street Years,* HarperCollins, 1993.
3. Quoted in Young, op. cit.
4. Thatcher, op. cit.
5. See Robert Harris, *The Making of Neil Kinnock,* Faber & Faber, 1983.
6. Denis Healey, *The Time of My Life,* Michael Joseph, 1989.
7. See Max Hastings & Simon Jenkins, *The Battle for the Falklands,* Michael Joseph, 1983; Lawrence Freedman, *Britain and the Falklands War,* Oxford U. P., 1988; Kevin Jeffreys, *Finest and Darkest Hours,* Atlantic Books, 2002; and Thatcher, op. cit.
8. Hugo Young & Anne Sloman, *The Thatcher Phenomenon,* quoted in Young, op. cit.
9. From Patrick Hannan, *When Arthur Met Maggie,* Seren, 2006.
10. Hannan, op. cit.
11. All this, and the preceding information, is taken from the fourth volume of David Kynaston's wonderful history of the City of London: *A Club No More, 1945–2000,* Chatto & Windus, 2001.
12. Interviewed in Kynaston, ibid.
13. Jill Treanor, *Guardian, 17* October 2006.
14. Kynaston, op. cit.

15. A comparison made by Christopher Harvie in *Fool's Gold,* Hamish Hamilton, 1994.
16. Keith Aitken in Magnus Linklater 8 Robin Denniston (eds), *Anatomy of Scotland,* Chambers, 1992.
17. See Harvie, op. cit.
18. Tony Benn, *The Benn Diaries,* Arrow, 1996 (entry for 7 January 1976).
19. Nigel Lawson, *The View from Number 11,* Bantam Press, 1992.
20. Ibid.
21. Quoted in *The Times,* 31 January 2006.
22. John Davies, *A History of Wales,* Allen Lane, 1990.
23. Martin Westlake, *Kinnock: The Biography,* Little, Brown, 2001.
24. Michael Fallon & Philip Holland, *The Quango Explosion,* Conservative Political Centre, 1978.
25. Quoted in Andrew Marr, *Ruling Britannia,* Michael Joseph, 1995.
26. Thatcher, op. cit.
27. Evan Davies, *Schools and the State,* Social Market Foundation 1993; see Marr, op. cit.
28. Simon Jenkins, *Thatcher and Sons,* Allen Lane, 2006.
29. Thatcher, op. cit.

Part 5: Nippy Metro People

1. See Andy McSmith, *John Smith: Playing the Long Game,* Verso, 1993.
2. McSmith, ibid.

3. John Major, *The Autobiography,* HarperCollins, 1999.
4. Christian Wolmar, *On the Wrong Line,* Aurum Press, 2005.
5. Simon Jenkins, *Thatcher and Sons,* Allen Lane, 2006.
6. Major, op. cit.
7. See Malcolm Balen, *Kenneth Clarke,* Fourth Estate, 1994.
8. See Mark Lawson, *Media Guardian,* 21 October 2006.
9. Anthony Seldon, *Blair,* The Free Press, 2004.
10. Robert Peston, *Brown's Britain,* Short Books, 2005.
11. All quotes from Peter Hyman, *1 out of Ten,* Vintage, 2005.
12. See Jenkins, op. cit.
13. Andrew Rawnsley, *Servants of the People,* Penguin, 2001.
14. Lance Price, *The Spin Doctor's Diary,* Hodder & Stoughton, 2005.
15. Peter Oborne, *The Rise of Political Lying,* The Free Press, 2005.
16. National Statistics website, 2006.
17. Peston, op. cit.
18. Robert Whelan of Civitas, interviewed *Daily Mail,* 3 November 2006.